Co-Teaching for English Learners

Co-Teaching for English Learners

Evidence-Based Practices and Research-Informed Outcomes

edited by

Maria G. Dove
Molloy College

Andrea Honigsfeld
Molloy College

INFORMATION AGE PUBLISHING, INC.
Charlotte, NC • www.infoagepub.com

Library of Congress Cataloging-in-Publication Data

A CIP record for this book is available from the Library of Congress
http://www.loc.gov

ISBN: 978-1-64802-225-8 (Paperback)
       978-1-64802-226-5 (Hardcover)
       978-1-64802-227-2 (E-Book)

We dedicate this book to our respective families, who are the source of our greatest support and inspiration: Tim, Dave, Jason, Christine, Sara, Meadow Rose, Gavin Joseph, and Rohnan Xavier; Howie, Benjamin, Jacob, and Noah

CONTENTS

PART I

TEACHER PROFESSIONAL LEARNING: CAPACITY BUILDING

PART II

SYSTEM-WIDE INITIATIVES: SCALING IT UP

PART III

COLLABORATIVE PLANNING AND CO-TEACHING PRACTICES

PART IV

CO-TEACHING TO ENHANCE INSTRUCTIONAL PRACTICE

PREFACE

Over more than a decade, we have been researching and publishing on the topic of co-teaching and collaborative practices for English learners (ELs), and so much has changed since we first began in the form of state and local policies and programs for the sake of this population of students. In particular, the practice of co-teaching for ELs has increased significantly across the United States, and co-taught instruction has become a part of approved, recommended, or mandated programs for English language development (ELD) in many school districts. Different states such as Colorado, Georgia, Hawaii, Idaho, Illinois, Indiana, Iowa, Massachusetts, Minnesota, Missouri, New Hampshire, New Jersey, New York, North Carolina, Oregon, Pennsylvania, Tennessee, Vermont, Virginia, and Washington all have schools that have embraced what we call integrated collaborative service delivery for ELD, a part of which is co-teaching. As collaborative teaching for ELs has increased, so has the research of these ELD programs.

Advocacy for integrated, collaborative instruction stems from the belief that ELs should not need to leave their general education classes or their English-speaking peers in order to learn to speak English. For students to have a sense of belonging and thrive academically, ELs need to be taught by subject-specific experts—content and grade-level teachers—along with developing their English-language skills with instruction provided by a language-development expert in order to learn the core curriculum. For this reason, co-teaching has become a preferred method of instruction to provide effective learning environments that will support ELs' academic, linguistic, social, and emotional growth.

Co-Teaching for English Learners, pages xi–xvi
Copyright © 2020 by Information Age Publishing
All rights of reproduction in any form reserved.

The focus of this book is on how different schools have conceived, implemented, and sustained their co-teaching practices for ELs, and in particular, what has been the impact of co-teaching on student outcomes and teacher learning. We have compiled a unique group of studies and documentary accounts which highlight the interactions of co-teaching partnerships, the influence of co-teaching on a variety of stakeholders, and the importance of leadership in fostering collaborative practices and instruction for the sake of ELs. In many ways, they chronicle the commitment that is necessary for ELs to succeed academically in co-taught instructional settings.

This volume closely explores co-teaching and integrated service delivery for ELs by (a) examining the collaborative instructional cycle—co-planning, co-instruction, co-assessment, and reflection practices—of co-taught programs for ELs; (b) presenting current, classroom-based, practitioner-oriented research related to all aspects of co-taught programs for ELs including curriculum mapping and alignment, co-development of instructional materials, building teaching partnerships in the ELD context; (c) offering authentic, evidence-based instructional practices that yield positive results for ELs; and (d) presenting practical recommendations for making instructional and program design decisions based on student outcomes.

We have organized the chapters contained in this volume into four separate categories to address the different aspects of the research presented. In Part I, *Teacher Professional Learning: Capacity Building*, we bring together a group of authors who offer discriminating accounts of how teachers develop their knowledge, insight, and skills about the instruction of English learners in the co-taught class. In the first chapter, Jennifer C. Norton explores the notion of ELD teachers as possible change agents for the academic success of ELs. She investigates the perceptions of elementary ELD teachers and general education teachers concerning their roles and responsibilities in the co-taught class and identifies a group of educators who emerge as capacity builders for the instruction of ELs. Focusing on collaboration as a means of teacher learning, Amanda K. Giles and Bedrettin Yazan examine how teachers reconcile their contradictions about diverse-needs students and how interactions between the English as a second language (ESL) teachers and content teachers are critical to student success. They argue how teacher agency is key to initiating and sustaining teacher collaboration. Investigating collaborative teaching practices and how they affect the way ESL teachers understand their professional roles and identities, Greg McClure harnesses his insight from the responsibilities he assumed as an ESL teacher and considers the sociopolitical context that ESL teachers must often navigate. He documents how teachers' identities are shaped in co-taught classes. Detailing how an embedded model of professional development (PD) impacted the instructional practices of co-teaching teams, Adam Cooper and Stephen Kroeger unfold some of the challenges of teaching partnerships and how an embedded model of PD supported co-teachers to implement data-informed instructional planning. Using reflection and reflective practice for self-study, Leia Bruton documents her journey as a developing co-teacher and examines the lessons she learned in order to make co-teaching an effective program model of instruction for ELs. Finally, the co-editors of this volume, Maria G. Dove and Andrea Honigsfeld, share their nationwide study on co-teaching implementation and reveal their insights and "aha" moments into what practices truly affect student outcomes.

In order to comply with or exceed national, state, and local mandates and guidelines for ELD, schools across the country have initiated, devised, or adopted innovative instructional programs and practices with ELs in mind. In Part II, *System-Wide Initiatives: Scaling It Up*, our authors recount how broad-scale initiatives bolstered the effectiveness of co-taught ELD programs. First, Joan R. Lachance focuses on a statewide initiative to support co-teaching for academic language and literacy development. She examines teachers' predictions about the benefits of co-teaching and collaboration as well as the impact these practices have on student outcomes and offers practical recommendations for successful co-taught programs. Considering the ever increasing immigrant and refugee population of students, Debra Cole highlights the role of instructional specialists who provide professional development as a countywide initiative for both EL and classroom teachers in the form of training, coaching, and technical assistance and analyzes the outcomes of co-taught programs for ELs. Examining a district-wide co-teaching initiative developed for ELs success, Holly Porter investigates the challenges of advancing co-taught instruction from exploring its possibilities to sustaining it as an inclusive program model for ELs. In our culminating chapter in this section, Lucia Perez-Medina uncovers how a district-wide professional learning community (PLC) involving co-teaching partners enhanced teacher capacity to instruct ELs in co-taught classes. She describes how the district-wide PLC served as a training ground for co-teaching pairs to turn key information and establish PLCs in individual schools in the district.

In Part III, *Collaborative Planning and Co-Teaching Practices*, we showcase the work of several authors who investigated parts of the collaborative instructional cycle—co-planning, co-instruction, co-assessment, and reflection—to determine paths to effective instruction for ELs in co-taught classes. To begin, Amy Frederick and Anne Ittner examine collaborative planning and illustrate its outcomes in terms of opportunities for professional learning, teacher inquiry, and reflective practice. With an interest in how to best implement new models of instruction, Felice Atesoglu Russell investigates the perceptions of teachers and school leaders concerning the purpose and implementation of co-teaching for ELs. Focusing on the systems of how teachers and students share physical space, Beth Clark-Gareca and David Mumper document in their descriptive case study how the use of classroom space affects student–teacher interactions in the co-taught class. Finally, Karrie S. Woodruff uncovers the successes and challenges of co-teaching in a dual immersion elementary school program. She reveals her findings which include the role experience plays in the co-teaching power dynamic and the importance of having proactive, direct, and compassionate communication in a teaching partnership.

In Part IV, *Co-Teaching to Enhance Instructional Practice*, we focus on authors who have investigated various practices for the sake of improving instruction for the academic success of ELs. Opening this section, Carrie McDermott, and co-editor Andrea Honigsfeld, report their findings concerning the positive outcomes of ELs in a co-taught high school social studies class. They investigate how a co-teaching team negotiated the integration of language and content instruction as well as joint professional learning through collaborative planning and teaching. Exploring co-planning, co-teaching, and shared reflective experiences for the sake of ELs, Marie Edgerton and Jane Charlotte Weiss use a technique known as lesson study to analyze their joint-teaching practices and their use of a workshop model routine for their co-taught lessons that bring about positive language and content knowledge growth for ELs. In a similar vein, Kathryn Toppel conducts a self-study to engage in meaningful reflection about her collaborative practices. She examines each aspect of the collaborative instructional cycle—co-planning, co-teaching, co-assessment, and reflection—within the framework of a consistent instructional routine known as SWIRL (speaking, writing, interacting, reading, and listening). Exploring how co-teachers empower ELs, Samantha Chung, Laura Baecher, and William Hargrove employ action research to uncover the process of collaborative planning using as a frame the Model United Nations (MUN) task-based curriculum and problem-based learning (PBL) to increase ELs' motivation and persistence with their studies. Considering the needs of twice exceptional students and the preparation of new and in-service teachers to meet their learning challenges, Ebony Terrell Shockley and Kia McDaniel investigate the instructional practices of teachers of ELs who are also identified as students with disabilities and examine the co-teaching models used by general, special education, and ESOL educators. Addressing the practical aspects of supporting students to write in different genres, Brandy Gibb, Guofang Li, and Teresa Schwartz reveal how students' consistent errors on science lab reports led to the development of specific collaborative and instructional strategies and resources to improve the writing skills of all students. In our final chapter, Jennifer Daddino, Kimberly Grogan, and Marina Moran focus on collaborative conversations that are guided by a three-point framework—differentiation and curriculum design, co-teaching, and making content comprehensible.

Various types of collaborative conversations and multi-level, differentiated resources that teachers created to meet the needs of ELs are outlined here.

This volume demonstrates that there is emerging evidence in support of co-teaching for English learners. It is our sincere hope that this volume will be a valuable resource to assist both novice and experienced teachers in their endeavors to provide effective integrated, collaborative instruction for ELs in K–12 schools.

—**Maria G. Dove** and **Andrea Honigsfeld**

ACKNOWLEDGMENTS

We would like to express our deepest appreciation to the authors who brought their rich and diverse talents to contribute to this volume. We are so very grateful for your time, insights, and revelations into the topic of collaborative teaching for English learners (ELs). As a result of your efforts, we have been able to further document authentic and innovative collaborative instruction for the sake of ELs as well as detail the positive outcomes of co-taught instruction for students and teachers. We would also like to thank you for your steadfastness and your patience as we finalized the manuscript.

Our friends and colleagues at Molloy College, Rockville Centre, New York, have always been a source of encouragement and support for our scholarship efforts. We would like to express our sincere gratitude for all that they do.

This project would not have been possible without the assistance of the staff at Information Age Publishing, to whom we would like to express our appreciation for the creation of this volume.

Last but not least, we are truly grateful for the ongoing support of our loving and kind families and friends who are always ready to applaud our endeavors, no matter what.

PART I

TEACHER PROFESSIONAL LEARNING:
CAPACITY BUILDING

CHAPTER 1

REDEFINING BORDERS THROUGH CO-TEACHING

ESL/ELD Teachers as Change Agents in K–5 Classrooms

Jennifer C. Norton
Office of the State Superintendent of Education

We have often heard co-teaching compared to a marriage with give-and-take between two teachers with unique expertise, but co-teaching also has the potential to empower English as a Second Language (ESL)/English Language Development (ELD) teachers as teacher leaders—change agents who leave a lasting impact on general education teachers, even when they are not present in the classroom co-teaching to serve English language learners (ELLs). Can ESL/ELD teachers redefine borders in an otherwise siloed profession, where teachers are typically physically separated into different classroom spaces (Lortie, 1975)? Survey data ($n = 61$) followed by semi-structured interview data ($n = 4$) were collected to investigate how elementary ESL/ELD and general education co-teachers across 38 schools (with about 11% ELLs) perceived one another's roles as co-teachers.

Co-Teaching for English Learners, pages 3–11
Copyright © 2020 by Information Age Publishing

Qualitative analysis results from this study suggest that when ESL/ELD teachers frame co-teaching as capacity building, they have the potential to develop relationships that are catalysts for improving instruction for K–5 ELLs in the general education classroom.

BACKGROUND

Based on the review of the literature, co-teachers' perceptions of one another's co-teaching roles can be attributed to district- or school-level factors or to teacher-level factors, as summarized in Figure 1.1. In this conceptual framework, at the district or school level, administrative leadership can help establish clear roles, responsibilities, and expectations, thereby affecting how co-teaching is carried out, and setting the tone for teachers' attitudes and expectations. Administrators can determine logistical supports, such as regularly scheduled planning time and reasonable co-teaching schedules. At the teacher level, preparation for co-teaching, knowledge of the subject matter, and the pressures of one's teaching position can affect how roles are perceived. Furthermore, communication style, teacher compatibility, teaching philosophy, and attitudes towards ELLs have been noted as affecting co-teaching (Davison, 2006; DelliCarpini, 2009; Weiss & Lloyd, 2003).

In the ideal scenario, co-teaching is designed based on students' linguistic and academic needs, the lesson's objectives, the type of activities in the lesson design, and co-teachers' preferences and styles (Cook & Friend, 1995; Dove & Honigsfeld, 2018; Honigsfeld & Dove, 2010). In addition,

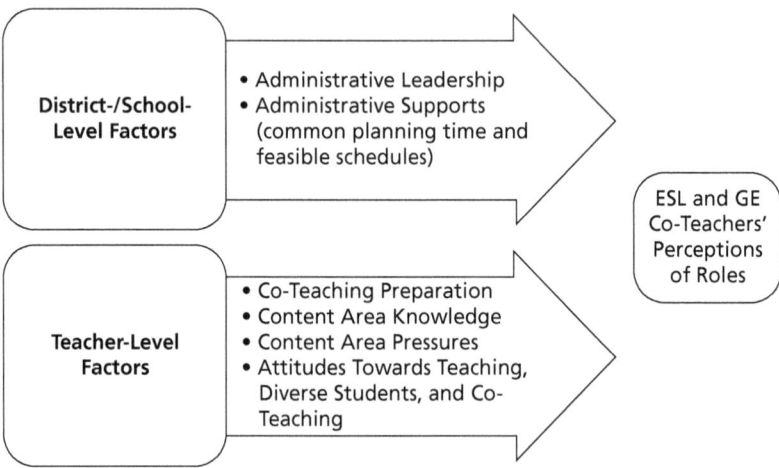

Figure 1.1 Conceptual framework of ESL/ELD and GE co-teachers' perceptions of roles.

co-teaching ideally involves co-planning, co-reflection on student progress, and teacher collaboration at a curricular level. Some co-teachers may share a single classroom all day every day, whereas others may co-teach on only certain days or at certain times.

STUDY CONTEXT AND RESULTS

In the district from which the study sample was drawn, co-teaching started as a small pilot program and expanded incrementally. Now, co-teaching is required for elementary ESL/ELD and general education teachers; no pull-out instruction in which ELLs are removed from their general education classrooms is done. The K–5 teaching team co-taught during regularly scheduled periods. Most general education teachers taught one grade only and co-taught with one or two teachers for less than half of a typical week, whereas most ESL/ELD teachers co-taught five to six different grades with at least five teachers for more than half of a typical week. Almost all respondents had shared planning time once a week. In the section that follows, first-hand accounts from qualitative interviews about co-teachers' perceptions of their roles shine the spotlight on teachers as leaders, who despite logistical challenges, redefine co-teaching as more than sharing teaching responsibilities. Their perceptions frame co-teaching as a larger call to action for teachers to serve as teacher leaders as they develop effective co-teaching relationships that can leave a lasting impact on teacher practice.

Equal Responsibilities or Mainstream/General Education as Primary Instructor?

Overall, the K–5 general education teachers in this study understood that ESL/ELD teachers' co-teaching roles involved using language development expertise and general education teachers' roles used their expertise in teaching academic curricular content. However, some disagreement over specific roles and responsibilities surfaced. For example, 11.5% of ESL/ELD teachers and 22.9% of general education teachers considered *teaching language to the ELLs* in the class *their* responsibility, not the other teacher's.

In addition, equal roles of co-teachers were not a reality, given the ESL/ELD teachers' presence in the classroom for one daily or weekly time block. For instance, one general education teacher, Lisa, did the majority of the planning because she taught the class all week, regardless of the ESL/ELD teacher's presence. She designed the classroom management procedures, created most of the assessments, and communicated with parents, although her ESL/ELD co-teacher shared ideas for classroom management and sometimes did grading. Similarly, Scott, also a general education teacher, called himself the "primary instructor," though he felt co-teaching brought "focus on students who were ELLs, but the ESL/ELD teacher could sometimes give instruction to all students, so the approach would benefit all students."

Olivia was the only ESL/ELD teacher who did not perceive the general education teacher as the primary instructor. She saw the goal of co-teaching as parity between teachers and strived to shift away from teacher-centered instruction towards a different way of teaching that involves two teachers and grouping students. Olivia's perceptions reflected her current context where co-teaching was vastly different from general education teachers' previous approach to instruction. Olivia felt that even introducing the concept of differentiation was a new way of thinking. Given that she sensed resistance to co-teaching from some general education teachers, she seemed to be focused on encouraging teachers to "release control" and be "in a posture for growth" that would allow the ESL/ELD teacher an equal role in the classroom.

General Education Co-Teachers as Resident Experts

The general education teachers tended to consider their knowledge of the academic content of the grade-level curriculum a key feature of their role in the classroom. Both Scott and Lisa expressed confidence in their ability to teach the general education curriculum for their assigned grades, referring to their years of experience teaching the academic content in their respective schools. Lisa used the term "resident expert" in reference to her knowledge of teaching academic content. For example, Scott talked about knowing the science program and the writing program very well, and Lisa indicated that she "can show [the ESL/ELD teacher] the content that we're going to need to present that are within the standards or within the curriculum, or even whatever the program that we're using is presenting, and how it's presenting it."

ESL Co-Teachers as Co-Teaching Coaches and Capacity Builders

Two ESL/ELD teachers, Olivia and Melanie, acknowledged their perceptions of their roles vary either depending on the student's level of need or on the general education teacher with whom they are co-teaching. They each perceived that co-teaching involves multiple purposes that they carry out in their practice. Three themes that emerged in the ESL/ELD teachers' perceptions of their roles are: (a) co-teaching coach/capacity builder,

(b) ESL/ELD specialist, and (c) ELL student and community advocate. As Olivia stated, "Of course it's supporting the ELLs and work you're doing with them directly. But the other component is building the capacity of classroom teachers and helping them have strategies for differentiating needs with a range of English language learners."

Working with multiple general education teachers every week, Melanie and Olivia recognized that working with each teacher is different, depending on personality and teaching style, as well as the extent that they have experience co-teaching. As Olivia stated, "Our co-teaching model is based on the idea that it's professional development to build capacity of the classroom teachers." The perceived goal was to have an effect on instruction, even outside of the time when the ESL/ELD and general education teacher are co-teaching. Melanie felt, "Not only are we the ELA specialists, but all of a sudden, we're the co-teaching specialists as well." She felt like through her co-planning and co-teaching, she was also a coach helping the general education classroom teacher, who was the expert in the content, to become "more secure" in her ESL/ELD strategies and skills.

Both Melanie and Olivia conveyed similar messages about the coaching role they felt responsible to take on when working with general education teachers. In particular, when co-teaching with general education teachers who were unfamiliar with co-teaching or with teaching ELLs, the ESL/ELD teacher was the "introducer" of both the collaborative aspect of co-teaching and the differentiation component. Melanie's approach to starting a relationship involved developing trust as the first step towards building the capacity of the general education teacher:

> It's about building capacity as well, and so for the team to be successful, you need to have a successful partnership, but then—just to get it started, you know, you need to show up when you say you're going to, and follow through with stuff. And then you build that trust, and then you kind of show some of your bag of tricks, and invite that person to try them also, and so it's not just oh, I'm the hoarder of the knowledge. And then the confidence in those skills increases, and therefore, the willingness to co-teach more increases.

Melanie noted that co-teaching is a district policy that has been met with some resistance, so "the only way to get people fully on-board is to show them how positive it can be." In this manner, Melanie felt it was critical to demonstrate respect for the general education teacher's space and adapt to existing systems. In her view, "Who am I to go in there and start changing things? So I need to be the adjustable one, and we'll see how that works, and then we build on it . . . see how the next part works, and then we build on it." For instance, building capacity required explicit conversations asking about the general education teacher's preferences, such as where Melanie should put her coat or set her materials when in the general education classroom. Adapting to the general education teacher's systems involved using the same language that the general education teacher used for classroom systems and implementing those systems as the general education teacher intended. As Olivia described it, "I'm voicing what they are voicing so that we can be united in that." For example, if one general education teacher used a "time out desk," then when in that classroom, the ESL/ELD teacher would also refer to the "time out desk." These actions were seen as trust-building strategies to enable co-teaching. From Melanie and Olivia's perspectives, building general education teachers' openness to co-teaching then lends itself to opening general education teachers' practice to differentiation for ELLs.

ESL/ELD Co-Teachers as Specialists in Language Development

Melanie and Olivia couched their perceptions of their roles in ensuring differentiation for ELLs' needs. Melanie talked about being someone "coming in with a different lens," similar to how Olivia described her role as:

> Providing support for [the general education teachers] to actually look at the language forms and functions that are embedded into that content and how we can extract that into that language objective and frame language so that students are aware of the role that language is playing in their learning and actually have that sort of in front of them in a way that's tangible and understandable.

The ideal result of their capacity building would be to teach *with* the classroom teacher, and to "look at the language components of what we're doing and the objectives around that." As explained by Olivia:

> By and large, most people haven't been trained to teach collaboratively. So a lot of what you have to work towards is beginning to reframe the classroom when there are two teachers. So that's a process in and of itself. And within that, you are helping to frame an understanding of how you scaffold instructions for English language learners.

Both ESL/ELD teachers perceived their co-teaching as an opportunity to affect instruction during the rest of the school day as well, as illustrated in how Melanie described her "agenda":

> Since I'm only in there for what, 35 to 45 minutes a day, you know, the big question is what happens the rest of the time? Do the students still have the support? I do have an agenda, so like when I'm co-planning with teachers or

whatever, sometimes I might suggest—you know, especially if they ask for it, but even when they don't ask for it necessarily, I might suggest hey, you know, I'll have to leave at this point, but maybe they could have some oral rehearsal with a partner.

As emerged in the data, Olivia and Melanie's overarching perception were as ESL/ELD specialists who build capacity in general education, able to affect change even when they were not physically in the classroom doing co-teaching. To them, the co-teaching relationship yielded more than co-operation; in fact, the general education teachers' practices became more responsive to ELLs' needs as a result of co-teaching.

ESL/ELD Co-Teachers as Student and Community Advocates

Melanie and Olivia both expressed their self-perception as advocates for ELL students and for the ELL community. Advocating for ELL students meant ensuring that language supports were present in the general education classroom, even when the ESL/ELD teacher was not, but it also referred to helping general education teachers understand the diverse backgrounds of their students. Furthermore, Melanie and Olivia both described their role in working with parents of ELLs to foster a positive understanding of multilingualism.

Understanding the positive impact that family involvement has on student achievement, Melanie expressed, "That's part of my job, to be the advocate with the ELL community. Anytime that you can bring the parents in really helps bridge some of the divide." She did this by submitting interpreter requests and calling parents whose home language she also speaks. The context for Olivia's co-teaching was an affluent, predominantly White school with a lower incidence of ELLs, where she felt that her advocacy work surrounded building a positive identity for multilingualism and multiculturalism. She has observed families upset that their children were placed in ELL services and Olivia strived to build "a positive identity for the idea of you can actually acknowledge that there is another language and that there is more than one background versus just kind of whitewashing things."

IMPLICATIONS AND RECOMMENDATIONS FOR PRACTICE

In this study, ESL/ELD teachers appeared to be the main messengers about co-teaching to general education teachers, and some self-identified as coaches or capacity builders whose goals included educating teachers about serving ELLs in the general education classroom. The range of perceptions regarding the details of co-teaching is likely due to the uniqueness of co-teaching pairs' working relationships. They may have the freedom to lay out their specific responsibilities depending on logistics, students' needs, or their teaching styles, or the range of perceptions may be due to confusion regarding who is truly responsible for various aspects of general education classroom teaching and how to share them accordingly.

The onus was on ESL/ELD teachers to make entries into the classroom and to coach or persuade general education counterparts to learn about co-teaching. As Honigsfeld and Dove (2010) described, the leadership of ESL/ELD teachers can help shape inclusive teaching models. Given that ESL/ELD teachers often do "make the first move" (p. 13) in co-teaching, developing ESL/ELD co-teachers as leaders of co-teaching can facilitate ongoing, effective co-teaching relationships.

Co-Teaching as Teacher Leadership

Although a limitation of this study is that it focuses on co-teacher relationship development, but not student achievement, the findings suggest that co-teaching has the potential to improve general education teachers' practices for ELLs. As ESL/ELD co-teachers redefine borders and their identities as leaders or change agents, they can consider how to (a) be proactive in grasping the general education curricula when co-teaching, (b) gently assist teachers in deepening their understanding of ELLs' needs, and (c) embrace the role of co-teaching initiator in many circumstances. On top of that, ESL/ELD teachers are encouraged to conceptualize co-teaching as a leadership opportunity. Their language development expertise, combined with their cultural sensitivity and advocacy, have the potential to change mindsets and practices. Conversely, general education teachers may consider (a) actively increasing their knowledge of language development for ELs, (b) offering curricular resources to assist ESL/ELD teachers with content knowledge gaps, and (c) shifting away from a single teacher mentality. Establishing clear roles and responsibilities is important for co-teaching (Arkoudis, 2006; Dove & Honigsfeld, 2018; Honigsfeld & Dove, 2010).

When leading a transition to co-teaching, policies must be established and disseminated in a coherent, strategic manner. Administrators need to coordinate across departments to ensure consistent messaging and joint training on co-teaching implementation and provide joint professional development for co-teaching pairs that includes:

- focusing on teaching academic content and on teaching ELLs,
- observing effective co-teaching, and
- being observed and receiving feedback.

School administrators can facilitate co-teaching efficacy by creating manageable co-teaching schedules and common planning time. Co-teaching should not be used to stretch ESL/ELD teachers to serve larger "caseloads." Limiting the number of co-teaching partners per person can facilitate substantive co-planning, co-teaching, and reflection on students' learning and how to tailor instruction to their needs. It is critical to ensure that both general education and ESL/ELD co-teachers are informed of and supported in the expectations of the co-teaching practice. In the long run, administrators are encouraged to make the most of co-teaching by supporting ESL/ELD teachers as leaders and capacity builders, in order to support improved outcomes for students.

REFERENCES

Arkoudis, S. (2006). Negotiating the rough ground between ESL and mainstream teachers. *The International Journal of Bilingual Education and Bilingualism, 9*(4), 415–433.

Cook, L., & Friend, M. (1995). Co-teaching: Guidelines for creating effective practices. *Focus on Exceptional Children, 28*(3), 1–16.

Davison, C. (2006). Collaboration between ESL and content teachers: How do we know when we are doing it right? *The International Journal of Bilingual Education and Bilingualism, 9*(4), 454–475.

DelliCarpini, M. (2009). Dialogues across disciplines: preparing English as a second language teachers for interdisciplinary collaboration. *Current Issues in Education, 11*(2). Retrieved from https://cie.asu.edu/ojs/index.php/cieatasu/article/view/1573

Dove, M. G., & Honigsfeld, A. (2018). *Co-teaching for English learners: A guide to collaborative planning, assessment, and reflection.* Thousand Oaks, CA: Corwin.

Honigsfeld, A., & Dove, M. G. (2010). *Collaboration and co-teaching: Strategies for English learners.* Thousand Oaks, CA: Corwin Press.

Lortie, D. (1975). *Schoolteacher.* Chicago, IL: The University of Chicago Press.

Weiss, M. P., & Lloyd, J. W. (2003). Conditions for co-teaching: Lessons from a case study. *Teacher Education and SPED, 26*(1), 27–41.

CHAPTER 2

"THEY SEE US TOGETHER"

Collaborative Activity in a Math Middle School Classroom

Amanda Giles
ESL Teacher

Bedrettin Yazan
University of Texas at San Antonio

I think it builds a relationship between the teachers and lets the kids know that we're working together too, that they see us together and not as two separate people or subjects or whatever. It's one big system for them.
—Interview 2, April 6, 2017

Given the necessity for collaboration as a means to increase teacher learning for favorable student outcomes, it is crucial to explore how content and English as a second language (ESL) teachers collaborate to meet the needs of English learners (ELs) in the secondary classroom (Dove & Honigsfeld, 2018; Giles, & Yazan, 2019). Departmental structures in secondary schools can further lead to the ESL teacher's relegated role as an assistant rather than a subject-specific teacher (Arkoudis, 2003; Pawan & Craig, 2011). Different schedules and inconsistent administrative support

Co-Teaching for English Learners, pages 13–24
Copyright © 2020 by Information Age Publishing
All rights of reproduction in any form reserved.

13

can also make collaboration challenging (Dove & Honigsfeld, 2018; Giles, 2018; Giles & Yazan, 2019; Peercy, Ditter, & DeStefano, 2016). As such, by using Engeström's (2001) cultural historical activity theory (CHAT), this study posed the following question: "How does an ESL teacher engage in collaborative activity with a math teacher to co-plan and co-teach lessons in a seventh grade math classroom in a suburban middle school in the southeastern United States?"

TEACHER LEARNING IN ACTIVITY

From a sociocultural perspective, scholars conceive teacher learning as "a long-term, complex, developmental process that is the result of participation in the social practices and contexts associated with learning and teaching" (Johnson, 2009, p. 10). In this lifelong and ever-changing process, teachers learn to teach as they challenge, reconsider, and reshape their beliefs, values, and teaching practices along with their "understandings of themselves as teachers, of their students, and of the activities of teaching" (Johnson & Golombek, 2003, p. 730). Teacher interactions are a critical component in this learning process by which teachers specifically learn through collaborative social interactions with their colleagues in job-embedded contexts (Darling-Hammond, Hyler, Gardner, & Espinoza, 2017).

Sociocultural-oriented research on teacher learning utilized Engeström's (2001) model to examine how teacher learning occurs through the connectivity and interrelatedness of various factors of individuals working in activity. His model includes the following components: subject, artefacts/tools, division of labor, object, rules, school community, and outcome. *Subjects* are agentive individuals who use culturally mediated *tools* and negotiate a *division of labor* to work together toward a specific *object* within a sociocultural *community* governed by *rules*; their involvement in activity ultimately transforms into a certain *outcome* that includes learning. Engeström (2001) extended this model to include multi-voicedness and contradictions. Multi-voiced subjects underscore how individuals have distinct positions and interests that influence their involvement in activity. Contradictions are "structural tensions within and between activity" (Engeström, 2001, p. 137) that are necessary and must be resolved for learning and development to take place.

When we applied CHAT to this study, we considered the subjects as the ESL and seventh grade math teachers with different positions and interests in the school community. The division of labor delineates each teacher's roles and responsibilities regarding their disciplinary positions. The object is to co-plan and co-teach two math lessons based on the content and language standards. The community is the larger context that includes other teachers, administrators, and school district personnel. The rules are the normative practices and the school, district, state, and federal regulations. The activity's outcome results in the math and ESL teachers' learning how to engage in collaboration to provide access to academic language and math content for ELs in the secondary content classroom.

METHODOLOGY

The study took place at a middle school that had approximately 800 students with 11% of its students classified as ELs. Students spoke many additional languages with Spanish being the most frequent additional language spoken. In this particular seventh grade math classroom, Lily,[1] the math teacher, taught around 24 students including four ELs and one student who recently exited the ESL program. Three students considered Spanish as their home language, and one student considered Vietnamese as his home language. Three of the four students also required special education services. This collaboration emerged at the beginning of the 2016–2017 school year when Amanda, the ESL teacher, delivered student information to Lily before school began. During this meeting, Lily expressed concern over working with ELs in her classes, and Amanda offered co-planning and co-teaching as a potential solution. Amanda arranged her schedule so that she could co-teach with Lily 2 days each week and continued to co-teach with Lily throughout the 2016–2017 school year.

Participants

Amanda worked as an ESL and Spanish teacher at this middle school. She began her teaching career at this school as a language arts (LA) teacher and transitioned into the role of ESL/Spanish teacher during her sixth year of teaching. She had been teaching ESL/Spanish for 4 years and had 9 years total teaching experience. Lily was one of the three seventh grade math teachers and had been at this school for 5 years. She had 21 years of total teaching experience and had taught both middle and high school throughout her teaching career. She spoke English only. While she previously taught both middle and high school, she reported that she had "a heart for middle school" (Interview 1, February 15, 2017).

Data Collection and Analysis

We collected data through three semi-structured interviews, three video recorded collaborative planning sessions, two reflective journals, and field notes to examine teacher learning in a collaborative activity that focused on enhancing student outcomes in this single qualitative case study. We coded the data using in vivo codes to emphasize the participants' own wording and descriptive codes to analyze the topic or events in the sentence or passage during the first cycle of coding (Saldaña, 2013). We categorized these initial codes using the following six categories from CHAT: subject, school community, rules, contradictions, tools, and outcome. After the first coding cycle, we categorized the initial codes by "theming the data" (Saladaña, 2013, p. 175). This analysis extended the categories into theme statements which made meaning of the data; the theme statements were our findings, which we explain in the next section.

FINDINGS

The CHAT framework allowed us to examine how subjects learn as they navigate contradictions through their engagement in activity. We found that contradictions arose from Lily's assumption that ELs were similar to other struggling students. This contradiction was resolved due to Amanda's knowledge of math content, her experience as a general education teacher, and her agency in this math classroom and the larger school community. Lily gradually developed an understanding that ELs have unique learning needs and re-conceptualized the ESL teacher's role. Amanda additionally grasped a better understanding of initiating and sustaining ESL and content teachers' collaborative efforts. In the following, we will discuss how teachers learned to (a) navigate the collaborative activity's contradictions, (b) understand ELs' unique learning needs, and (c) re-contextualize the ESL teacher's role at this school. After an explanation of teacher learning in activity, we will discuss how the teachers believe their collaboration is impacting ELs' learning.

"Just Like Any Struggling Student": The Contradiction

Contradictions arose as Lily believed that ELs' learning needs were the same as any struggling student. In an interview, Lily categorized ELs as struggling students:

> **Amanda:** How do you plan lessons specifically for ELs?
> **Lily:** Honestly, this year I don't... I plan more for learners that struggle rather than particularly ESL or LD. I kind of think of it a little more broad.

Amanda: Okay. So let's talk about this then. What would be a different accommodation for an EL student versus a struggling student? Do you see a difference? Talk to me a little bit about that.

Lily: The only difference I see is this year I have students that struggle a lot more than in the past. Those strugglers are also ELs (Interview 2, April 6, 2017).

Because Lily categorized ELs in one "broad" category of struggling students, she had a difficult time planning lessons with ELs in mind. Throughout the collaborative activity, this broad categorization inhibited her ability to understand how academic language is more challenging for ELs and then plan accommodations accordingly. She identified the ELs in her class as "high functioning," implying that students understood conversational English. She believed they did not need specific language accommodations since they understood conversational English. Lily's misunderstanding of the difference between academic and conversational English yielded a twofold contradiction during the activity. First, Lily was unable to identify Amanda's vocabulary suggestions as specific language accommodations. After the first collaborative cycle, Lily concluded that she "didn't learn anything directly ESL because our ESL kids are pretty high functioning, so there were not ESL strategies [in the lesson]" (Reflective Journal, April 6, 2017). Second, this contradiction led to an unequal division of labor where Amanda became the lead teacher in designing and teaching the lesson. Lily acknowledged these unequal roles as she admitted that Amanda was "the head-lead teacher," and she "did it all" (Interview 2, April 2017).

Thus, Amanda's math content knowledge, classroom management, and understanding of the general classroom's structure resolved this contradiction. Lily explained Amanda's contribution in the collaborative activity:

Lily: Your knowledge of classroom management, organization, and the math itself. It's nice that you know math. I don't have to worry about teaching you the math, or you know, that kind of thing, so that's definitely a benefit (Interview 2, April 6, 2017).

Lily's acknowledgement that Amanda's content knowledge and "classroom management" were "a benefit" indicated her satisfaction to the point where she did not feel as if she had to intervene to ensure that the students understood the math concept during class. As such, Amanda's math content knowledge, classroom management, and organization sustained the collaborative activity, which led to Lily's gradual understanding of ELs' unique learning needs and the ESL teacher's reconceptualized role in the school community.

"More Aware of Individual Language Learning": The Math Teacher's Learning

By the end of the second collaborative cycle, Lily began to articulate an understanding of ELs' individual language needs in the math classroom. During an interview, Lily acknowledged her own learning by giving an example of the challenges that a "high functioning" student faced in her class:

> **Lily:** It's made me more aware of their individual language learning whether it be students who speak the same language or different languages.
> **Amanda:** Okay, you talked about their individual needs. Can you give me an example of what an individual need would be?
> **Lily:** [The student's name] from Russia seems to need more of the American terms that we use that aren't really words . . . or good words . . . So you can't treat them all the same especially with different language backgrounds (Interview 3, May 22, 2017).

Lily's awareness of ELs' language needs and her realization that ELs cannot receive the same treatment suggested that she was beginning to distinguish unique differences in students. Acknowledgement of individual learning needs is the first step in being able to identify and then plan to accommodate to better serve ELs. Her words (e.g., "more aware," "student needs more American terms," "you can't treat them all the same") also were noticeably different in this interview than in the previous example where she did not think she learned strategies for ELs. This difference indicated Lily's learning progress that one suspects will continue to grow through her continued collaborative partnership with the ESL teacher. She admitted that she learned more about working with diverse students and credited this learning to working in collaboration.

"I Know That You Know the Kids": The ESL Teacher's Re-Conceptualized Role

In addition to learning about students' diverse needs, Lily also changed her perception about the ESL teacher's role at school. Prior to this collaborative experience, Lily cited infrequent interactions with the former ESL teacher. She explained that she met the former ESL teacher at the beginning of the year and talked briefly with her, but because of these limited interactions, she did not have expectations regarding the ESL teacher's responsibilities in helping ELs learn English and/or collaborating with content teachers. Due to her participation in this collaborative experience, she conceptualized the role of the ESL teacher differently. In an interview, Lily explained:

> **Lily:** Now that I have a comparison, [my perception of the ESL teacher] would be a little different... It just wasn't content related [before], and I didn't know to expect or not to expect that.
>
> **Amanda:** So now your ideal role of the ESL teacher would be what?
>
> **Lily:** Ideally, what it is now, for sure. You...just having you come in the classroom is huge because I know that you know the kids, and I feel comfortable coming to you about the content as well as just the child (Interview 2, April 6, 2017).

Lily's perception of the ESL teacher now is someone who has content knowledge and an understanding of ELs' language needs. This magnified Lily's comfort in coming to Amanda to discuss the students' needs, which strengthened the teachers' partnership and ability to collaborate.

Lily also mentioned Amanda's comfort in knowing math and teaching students, which contributed to this reconceptualization. Lily described Amanda's contribution to the co-teaching session:

> **Lily:** You were the main teacher even though it was a co-teaching session. You were the teacher for that day so to speak...the head lead teacher might be a better word I don't know. And you being comfortable with it... the content area and the kids and taking that role, and that it's okay to just bounce back and forth. And not have to feel like you have to ask me, "Is this okay to show them this way?" No, whatever...I mean it's okay. Just do it (Interview 2, April 6, 2017).

Lily perceived that Amanda was comfortable in her role as the lead teacher, and Lily also appreciated a co-teacher who did what she thought was best without asking permission. Amanda's willingness to lead showed her agency in the classroom, contributing to a fruitful collaborative experience. Lily also discussed her thoughts of the potential challenges in co-planning and co-teaching. In this discussion, she explained another instance where Amanda answered a student's question during an impromptu co-teaching session without waiting for Lily's approval which further highlighted Amanda's agency:

> **Lily:** The planning time. The common planning time [can be a potential challenge]. You know ideally, you would co-teach every day. Or, just when you were in here yesterday, and we didn't really plan anything, and the kids had a question, and you just went to the board and showed something, and that was great. And I think that that's another benefit (Interview 2, April 6, 2017).

Lily acknowledged that planning time could be a potential contradiction in collaborating to meet ELs' needs. However, Lily gave an example of Amanda's agency as a way to overcome collaborative challenges. Her example suggested that the ESL and content teachers may not have to meet to discuss each lesson plan fully if the ESL teacher exhibits agency to help ELs and all students when needed. Lily ultimately indicated that this agency is another benefit in this collaborative experience.

The Impact of Teacher Collaboration on ELs

The math and ESL teachers believed that the ELs began to see the math and ESL teachers working together as a unified team with the collective purpose of helping students learn because of their involvement in collaborative activity. Lily describes the ELs' responses to their collaboration, saying,

> **Lily:** I think it builds a relationship between the teachers and lets the kids know that we're working together too, that they see us together and not as two separate people or subjects or whatever. It's one big system for them (Interview 2, April 6, 2017).

During the collaborative activity, Lily's perception was that the ELs did not see Lily and Amanda as the math and ESL teacher separately. Instead, she thought the students believed both teachers were working together for the shared purpose of student learning. Lily's use of the word, "system," additionally indicates that she saw this collaboration as a model in which both teachers were equally dedicated to student learning.

After the first co-teaching cycle during the second interview, Lily additionally commented that the students benefited from seeing another teacher instructing students with the math teacher's support. She explained:

Lily: I didn't have to leave a kid, or I could still just intermingle with the kids. And for them to know that I'm comfortable with you teaching it, and then I'm not interrupting you or saying anything. I think that's good for them to see as well (Interview 2, April 6, 2017).

Lily's description specifically addressed how students benefited during the co-teaching session because they viewed another teacher (e.g., the ESL teacher) as willing and capable of teaching math concepts. Lily also stated that with two co-teachers, she could help students and spend as much time as needed with them because her co-teacher provided the daily instruction. This co-teaching scenario afforded her the opportunity to provide "instant feedback" (Dove & Honigsfeld, 2018, p. 17) to students because she trusted Amanda to teach math.

Amanda additionally observed that the ELs participated more during the co-teaching sessions. Due to her role as the "main teacher," she observed that the ELs answered more questions during the whole-group part of the teaching session because she looked for ways to engage them in the discussion and allowed them to answer questions to highlight ELs' strengths. For example, in a co-teaching session about central tendency, Amanda reviewed mean, median, mode, and range separately and used scaffolded instruction to emphasize key concepts. In her review of mean, she reminded students that the mean is the average of the data set, and then she worked an example on the whiteboard. After modeling how to find the mean, she selected another example and chose an EL to work the problem with her assistance. This student recited the steps in finding the mean and found the mean as Amanda worked the problem out on the board. Lily and Amanda circulated the room when students worked independently, and Amanda observed that ELs were able to calculate the mean in a data set. This example shows ELs' increased participation and enhanced learning outcomes when two teachers are engaging in collaboration.

DISCUSSION

Sociocultural learning theory purports that teachers' learning extends beyond initial teacher preparation to include the ways in which teachers negotiate and mediate meanings in educational activities. Through this negotiation and mediation, they come across contradictions whose resolution leads them to revised or renewed understandings of their teaching roles, student perceptions, and professional responsibilities (Johnson, 2009). Teachers' agency, commitment, and intentionality direct the ways in which they grapple with these contradictions (Giles, 2018). With these theoretical considerations, this study stands out as an important examination of teacher learning through two teachers' engagement in collaborative planning and teaching and contributes to two main conversations in prior research: (a) the negotiation of meanings in teacher collaboration and (b) teacher agency in collaboration.

Negotiation of Meanings in Teacher Collaboration

The findings attend to the complexities and challenges involved in teacher collaboration (Dove & Honigsfeld, 2018; Giles & Yazan, 2019; Peercy, Martin-Beltrán, Yazan, & DeStefano, 2017). Teachers need to overcome various contradictions when engaging in effective and sustainable collaboration that is focused on improving ELs' learning outcomes (Giles, 2018). Having distinct positions and interests, the two subjects had to confront contradictions, specifically regarding the object and the division of labor in the activity system of teacher collaboration. To explicate, throughout their collaborative interactions, Lily and Amanda negotiated ELs' academic needs and how to best serve them in the math content classroom, which helped Lily better understand the object. They engaged in a mediational process in which they had to agree upon meanings of who ELs are and what they need. A similar mediational process occurred when they negotiated meanings about the ESL teacher's roles, responsibilities, and capabilities which are socially, culturally, and historically situated in the school context. In both cases, the meaning negotiations and mediations are part of the resolution and thereby, indicative of the development and transformation taking place in the activity system.

The ESL Teacher's Agency

The study's findings also lead us to argue that teacher agency is a key component in the initiation and sustenance of teacher collaboration (Giles & Yazan, 2019). In the case we investigated, Amanda challenged the earlier ESL teacher's practices about how to serve ELs in the school. That is, collaboration between ESL and content teachers was unknown to the content teachers since they had never been asked to do so before, and this became a norm in teachers' understanding. Therefore, Amanda had to assert her agency to approach Lily and ask about potential collaboration to enhance ELs' learning outcomes in math classes, and Lily's positive response made the collaboration possible in the first place. Breaking the mold, Amanda had to introduce a teacher/teaching practice that was completely different from any content teachers' expectations of the ESL teacher in this school.

In this endeavor, Amanda's agency was fueled by her social capital, that is, her strong relationships with content teachers and her experience as an established teacher at this school.

CONCLUSION AND RECOMMENDATIONS

The population of ELs in U.S. schools continues to grow at unprecedented rates, and the necessity to collaborate to meet ELs' needs is needed to effect positive and equitable educational opportunities for ELs (Giles & Yazan, 2019; Peercy, DeStefano, Yazan, & Martin-Beltrán, 2016). As such, administrators need to reconceptualize the potential for teacher learning through collaborative efforts. Content teachers additionally need assistance in identifying and providing language accommodations for ELs. ESL teachers likewise should seek to understand content teachers' needs, specifically addressing their desire for the ESL teacher's content knowledge. ESL teachers also need opportunities to exercise their agency in the content classroom and broader school community to best serve ELs' needs in a particular school.

Therefore, a reconceptualization of the division of labor is needed that includes challenging traditional notions of ESL and content teachers' expertise in secondary schools. This will also include a shared responsibility of ELs' education by the entire school community, such as teachers and administrators with power and resources to sustain collaborative efforts for the equitable education of ELs. This reconceptualization can be achieved through:

- the increased awareness of content teachers on ELs' language and academic needs;
- opportunities for the ESL teacher to learn content knowledge and exercise his/her agency in the content classroom and school; and
- more collaborative partnerships and co-teaching experiences where ESL and content teachers work together to teach ELs language and content.

IMPLICATIONS FOR FUTURE RESEARCH

The potential for teacher learning and positive student outcomes through collaborative efforts in secondary classrooms warrants further examination. In order to provide for this nuanced understanding, future researchers might (a) investigate how job-embedded professional development opportunities lead to teacher learning and positive student outcomes, (b) extend this investigation to scrutinize teacher learning in collaborative efforts across additional content areas (e.g., language arts, science, and social studies) in secondary schools, and (c) examine how the ESL teacher exercises her agency to redefine this teaching role in secondary schools.

NOTE

1. All names are pseudonyms except Amanda, who is this chapter's first author. The Institutional Review Board granted research approval (Reference #17-OR-002). All participants voluntarily agreed to participate in this study by signing an informed consent form.

REFERENCES

Arkoudis, S. (2003). Teaching English as a second language in science classes: Incommensurate epistemologies? *Language and Education, 17*(3), 161–173.

Darling-Hammond, L., Hyler, M. E., Gardner, M., & Espinoza, D. (2017). *Effective teacher professional development.* Palo Alto, CA: Learning Policy Institute.

Dove, M. G., & Honigsfeld, A. (2018). *Co-teaching for English learners: A guide to collaborative planning, assessment, and reflection.* Thousand Oaks, CA: Corwin.

Engeström, Y. (2001). Expansive learning at work: Toward an activity theoretical reconceptualization. *Journal of Education and Work, 14*(1), 133–156.

Giles, A. (2018). Navigating the contradictions: An ESL teacher's professional self-development. *TESL Canada Journal. 35*(2), 104–127.

Giles, A., & Yazan, B. (2019). ESL and content area teachers' collaboration. *Indonesian Journal of English Language Teaching, 14*(1), 1–18.

Johnson, K. E. (2009). *Second language teacher education: A sociocultural perspective.* New York, NY: Routledge.

Johnson, K. E., & Golombek, P. R. (2003). "Seeing" teacher learning. *TESOL Quarterly, 37*(4), 729–737.

Pawan, F., & Craig, D. A. (2011). ESL and content area teacher responses to discussions on English language learner instruction. *TESOL Journal, 2*(3), 293–311.

Peercy, M. M., DeStefano, M., Yazan, B., & Martin-Beltrán, M. (2016). "She's my right hand...she's always there": Teacher collaboration for linguistically diverse students' equitable access to curriculum. In J. C. Richards & K. Zenkov (Eds.), *Social justice, the Common Core, and closing the instructional gap: Empowering diverse learners and their teachers* (pp. 39–56). Charlotte, NC: Information Age.

Peercy, M. M., Ditter, M., & DeStefano, M. (2016). "We need more consistency": Negotiating the division of labor in ESOL–mainstream teacher collaboration. *TESOL Journal, 8*(1), 215–239.

Peercy, M. M., Martin-Beltrán, M., Yazan, B., & DeStefano, M. (2017). "Jump in any time": How teacher struggle with curricular reform generates opportunities for teacher learning. *Action in Teacher Education, 39*(2), 203–217.

Saldaña, J. (2013). *The coding manual for qualitative researchers.* Thousand Oaks, CA: SAGE.

CHAPTER 3

"THEY SEE ME AS A REAL TEACHER NOW"

ESL Teacher Identity in Collaborative Contexts

Greg McClure
Appalachian State University

I began my career in education as an English as a second language (ESL) teacher in the mid-1990s in North Carolina, and I can relate to the idea of wanting to be treated "like a real teacher." I had a teaching license and a master's degree, but my "classroom" had four wheels instead of walls and was jokingly referred to as the "language buggy." The language buggy housed all the essentials for a traveling ESL teacher: bilingual dictionaries, CD player, crates of pens, markers, and other art supplies, as well as tissues, water bottles, my lunch box, and other personal items. I was not completely homeless though; each period I relocated to a different space, taking advantage of colleagues who would willingly give up their classroom during their planning period. While my knowledge about language pedagogy and second language acquisition were appreciated, when it came to physical

Co-Teaching for English Learners, pages 25–32
Copyright © 2020 by Information Age Publishing

resources and professional credibility, ESL was peripheral. My colleagues valued me—especially when they needed someone to translate—but, as evidenced by my four-wheeled classroom, I was not an equal.

The marginalization of ESL teachers and their struggle for professional legitimation is not a new phenomenon. Even in 2019, it is not uncommon to encounter ESL teachers conducting their important work in repurposed storage rooms or in some small corner of a school's media center. However, this situation deserves renewed attention as teaching contexts have shifted towards more collaborative approaches, and ESL teachers find themselves working alongside classroom teachers in mainstream classrooms.

English learners (ELs) continue to represent one of the fastest growing segments of the K–12 student population in the United States. In North Carolina for example, the EL population increased by 395% between 1990 and 2010 (Pandya, Batalova, & McHugh, 2011). In recent years, many school districts in the state have attempted to improve educational outcomes for ELs by implementing collaborative instructional models like co-teaching. Co-teaching for ELs pairs the general education teacher with an ESL teacher in order to provide instructional support that focuses on language development for ELs in the mainstream setting (Honigsfeld & Dove, 2010). Co-teaching research has demonstrated how the practice promotes EL engagement in the mainstream classroom (Dove & Honigsfeld, 2010) and facilitates prolonged teacher learning and professional development (Peercy & Martin-Beltran, 2012). These studies illustrate how co-teaching can foster collaborative learning environments for students as well as teachers engaged in the model.

Scholars have also examined some of the challenges associated with co-teaching. At its heart, co-teaching is a relationship between two professionals, and as such, requires an investment of time and resources. Of course, these may not always be present. In an interview study of a kindergarten co-teaching partnership, Peercy, Ditter, and Destefano (2017) documented the importance of having an organizational structure and routines in co-teaching. Although the teachers in the study were committed to the partnership, the lack of a routine and consistent schedule made it difficult for the partnership to flourish.

Other challenges to co-teaching arise when co-teachers are afforded different levels of power and status in the school setting. McClure and Cahnmann-Taylor (2010) noted that when dominant attitudes in schools and classrooms privilege English at the expense of Spanish and other languages, ESL teachers (and students) are positioned as peripheral and less important. Learning mainstream content takes precedence over navigating language and culture. When this occurs, co-teaching relationships can suffer because this privileging of content over language challenges core aspects of the ESL teacher identity. Historically, as ESL teachers worked in isolated pullout settings, this marginalized positioning was visible and obvious. ESL teachers could be seen setting up shop in libraries and alcoves, or, in my case, pushing the language buggy from room to room throughout the day. Co-teaching brings ESL teachers out of the hallway and into the mainstream classroom. This shift in teaching practice creates opportunities for collaborative partnerships, but it also disrupts how, when, and where ESL teachers conduct their work. Therefore, in what ways has this emphasis on collaborative teaching practices affected how ESL teachers understand their professional roles and identities?

CO-TEACHING IN NORTH CAROLINA

In this chapter, I explore this question from the context of North Carolina, a state that continues to invest in co-teaching for ELs. To get a broad sense of co-teaching in North Carolina, I conducted an online survey of ESL and classroom teachers who were working in co-teaching models. Over a 3-week period, 234 ESL teachers and 202 classroom teachers participated in the survey. The survey data provided a broad view of co-teaching in North Carolina, but in order to gain a deeper understanding of how co-teaching shapes the way ESL teachers think about their professional identities, I conducted in-depth interviews with eight ESL teachers at eight separate schools in North Carolina. All eight participants identified as female, and evenly represented urban and rural schools. Table 3.1 provides further descriptive data on the participants.

The interviews occurred during a 2-day visit to each school site. Day 1 of each visit included a tour of the school, informal meetings with the principal and co-teachers, and a formal one-on-one interview with the ESL

TABLE 3.1 Interview Participants						
Pseudonym	Race/ Ethnicity	Years Teaching	Years Co-Teaching	Languages	Grades	Subject
Ana	African American	>3	2	English, Spanish	3–5	Math/Sci
Elena	Mixed	>10	1	English, Spanish	K, 2, 5	ELA
Harmon	White	>3	>3	English, Spanish	6–8	ELA/Math
Magda	White	>10	>3	English, Spanish	4–5	ELA/Math
Marta	Latina	>3	2	English, French, Spanish	K–2	ELA/Math
Reese	White	>10	2	English	K–3	ELA/Math
Sara	Latina	>10	>3	English, Spanish	2–3	ELA
Talia	White	>10	>3	English	K–5	ELA

teacher. During the second day of each visit, I shadowed the ESL teacher throughout the school day, taking extensive field notes on the range of activities the ESL co-teachers experienced in a typical school day. Each of the teachers described unique co-teaching experiences due to a variety of factors; however, three major themes were evident across all interviews: ESL teachers worked as diplomats; they felt their core focus shift from teaching language to teaching content, and co-teaching provided a sense of professional validation. Below I elaborate on each of these themes, highlighting individual experiences from the participating teachers.

Sure, I Can Do That: ESL Diplomacy

Like all teachers, ESL teachers are adept at tackling a wide range of tasks and roles. I recall from my own years of teaching ESL how I frequently morphed from being a teacher to being an advocate, translator, and cultural broker, often all in the same school day. These are day-to-day concerns that many teachers must deal with; however, ESL teachers also often find themselves at the center of charged sociopolitical issues in their schools and communities. For example, it is not uncommon for ESL teachers to be actively working with immigrant and refugee children in a community that is openly resistant to immigrants and refugees. In fact, many ESL teachers are immigrants themselves. Navigating these issues is challenging work, particularly as local and national attitudes towards language diversity, immigration, and refugee concerns have become less tolerant. While these sociopolitical tensions represent broader concerns, ESL teachers in collaborative contexts are also often faced with the challenge of advocating for ELs while simultaneously working to maintain a positive work environment with colleagues. Navigating these tensions and challenges requires a unique skill set, what I call here ESL diplomacy. ESL diplomacy refers to the ways that ESL teachers strategically balance the array of competing and conflicting expectations placed on them in order to achieve the best outcomes for the ELs they serve.

The most common way that participants engaged in ESL diplomacy was by making compromises and relinquishing some of their instructional priorities in order to "keep the peace," as Sara put it. Sara is an ESL teacher who identifies as a bilingual immigrant from Mexico; she had been co-teaching in the same rural elementary school for 4 years. She enjoyed co-teaching and described her relationship with her co-teacher as "very strong and communicative," but like all relationships, it had its struggles. She recounted a recent lesson when she felt forced to make some concessions for her co-teacher:

> I came into the classroom, and it was clear that she wasn't ready or prepared to do what we had discussed. She avoided making eye contact and kept plow-

ing ahead with her lesson. I gave it a few minutes, thinking, "We'll transition," but it never came. Now what am I supposed to do with that? I'm prepared with materials and a plan that we discussed. So, I just rolled with it. That's happened before, and I know it'll happen again. Most of the time, I'll just try to do whatever she needs, you know, to help the kids.

When I asked how she felt about this, Sara acknowledged that it frustrated her, and she felt that it disregarded her expertise; she said she "felt like a tutor." However, she was clear on her motives, adding, "I know the most important resource for those kids [ELs] is that we [co-teachers] have a good working relationship. If we're on good terms, then I have better access. There's no pullout anymore." Here, Sara reveals how she is willing to strategically compromise in order to maintain standing with her co-teacher. Further, she recognized that without the opportunity to serve ELs in pullout, that she was trapped in a sense, and worked to make sure that her co-teaching environment ran smoothly. This act of diplomacy was a calculated one, and other ESL teachers like Reese, took a similar stance. When talking about what she perceived as a lack of time to focus on language, Reese said, "I choose my battles. I can't have her [co-teacher] upset with me; then we don't work. But I have my limits, and I'll only bend so far before the tiger comes out to protect these kids!" Reese was laughing loudly as she said this, and further explained that she and her co-teacher enjoyed a great working relationship. She made it clear that she was willing to do what was necessary to ensure a positive co-teaching partnership. However, like Sara and others, Reese also indicated that she "felt guilty, or sometimes like an aide," when she conceded focusing on language.

But What About Language?

ESL teachers interviewed in this study felt that co-teaching had shifted the focus of their work from teaching language to teaching content. All of the teachers indicated that the nature of their work—what they actually *did*—was quite different in mainstream classrooms compared to the pullout settings in which they were used to working. While they continued to work with ELs and still supported language learning, the emphasis was clearly on teaching grade level content. Ana, who was in her second year of co-teaching, struggled with this shift. She had worked for 6 years in the same rural school and demonstrated great pride in being the only bilingual professional at the school. For her, the changes to her work as a result of co-teaching had a significant impact on her professional identity. It fundamentally changed how she viewed her teacher self. During her interview, she shared the following:

> There's lots of times when I don't even feel like an ESL teacher anymore, just another body in there to push the content... Inclusion is really great sometimes because I can support their classroom learning, but my real strengths are in language development. Lots of times I feel like I need more time to focus on language and even encourage the kids to use their Spanish too.

Other teachers I interviewed also mourned this loss of emphasis on language development. Harmon co-taught English language arts and math in middle school. When I observed her co-teaching during a 6th-grade math lesson, the pair seemed to have a strong rapport with one another, sharing instructional space at the front of the room and taking turns leading instructional sequences. However, although I was only able to observe one lesson, it was difficult to discern if/when Harmon's expertise in language development was utilized. During her interview, she echoed Ana's comments regarding her own identity, as well as concerns about teaching content:

> I've changed for sure. I'm not concentrating so much on language understanding. I'm placing more emphasis on just getting through content. This has helped my students understand their classroom world, but at what cost? I don't have the time and space to promote language anymore—it's all content, all the time and I think my students will suffer in the long run. You know what else, I'm running ragged trying to remake myself into a math teacher.

Ana's and Harmon's comments speak to how ESL teachers' professional identities are closely connected to their expertise regarding language acquisition and pedagogy, but they are also shaped by interactions with other peers (Tsui, 2007). When their skills went underutilized, they experienced a shift in how they viewed themselves as professionals. This was borne out in the statewide survey as well. To the statements, "Co-teaching has changed how I view myself as an ESL teacher," and "Co-teaching has changed my work as an ESL teacher," 81% of ESL teachers either agreed or strongly agreed. Harmon's concern about remaking herself as a math teacher further indicates how the co-teaching context influenced her identity development. Being a language specialist and not a content expert, she expressed feeling intimidated and stressed about having to work in mainstream classrooms.

They See Me as A Real Teacher Now!

While the ESL teachers I interviewed struggled with some of the shifts that occurred from working in co-teaching settings, a majority (six of the eight) of the teachers indicated that co-teaching was validating for them, both in their co-teaching partnerships and in their schools. For some teachers, this validation came from having access to the physical resources previously only available to classroom teachers. Talia and Magda both spoke at length about how co-teaching changed the physical realities of their teaching. Magda had taught ESL pullout for more than 10 years in a variety of temporary settings. She summed up this position, saying, "So this is what it's like—I mean now I've got access to a projector, smart board, computers, even a locking cabinet for my purse!"

Other participants explained that co-teaching provided external validation, as their co-teaching partners witnessed the knowledge and expertise that they brought to their classrooms. Six of the teachers I interviewed described this external validation from co-teaching colleagues as having a significant effect on how they viewed themselves. Elena, who was in her first year of co-teaching in an urban elementary school, shared the following:

> You know at first, it was very intimidating to go in there [a 2nd grade classroom]. I've never taught a whole classroom before, and that's her space. But after, I think, the third or fourth day, she came up to me and said, "You are *amazing*!" She talked about how she really had no idea what ESL teachers did before. I don't know, I think she maybe thought we just translated or something, but it was good to hear that from her. Other teachers too, they see the actual work I do . . . I think one of the best things is that I know they see me as a *real* teacher now, and I don't worry anymore about it being "their space."

CONCLUSION

Teachers' identities are shaped by myriad experiences and factors. Geography, education, gender, and social attitudes—these are but a few of the elements that affect how we move through the world, and importantly, how others receive and treat us. Remembering my days of pushing the language buggy down the hall, I recall how easy it is to second-guess one's professional identity. Like me, many of the ESL teachers I interviewed navigated complicated arrangements regarding physical resources, content curriculum, and other priorities. Having to frequently adjust to changing spaces, partners, or content expectations can affect one's self-confidence. In responding to some of the challenges they faced in co-teaching, the ESL teachers engaged in a range of diplomatic responses in order to maintain positive relationships with their co-teachers. For many, a fractured partnership meant limited access to the ELs they needed to serve. As a result, ESL teachers made compromises in the short term, such as eschewing well-developed lesson plans and doing "whatever the teacher needs." These calculated moves facilitated positive co-teaching partnerships, but they also marginalized ESL teacher knowledge (Harper, de Jong, & Platt, 2008) and affected how ESL teachers felt about themselves as professionals.

On the other hand, we see here how co-teaching can create unique opportunities for ESL teachers to shine in the spotlight on the mainstage of the regular classroom. When this occurs, mainstream colleagues often see, and even acknowledge, the disciplinary expertise that ESL teachers bring to the classroom and school setting. The ESL teachers interviewed here presented a strong, sometimes fierce, dedication to their professional responsibilities of promoting language and academic success for ELs. Their experiences lend further support to the notion that co-teaching is a complex act, one that is shaped by nuances of context, professional knowledge and dispositions, and the social markers that frame one's identities. While much of the literature and professional development on co-teaching focuses on the utilitarian elements of the practice—models of collaboration like team teaching and station teaching, structures for planning, and so on—the findings here suggest that it is equally important to consider the ways co-teaching contexts are implicated in ESL teacher identity development. Finding ways to instill confidence in one's professional role and identity will strengthen efforts to develop strong collaborative instructional approaches for educating ELs.

REFERENCES

Dove, M. G., & Honigsfeld, A. (2010). ESL coteaching and collaboration: Opportunities to develop teacher leadership and enhance student learning. *TESOL Journal, 1*(1), 3–22.

Harper, C. A., de Jong, E. J., & Platt, E. (2008). Marginalizing English as a second language teacher expertise: The exclusionary consequence of No Child Left Behind. *Language Policy, 7*(3), 267–284.

Honigsfeld, A., & Dove, M. G. (2010). *Collaboration and co-teaching: Strategies for English learners.* Thousand Oaks, CA: Corwin.

McClure, G., & Cahnmann-Taylor, M. (2010). Pushing back against push-in: ESOL teacher resistance and the complexities of coteaching. *TESOL Journal, 1*(1), 101–129.

Pandya, C., Batalova, J., & McHugh, M. (2011). *Limited English proficient individuals in the United States: Numbers, share, growth, and linguistic diversity.* Washington, DC: Migration Policy Institute.

Peercy, M. M., Ditter, M., & Destefano, M. (2017). "We need more consistency": Negotiating the division of labor in ESOL–mainstream teacher collaboration. *TESOL Journal, 8*(1), 215–239.

Peercy, M. M., & Martin-Beltran, M. (2012). Envisioning collaboration: Including ESOL students and teachers in the mainstream classroom. *International Journal of Inclusive Education, 16*(7), 657–673.

Tsui, A. (2007). Complexities of identity formation: A narrative inquiry of an EFL teacher. *TESOL Quarterly, 40*(4), 657–680.

CHAPTER 4

EMBEDDED PROFESSIONAL DEVELOPMENT FOR THE COLLABORATIVE WORK OF CONTENT AREA TEACHERS AND TEACHERS OF ENGLISH TO SPEAKERS OF OTHER LANGUAGES

Adam Cooper
Xavier University

Stephen Kroeger
University of Cincinnati

Kelly and Daniel taught 6th grade science to an inclusion English to speakers of other languages (ESOL) class with nearly 44% English learners (EL). The room was composed of a series of group stations. Dispersed among the 27 students in the classroom were 12 ELs. On any given day, students might find

Co-Teaching for English Learners, pages 33–48
Copyright © 2020 by Information Age Publishing
All rights of reproduction in any form reserved.

the stations rearranged to fit a new purpose of the lesson. The stations might line the back edge of the room, serving as a crime lab for small groups, or arranged in the center of the room as tables for a unique vocabulary game.

By helping her EL students, Kelly, the ESOL teacher, also helped native English speakers, fulfilling a reciprocal role with her co-teaching partner, Daniel. Kelly celebrated other accommodations the team implemented in the science classroom, including guided notes and highlighted text. She also played a crucial role in facilitating formative assessments, credited with raising students' scores on summative exams. Kelly described her co-teaching experience as follows: "We help each other around here a lot. I help the gen ed. kids too." Kelly referred to native English-speaking students in general education in order to emphasize her point that all students benefited from the accommodations she helped implement in her content-based ESOL classes.

There was ample evidence that the content teacher, Daniel, fulfilled a reciprocal role, as well. Over 44% of the students enrolled in their inclusion ESOL classes were ELs who required accommodations to make grade level academic content material accessible. This occurred as Daniel assumed responsibilities for some of the accommodation procedures typically assigned to Kelly as the ESOL teacher. As this study began, Daniel already used graphic organizers that he placed in the back of students' binders, often using instructional time to direct students to them. Students recorded their responses to content material with prompts such as, "This reminds me of . . ." and "Draw a picture . . ." Additionally, Daniel increasingly referenced the word wall, which became more of an active part of the class. This also prompted him to use the vocabulary when he was speaking, rather than opting for language that was below grade level.

Despite not having common planning time, this team successfully modified instruction and engaged students in classroom activities. The team consisted of a science teacher, referred to here as Daniel, and his co-teaching partner, referred to as Kelly. Though Daniel possessed the smaller amount of total teaching experience, just 3 years, his pre-teacher training as well as his expertise in grade-level curriculum and content material provided him with invaluable tools for classroom management and for designing meaningful learning opportunities for his students. He was also familiar with action research, and therefore adept at some of the practices employed throughout the planning, action, and reflection cycles that guided professional development activities in this study.

Daniel's co-teaching partner, Kelly, was a TESOL endorsed, Spanish-speaking teacher with experience, practice, and a desire to improve the lives and education of this particular population of students. Since this team lacked common planning time, opportunities for reflection and planning meetings facilitated by the researcher were limited. Kelly and Daniel conducted much of their planning in the halls, at pre-planned lunch meetings, or in the classroom during student learning activities. Each teacher most often participated in reflection meetings with the researcher in isolation from the other member. In this respect, reflection meetings with Kelly resembled one-on-one interviews where the researcher could ask clarifying questions of one person without that person's fear of speaking frankly in front of others.

During these reflection meetings, Kelly would often describe her own background in order to articulate the kinship she felt with the Spanish speakers in this school. It was a kinship grounded in both language and class. The working-class urban fringe culture of the student participants in this study was similar, in her view, to the working-class urban culture of her youth. She used these opportunities to describe her upbringing so that she could also highlight her current role as a mother figure and a champion of bilingual students in her own community. These reflections did much to express her belief in the students' abilities to achieve, though they were often accompanied with lamentations about her students' lack of motivation to achieve in school. Kelly's one-on-one reflection meetings revealed other negative perceptions that would uncover challenges for her co-teaching team.

THE CHALLENGE

Regarding educational opportunities of English learners (ELs), there is a discrepancy between program designs showcased in the professional literature and those actually implemented by school personnel. Much of the large-scale research about bilingual program design favors bilingual enrichment education with opportunities to develop literacy skills in native and second languages (L2). In ideal settings, ELs have options to display competence in cognitively demanding academic settings. In a progression from this ideal toward less effective programs, students receive short-term intensive English instruction at the expense of grade level content courses, transitional bilingual education programs, content-based ESL instruction, or ESL pullout instruction (Collier & Thomas, 2007; Rolstad, Mahoney, & Glass, 2005; Slavin & Cheung, 2005; Willig, 1985). The variation between what is recommended and what is implemented depends on the availability of resources required for any given program design.

Districts with high EL enrollment are better prepared to allocate the training resources necessary to enact the highest quality EL programs (Gandara, Rumberger, Maxwell-Jolly, & Callahan, 2003). In many instances, circumstances place teachers and administrators in a reactionary position. With inadequate resources, they still must respond to the unique needs of a growing number of ELs, oftentimes by turning to prescribed plans that provide easily accessible materials. In the United States, this plan almost invariably includes the Sheltered Instruction Observation Protocol (SIOP; Echevarria, Vogt, & Short, 2017). SIOP is a patented approach to TESOL that has produced numerous texts devoted to providing teachers with printable materials and easy-to-follow instructions (Vogt & Echevarria, 2008). The primary purpose of SIOP is to provide content teachers with the tools to make content material more accessible for ELs in the inclusion classroom. Still, planning teams need additional guidance for schools that choose robust program designs, where ELs are afforded extensive resources, such as state endorsed co-teachers.

This chapter proposes an embedded model of professional development (PD) that provides co-teachers with sustained support to implement data-based instructional planning while capturing evidence from planning meetings and classroom practice for descriptive analysis. This level of support is required for teachers to respond adequately to directives from administrators, engage in co-taught instruction, and meet the unique needs of emerging bilingual students. The embedded PD in this study allowed teachers to sustain and develop research-based teaching strategies for ELs. For novice teachers, this PD addressed an urgent need. For veteran teachers like Kelly, embedded PD also fostered increased support for their emergent bilingual students.

CONTENT-BASED LANGUAGE LEARNING RESEARCH

Content-based language learning (CBLL), in its broadest sense, is the simultaneous teaching of English language development (ELD) and content material. More specifically, it is an attempt to teach language through the presentation of grade-level academic content. Though CBLL research supports integration of ELs, circumstances often prohibit full participation in grade-level content courses. Content teachers are not adequately trained (Byrnes, Kiger, & Manning, 1997); they lack time to implement what they know (Reeves, 2006) and miss opportunities to attain self-efficacy. Resistance from teachers, who feel neither prepared nor entrusted to address EL needs, poses risks to encouraging full participation. When schools make resources available, co-teaching affords content teachers the ability to mitigate these risks. This work aims to promote CBLL practices and build professional relationships between co-teachers.

Research in CBLL supports simultaneous acquisition of language and content knowledge because it integrates the language learner into a new culture, in this case an academic culture with unique ways of speaking and acting (Mohan, 1986). Theories of language socialization (Schieffelin & Ochs, 1986; Watson-Gegeo, 2004) suggest that we acquire language via interaction with a community that uses it for similar purposes; it is impossible to separate language from the knowledge it represents. Neither can we separate language from the knowledge it constructs.

English learners need to use the language of particular content areas. In the field of systemic functional linguistics (Achugar, Schleppegrell, & Oteiza, 2007; Aguirre-Muñoz, Park, Amabisca, & Boscardin, 2009; Halliday, 2004), ELs are able to acquire language when they can assess such linguistic structures as word parts, vocabulary, and syntax as it is used in its authentic social context. Additionally, they can analyze the role of these structures in the accomplishment of particular functions of language in the target community, description, sequencing, classification, and causal explanations (Huang & Morgan, 2003; Huang, & Normandia, 2007; Mohan & Beckett, 2001; Schleppegrell, 1998; Schleppegrell, Achugar, & Oteíza, 2004; Vickers, 2007). Facilitating the socialization of ELs into an academic community requires explicit instruction in the language of particular content areas. The co-teaching vignette that opened this chapter demonstrates the potential for a content and literacy specialist to meet this complex set of needs. When done well, co-teaching ensures that ELs benefit from a teacher's expertise in both content material and the cultural and linguistic practices of that academic community.

EMBEDDED PROFESSIONAL DEVELOPMENT

When professional development is embedded and situational, it is more likely to create sustained results (Darling-Hammond, Hyler, & Gardner, 2017; Desimone & Pak, 2017; Glazer & Hannafin, 2006; Shulman & Shulman, 2010). As Cox (2004) explains, without the benefit of collaborative knowledge, expertise, and responsibility for meeting the needs of all learners, teachers operate in isolated silos by default. Dove and Honigsfeld (2010) emphasized the need for sustained professional development in collaborative practice to reduce this tendency toward isolation.

Still, context matters in collaborative relationships. There is no guarantee of success when teachers are assigned to teach together. In the past, collaborations among content and language teachers achieved varying degrees of success due to distinct contextual factors (Pawan & Ortloff, 2011; Russell, 2012). Davison's (2006) study of elementary and English as a second language (ESL) teachers identified five levels of collaboration in an ESL classroom: passive resistance, compliance, accommodation, convergence, and creative co-instruction. Though partnerships experience varying levels of success, the most effective collaborations yield a heightened concern among teachers for achieving curricular objectives (Davison, 2006) and higher ratings in satisfaction surveys of students with co-teachers (Stewart & Perry, 2005).

Embedded professional development for co-teachers provides structures of accountability, where instructional products and performance outcomes are the goals. It requires significant commitment from teachers, but the structural support it provides addresses challenges to the viability of co-teaching endeavors (Aguirre-Muñoz et al., 2009). The professional development provided in this study, therefore, challenged common pitfalls in co-teaching and likewise supported teachers' efforts to reach higher levels of collaboration.

METHODOLOGY

We used a multiple case study design in order to explore the complex human and environmental factors at play in a co-taught CBLL classroom. A case study is qualitative research that includes an intensive analysis and descriptions of a system bounded by space and time. It defines what is known based on careful analysis of multiple sources of information about the case (Hancock & Algozzine, 2006). A case study is employed to gain an in-depth understanding of a situation and meaning for those involved. It is about discovery more than confirmation. Insight gained can directly influence policy, practice, and future research (Merriam, 2001). Three case studies were employed in this research project, each occurring within inclusion science classrooms in the same building (a bounded system), thus this multiple case study approach provided opportunities for in-depth comparative analysis.

Setting

The researcher conducted this study at a middle school in a midwestern urban fringe district. Proximity to a much larger network of city schools as well as its incorporation of affluent, working class, and impoverished suburban communities contributed to a diversity lacking in many urban and suburban districts of comparable size. According to statistics provided by the state's department of education, the district enrolled 5,238 students in the year prior to this study, and 1,133 of those students attended the middle school. Across the district, 585 students, 11.2% of the total student population, were classified as limited English proficient (LEP). Of the 609 public school districts in the state, the district ranked fifth for the percentage of the total student body classified as LEP. Because of its historical experience with English language learners, the district had a reputation for adhering to nationally recognized recommendations for program design (Collier & Thomas, 2004).

Participant Co-Teaching Teams

The three co-teaching teams in this study taught in science-based language classrooms across the sixth, seventh, and eighth grades, respectively. At least one member of each team was a veteran teacher with ten or more years of experience. Table 4.1 shows the three teams, their area of expertise, and number of years teaching.

Action Research Cycle

The action research cycle of reflection, planning, and action guided the teachers' participation in the co-teaching experience, their lesson plans, and their instructional practice. The researcher who served as a professional development provider facilitated as a critical friend at each stage of the action research cycle. In the reflection stage, the team used the collaborative assessment log (CAL; see Figure 4.1) to articulate the celebrations and challenges in their instructional practice. During the planning stage, the team developed plans for building on celebrations and addressing challenges during co-teaching. Finally, the action stage was the actual implementation of those plans in the classroom. This cycle was repeated three times throughout the study, allowing the teachers to refine their practice.

Professional Development Activities

All professional development activities, including initial meetings with all participants, classroom observations of individual teams, and facilitation of planning and reflection meetings, fulfilled their own distinct roles in the action research cycle. Training included descriptions of co-teaching models

TABLE 4.1	Co-Teaching Teams		
Grade Level	Expertise	Pseudonym	Teaching Experience
Sixth	EL	Kelly	24 years
	Science	Daniel	3 years
Seventh	EL	Robert	15 years
	Science	Michelle	4 years
Eighth	EL	Liliana	6 years
	Science	Joseph	13 years

Note: Three co-taught science classrooms were affected by these research activities, at sixth, seventh, and eighth grade level. Of this group, Liliana was an instructional aide; all others were licensed teachers.

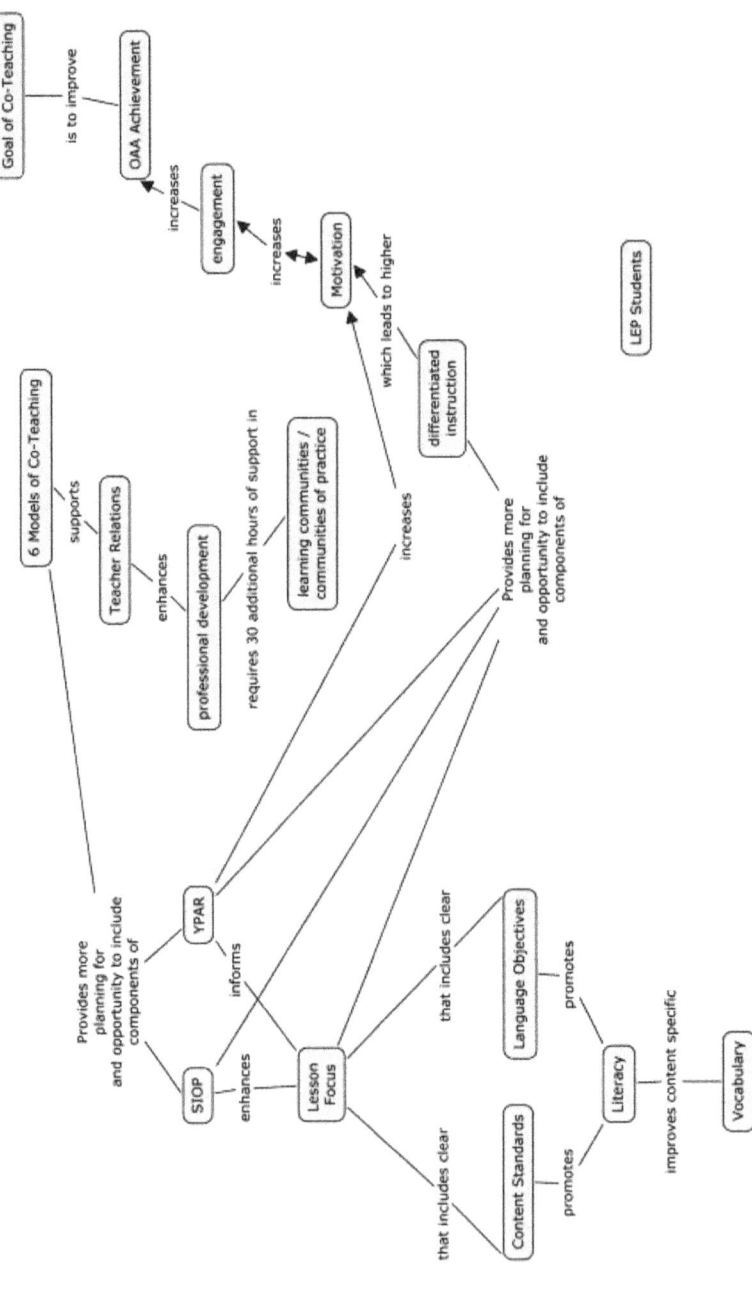

Figure 4.1 Concept map of teacher foci. *Note:* During the initial professional development session, all six teacher/participants collaborated to create this concept map of focus areas in a co-taught ESOL science classroom.

and discussions about increased parity and wider functionality associated with having two teachers in the classroom (Dove & Honigsfeld, 2010). The models included instructional arrangements such as alternative, team, parallel, and station teaching (Cook & Friend, 1995). Teachers also engaged in conversations about core beliefs, prerequisite skills, and administrative supports recommended for co-teaching success.

Data Collection Tools

The teams used conceptual tools to capture their thinking in visual formats. In addition to the CAL, which helped guide and record reflection and planning meetings, each team also employed concept maps and fishbone diagrams. All of the tools used in this study were chosen because of their potential for facilitating collaboration among academic peers, and they had the added benefit of making explicit connections between a variety of concepts and practices that are at play in a co-taught content-based classroom for English learners. Novak and Cañas (2008) describe how concept maps provide teams the opportunity to concisely represent knowledge as well as describe relationships between the concepts represented on the map.

Concept Maps
Teachers completed a concept map that represented their knowledge of teaching and learning strategies, as well as their purpose for a co-taught CBLL classroom. The concept map as a data collection tool facilitated conversations by the teachers about their relevant knowledge base (Artiles & McClafferty, 1998; Beyerbach & Smith, 1990; Kinchin, Hay, & Adams, 2000). See Figure 4.2 for the concept map of teacher foci collaboratively developed by the six participating teachers.

Fishbone Diagrams
Participants used the cause-and-effect fishbone diagram as a data collection tool during initial professional development activities. The cause and effect (fishbone) diagram, conceptualized by Kaoru Ishikawa, is a tool of causal analysis at a systems level. The tool assists in the identification of a specific problem to be addressed by answering the question, "Why do we get the outcomes that we currently do?" (Bryk, Gomez, Grunow, & LeMahieu, 2017). Each major bone represents a key factor thought to contribute to an unsatisfactory outcome. Smaller bones capture the details that emerge from the conversations about these factors.

The fishbone diagram allowed each team to identify one goal they wished to accomplish via collaborative practice. Then, teachers considered *causes* they needed in order to attain this goal. Sixth-grade co-teachers,

Formative Assessment Tool Collaborative Log	
Date:	
Teachers:	
Subject/Content Areas:	
Purpose of Today's Meeting:	

What's Working	Current Focus, Challenges, Concerns
Teacher's Next Steps	Resources & Activities
Next Meeting Date	Focus

Figure 4.2   Collaborative assessment log template. *Note:* This framework was used to guide and record collaborative planning and reflection meetings. Conversations were recorded with a digital pen, which provided an audio recording of the meeting, as well as a video recording of notes and transcriptions.

Kelly and Daniel, used the fishbone diagram to identify "student articulation of ideas/vocabulary acquisition and application" as a goal for their co-teaching efforts. They noted materials, school culture, external forces, and mental processes in second-language acquisition (SLA) as challenges to address in order to achieve their self-identified goal. Using the same type of diagram, Michelle and Robert identified "motivation to learn" as a goal for their co-teaching efforts in the seventh grade. They noted their own degree of knowledge and experience about models of co-teaching, instructional strategies, the SIOP model, and resources, materials, and technology as challenges to address in order to achieve their self-identified goal. Similarly, Joseph and Liliana used the fishbone diagram to identify "motivation" as a goal for their own co-teaching efforts in the eighth-grade context. They noted sociocultural influences, academic support, and access to materials as challenges to address in order to achieve their self-identified goal.

Digital Recordings

Using a digital pen, the researcher recorded teachers' bi-weekly meetings to plan classroom instruction. Teachers employed a CAL as a data collection tool during reflection and planning (Athanases et al., 2008). The CAL captured perceptions of co-teaching practice and problem-solving strategies for addressing emergent concerns. Digital recordings were used for field notes of classroom observations during lesson implementation that occurred on a bi-weekly basis throughout the quarter. Audio recordings supplemented written notes.

FINDINGS

Several sets of indicators were identified from the varied data collection tools used in this study. Together, these tools captured teachers' stated goals, key concepts, instructional practices, and extenuating factors, such as administrative decisions that influence the co-taught classroom. A set of consistent assets and challenges emerged from the findings, providing a preliminary list of needs and focus areas for future teams.

Classroom Observations

Overall, classroom observations of the three co-teaching partnerships exposed a set of consistent assets that supported growth toward reaching co-teaching goals. Assets possessed by teams included specific manifestations of prerequisite conditions required for successful co-teaching, evidenced by instances of trust, support, and parity. Other assets reported by teachers who found success with this embedded PD included training in co-teaching models and SIOP strategies, expanded instructional roles, deepened collaboration, and increased capacity to meet the instructional needs of the students. Nevertheless, significant challenges emerged.

Differences among these respective teams revealed challenges that require attention in future embedded professional development programs. Study participants recognized that multiple variables, such as the skill set of individual teachers and students, as well as characteristics of school culture, social culture and administrative constraints, influenced the degree of success in co-teaching ELs. There was evidence that professional development required greater focus on instruction related to linguistic development. Teachers concluded that in order to make gains in linguistic development, they needed more preparation in pedagogical content knowledge (Shulman, 1986), including content literacy, linguistic analysis skills, and CBLL strategies.

Prerequisites

Parity
The extent to which parity existed among team members was consequential. The teams acknowledged that parity was the ability of one partner to

respect the knowledge, experience, and contributions of the other partner and to engage in honest talk about instruction. Parity was apparent within two of the three teams as members of the sixth and seventh grade teams explicitly noted their respective teammate's value. Conversely, parity was impeded for the eighth-grade team because the ESOL professional rarely asserted her views about instructional design. This lack of communication and respect among members of the team resulted in the content teacher making decisions about services provided in the classroom. For this co-teaching dyad, the absence of parity hindered growth in co-teaching strategies.

Administrative Support

Indicators of administrative support for co-teaching were highlighted by the provision of common planning time, professional development training, and embedded support from the researcher. Administrators recognized the value of collaboration to improve students' academic literacy. When constraints obstructed indicators, other assets compensated for their loss. For instance, the team without common planning time profited from their parity and sustained PD. When compared with other case studies participating in this PD, both members of this team assumed responsibility for the academic and linguistic growth of all students in their classroom and more regularly applied research-based strategies for teaching ELs.

Barriers to Success

Teams experienced barriers to success, such as Kelly's and Daniel's lack of access to common planning time, an indicator of prerequisite conditions. Barriers to previously conceived notions of parity were evident. Although parity may have existed between two members of a team, it did not exist among all department colleagues or administrative staff. Kelly offered reflections that revealed a lack of confidence and trust in administrative actions and motives. These suspicions were mirrored by the seventh grade's team reflections and impeded their commitment to the process. Because of these challenges to prerequisite conditions, future research needs to explore the specific anatomy of team development, including the role of administration.

CONCLUSION

Embedded professional development for co-teaching English learners is supported in the literature (Darling-Hammond et al., 2017; Desimone & Pak, 2017; Dove & Honigsfeld, 2010; Glazer & Hannafin, 2006; Shulman & Shulman, 2010). We affirm the need to include embedded professional development that is available to co-teachers as they reflect, plan, and deliver instruction. Embedded support is required if teachers are expected to respond to directives from administrators and colleagues while engaging in co-teaching practice. The ultimate aim is to meet the unique needs of emerging bilingual students. Therefore, we propose the following recommendations:

- Ground co-teaching in basic prerequisites conditions (Davison, 2006; Scruggs, Mastropieri, & McDuffie, 2007). These include access to common co-planning time, operationalized and enacted behaviors of parity, and essential administrative support.
- Instances of parity include the identification of each partner's contributions and the assumption of interchanging roles. Teachers must be able to reach parity with departmental colleagues and administrators in order to fully implement new instructional strategies.
- Evidence of administrative support include provisions for CBLL classrooms, co-planning time, and resources for PD. Threats to administrative support can be mitigated with defined roles for administrators for the purposes of building trust.
- Co-teaching for CBLL classrooms requires systemic support. Partnerships possess unique characteristics, assets, and constraints. When resources are defined, perhaps in individual co-teaching plans, then full engagement will be more possible.

Co-teachers who seek support for their endeavors require a robust professional development that addresses core needs. In order for teachers to identify the factors that closely match their setting, it is essential that contextual factors that influence their co-teaching are voiced. Embedded support, with its attention to student success, creates a sanctioned space that empowers teachers to address the unique needs of each of their students. Collaboration is not a luxury; it is a moral imperative in our practice. Enlisting and undergirding new collaborative structures that systematically address student success points us to the end—the development of self-determined critical thinkers ready to join as citizens in a democratic society.

REFERENCES

Achugar, M., Schleppegrell, M., & Oteiza, T. (2007). Engaging teachers in language analysis: A functional linguistics approach to reflective literacy. *English Teaching: Practice and Critique, 6*(2), 8–24.

Aguirre-Muñoz, Z., Park, J. E., Amabisca, A., & Boscardin, C. K. (2009). Developing teacher capacity for serving ELLs' writing instructional needs: A case for systemic functional linguistics. *Bilingual Research Journal, 31*(1–2), 295–322.

Artiles, A. J., & McClafferty, K. (1998). Learning to teach culturally diverse learners: Charting change in preservice teachers' thinking about effective teaching. *The Elementary School Journal, 98*(3), 189–220.

Athanases, S. Z., Abrams, J., Jack, G., Johnson, V., Kwock, S., McCurdy, J., . . . Totaro, S. (2008). Curriculum for mentor development: Problems and promise in the work of new teacher induction leaders. *Journal of Curriculum Studies, 40*(6), 743–770.

Beyerbach, B. A., & Smith, J. M. (1990). Using a computerized concept mapping program to assess preservice teachers' thinking about effective teaching. *Journal of Research in Science Teaching, 27*(10), 961–971.

Bryk, A. S., Gomez, L. M., Grunow, A., & LeMahieu, P. G. (2017). *Learning to improve: How America's school can get better at getting better.* Cambridge, MA: Harvard Education Press.

Byrnes, D. A., Kiger, G., & Manning, M. L. (1997). Teachers' attitudes about language diversity. *Teaching and Teacher Education, 13*(6), 637–644.

Collier, V. P., & Thomas, W. P. (2004). The astounding effectiveness of dual language education for all. *NABE Journal of Research and Practice, 2*(1), 1–20.

Collier, V. P., & Thomas, W. P. (2007). Predicting second language academic success in English using the Prism Model. In J. Cummins & C. Davison (Eds.), *International handbook of English language teaching* (pp. 333–348). Boston, MA: Springer.

Cook, L., & Friend, M. (1995). Co-teaching: Guidelines for creating effective practices. *Focus on Exceptional Children, 28*(3), 1–16.

Cox, M. D. (2004). Building faculty learning communities. *New Directions for Teaching and Learning, 97,* 5–23.

Darling-Hammond, L., Hyler, M. E., & Gardner, M. (2017). *Effective teacher professional development.* Palo Alto, CA: Learning Policy Institute.

Davison, C. (2006). Collaboration between ESL and content teachers: How do we know when we are doing it right? *International Journal of Bilingual Education and Bilingualism, 9*(4), 454–475.

Desimone, L. M., & Pak, K. (2017). Instructional coaching as high-quality professional development. *Theory Into Practice, 56*(1), 3–12.

Dove, M., & Honigsfeld, A. (2010). ESL coteaching and collaboration: Opportunities to develop teacher leadership and enhance student learning. *TESOL Journal, 1*(1), 3–22.

Echevarria, J., Vogt, M. E., & Short, D. (2017). *Making content comprehensible for English language learners: The SIOP model* (4th ed.). Boston, MA: Allyn & Bacon.

Gandara, P., Rumberger, R., Maxwell-Jolly, J., & Callahan, R. (2003). English Learners in California schools: Unequal resources, unequal outcomes. *Education Policy Analysis Archives, 11*(36), 1–52.

Glazer, E. M., & Hannafin, M. J. (2006). The collaborative apprenticeship model: Situated professional development within school settings. *Teaching and Teacher Education, 22*(2), 179–193.

Halliday, M. A. K. (2004). *Introduction to systemic grammar* (3rd ed.; Revised by C. M. I. M. Matthiessen). London, England: Oxford University Press.

Hancock, D. R., & Algozzine, B. (2006). *Doing case study research: A practical guide for beginning researchers.* New York, NY: Teachers College Press.

Huang, J., & Morgan, G. (2003). A functional approach to evaluating content knowledge and language development in ESL students' science classification texts. *International Journal of Applied Linguistics, 13*(2), 234–262.

Huang, J., & Normandia, B. (2007). Learning the language of mathematics: A study of student writing. *International Journal of Applied Linguistics, 17*(3), 294–318.

Kinchin, I. M., Hay, D. B., & Adams, A. (2000). How a qualitative approach to concept map analysis can be used to aid learning by illustrating patterns of conceptual development. *Educational Research, 42*(1), 43–57.

Merriam, S. B. (2001). *Qualitative research and case study application in education*. San Francisco, CA: Jossey-Bass.

Mohan, B. (1986). *Language and content*. Reading, MA: Addison-Wesley.

Mohan, B., & Beckett, G. (2001). A functional approach to research on content-based language learning: Recasts in causal explanations. *Canadian Modern Language Review, 58*(1), 133–155.

Novak, J. D., & Cañas, A. J. (2008). *The theory underlying concept maps and how to construct and use them*. Retrieved from https://web.stanford.edu/dept/SUSE/projects/ireport/articles/concept_maps/The%20Theory%20Underlying%20Concept%20Maps.pdf

Pawan, F., & Ortloff, J. H. (2011). Sustaining collaboration: English-as-a-second-language, and content-area teachers. *Teaching and Teacher Education, 27*(2), 463–471.

Reeves, J. (2006). Secondary teacher attitudes toward including English-Language Learners in mainstream classrooms. *Journal of Educational Research, 99*(3), 131–142.

Rolstad, K., Mahoney, K., & Glass, G. V. (2005). The big picture: A meta-analysis of program effectiveness research on English language learners. *Educational Policy, 19*(4), 572–594.

Russell, F. A. (2012). A culture of collaboration: Meeting the instructional needs of adolescent English language learners. *TESOL Journal, 3*(3), 445–468.

Schieffelin, B. B., & Ochs, E. (1986). Language socialization. *Annual Review of Anthropology, 15*, 163–246.

Schleppegrell, M. J. (1998). Grammar as resource: Writing a description. *Research in the Teaching of English, 32*(3), 182–211.

Schleppegrell, M., Achugar, M., & Oteíza, T. (2004). The grammar of history: Enhancing content-based instruction through a functional focus on language. *TESOL Quarterly, 38*(1), 67–93.

Scruggs, T. E., Mastropieri, M. A., & McDuffie, K. A. (2007). Co-teaching in inclusive classrooms: A metasynthesis of qualitative research. *Exceptional Children, 73*(4), 392–416.

Shulman, L. S. (1986). Those who understand: Knowledge growth in teaching. *Educational Researcher, 15*(2), 4–14.

Shulman, L. S., & Shulman, J. H. (2010). How and what teachers learn: A shifting perspective. *Journal of Curriculum Studies, 36*(2), 257–271.

Slavin, R. E., & Cheung, A. (2005). A synthesis of research on language of reading instruction for English language learners. *Review of Educational Research, 75*(2), 247–284.

Stewart, T., & Perry, B. (2005). Interdisciplinary team teaching as a model for teacher development. *TESL-EJ, 9*(2), 1–17.

Vickers, C. H. (2007). Second language socialization through team interaction among electrical computer engineering students. *Modern Language Journal, 91*(4), 621–640.

Vogt, M., & Echevarria, J. (2008). *99 ideas and activities for teaching English learners with the SIOP Model.* Boston, MA: Allyn & Bacon.

Watson-Gegeo, K. A. (2004). Mind, language, and epistemology: Toward a language socialization paradigm for SLA. *Modern Language Journal, 88*(3), 331–350.

Willig, A. C. (1985). A meta-analysis of selected studies on the effectiveness of bilingual education. *Review of Educational Research, 55*(3), 269–317.

CHAPTER 5

MISTAKES MADE, LESSONS LEARNED

Leia Bruton
Rowan Salisbury Schools

During my first year co-teaching, I made a great many mistakes, as you can imagine. My biggest mistake was that I tried to co-teach in the exact same way in different classes. This chapter includes an examination of a few of the mistakes I made in the hopes that others might benefit from the lessons I learned and improve their co-teaching practices. The following action research occurred at a rural elementary school in Salisbury, NC. The school has approximately 650 students and almost 30% of them are English learners (ELs). This school prides itself on having the highest EL population of all of the elementary schools within the district. As such, each classroom has a large number of ELs and almost 50% of the student population speak an additional language at home, primarily Spanish.

The EL teachers at the school, as per the district's expectations, were providing EL support largely through a pullout model, in which ELs were taken out of class for approximately 45 minutes each day (typically during English language arts). Due to the high number of ELs in each room, as well as other non-ELs who needed extra support, I chose to try co-teaching instead of the

Co-Teaching for English Learners, pages 49–60
Copyright © 2020 by Information Age Publishing
49

pullout model. I was assigned to one grade level, so I was able to split my time among four classes during the day. By co-teaching, I was spending 45 minutes to 1 hour every day in each class, providing support for the needs of all learners. After much reflection, these are the lessons I learned.

MISTAKE #1: ASSUMING THAT MEETING WITH A TEACHER IS THE SAME AS CO-PLANNING

Before co-planning can begin, both teachers need to be aware of the expectations and understanding of what co-teaching is going to be like in the classroom. One expectation should be that when two co-teachers plan together, lesson plans are created and *used* in the co-taught class. One of the co-teachers should not deviate greatly from the plans without letting the other co-teacher know in advance. When this happens, the co-teachers are no longer in sync with what is to be taught. The problem with this is that one of the co-teachers comes in prepared for one lesson and then must scramble to find effective ways to support a completely different lesson. Unfortunately, this often leads to one teacher "sitting out" the lesson or taking on more of an assistant role, instead of providing specific planned instruction or support to the students.

Another challenge with co-planning occurs when one teacher agrees to execute the jointly created plans but may not fully understand the lesson contents or how to implement the plans that have been made. As with the previous scenario, this typically results in one teacher taking over the lesson and the other person becoming simply an extra body in the classroom. At best, one teacher leads the lesson while the other teacher rushes to create on-the-spot supports for the lesson, using her expertise to benefit the students.

Lack of expectations also can lead to one teacher planning and coming up with ideas while the other co-teacher agrees obediently without voicing his or her opinion. When this happens, it becomes one teacher's lesson with no joint ownership of instruction, which defeats the purpose of co-planning to co-teach. There are several issues attached to this particular misstep. One is that the teacher who simply agrees could potentially create his or her own plans (outside of the co-planning session) to then take the place of the plans in which both teachers supposedly created during the co-planning session. Consider the following scenario:

> When meeting with one of my co-teachers, we sat down to discuss lessons for the upcoming week. As the support specialist, I provided ideas of what I felt the lesson should include in the coming week. Instead of the classroom teacher adding her own ideas, she simply nodded her head in agreement

and wrote down what was said. My co-teacher then claimed that she would be following these plans in our co-taught class the coming week. However in reality, that same teacher spent the entire weekend rewriting our plans. She came to school on Monday and had completely new lessons written for the entire week. I was caught off guard, and was left to determine the best supports to use for the students as the lesson was being taught. My expertise in language learning was not adequately utilized for the benefit of students, due to not knowing the material that was being covered. It also hindered our relationship as a co-teaching team because I began to feel that my thoughts and ideas didn't matter and lost some trust that plans would be carried out according to plan. In this case, co-planning was ineffective because both parties weren't voicing their opinion or taking full ownership of the plans created.

Lesson Learned: Effective Co-Planning

For co-planning to be successful, both teachers should verbalize their thoughts and ideas to one another and offer appropriate strategies for specific students in the classroom. When disagreements occur (and they will), each teacher should voice his or her opinion respectfully and work through it together to modify lesson plans to meet not only the needs of all learners in their classroom, but also to take into account each other's ideas and teaching styles. Disagreement with co-planning is actually beneficial. You have two teachers who may be co-teaching with two different opinions and experiences. Instead of focusing on where they may disagree, co-teachers should see co-planning as an opportunity for both teachers to provide their expertise on the subject.

MISTAKE #2: ASSUMING ONE CO-TEACHING MODEL IS EQUALLY EFFECTIVE IN DIFFERENT CLASSROOMS

When co-teaching, it is vital to try different models or modes of co-teaching in order to meet the needs of the students as well as meet the comfort level of both teachers. As special educators, Friend and Cook (2010) reported that there are six different types of co-teaching models that can be used to meet the needs of learners. The models they recommended for meeting the needs of students with varying abilities are also applied to meeting the needs of ELs. Those models include: team teaching, alternative teaching, station teaching, one teach one assist, one teach one observe, and parallel teaching. Some co-teachers may be more comfortable with the station-teaching model (in which one teacher plans and delivers instruction at a station with students) as opposed to a team-teaching model (in which both teachers are in front of class teaching at the same time as a "team"). In order for co-teachers to carry out instruction with a selected co-teaching model, expectations must be set initially.

There are several factors to consider when determining the model of co-teaching. One factor is student data including the number of English learners (ELs) in the classroom, the achievement levels of the ELs and other students in the class, and the proficiency levels as well as specific language and content goals that have been planned. For example, when ELs are more than half of the class, teachers may want to try a team-teaching approach (two teachers teach the same content together) or an alternative teaching approach (one teaches, the other pre-teaches or reteaches). However, teachers that have fewer EL students may want to try a station teaching approach (multiple groups) so that different groups of students are given specific and tailored instruction and activities to meet their needs. The following scenario elaborates on using the same co-teaching model in two different classes:

> Early in the school year, one of my co-teachers and I decided we wanted to try a team-teaching approach, with both of us teaching the lesson together. This decision was born out of how our teaching relationship had developed to the point in which we planned every lesson together (even ones we weren't co-teaching) as well as the complementary nature of our personalities. Due to consistently planning lessons together and having a similar level of understanding about standards and supports, we transitioned easily into a team-teaching duo. We both knew the lesson and each brought our own expertise into the teaching. Since this model was so successful with this co-teacher, I wanted to quickly jump into team teaching with my other co-teacher. We did not plan together consistently nor did we both have the same comfort level with the material. So when we tried to team teach, it rapidly turned into one of us teaching and the other teacher standing by awkwardly, grappling for ways to add to the lesson. The students weren't receiving the level of support they could be if another model was used because team teaching, in this case, wasn't being utilized to its fullest potential.

Lesson Learned: Co-Teaching Model Effectiveness

When co-teaching, there is no "one size fits all" model. The needs of students as well as the dynamics of the co-teaching team should be considered when determining co-teaching models. Also, the nature of the lesson should be considered, evaluating which model would best meet the needs for that particular lesson. In order for any co-teaching model to be effective, co-planning must occur in that both teachers should know the material being taught as well as how the chosen co-teaching model should be carried out.

MISTAKE #3: ONLY USING STUDENT DATA TO DETERMINE INSTRUCTIONAL MODELS

Determining co-teaching models is a complex task with many factors that need to be considered. One essential factor most certainly is student data. However, teacher comfort level as well as individual teaching styles should be taken into consideration. With one co-teaching team, team teaching might appear to be a natural and authentic way to teach together. This model allows students to experience both teachers and their expertise in action. However, team teaching may not be the first choice of co-teaching models for some co-teaching teams. Prior to lesson delivery, different co-teaching models should be discussed, and the co-teachers should decide on the model or multiple models to try in their classroom.

Another factor to consider is teacher comfort levels. Some grade-level or content area teachers may not be comfortable with another teacher coming into their classroom and taking control of their class. For this reason, some co-teachers may be more comfortable with station teaching so that the classroom teacher is still able to teach the whole group lesson, but the EL or other co-teacher can still provide support for students through small-group instruction.

In addition to teacher comfort level, teachers may have a different style of teaching than their co-teacher. Disagreeing on lesson delivery or teaching styles should not hinder a team from co-teaching. This may be an opportunity for that team to explore different co-teaching models. One teacher may teach the whole group lesson, while another has a small group of students and is teaching the same lesson but with more scaffolding and language supports.

Consider the following scenario that illustrates various factors for determining co-teaching models:

In one of my co-teaching classes, the grade-level teacher and I effortlessly worked well together. We quickly became comfortable with each other to the point of finishing each other's sentences. Team teaching became a common practice for us and was successful due to our compatibility with each other. I believe our compatibility was born out of our opposite personalities but common goals for students as educators. Team teaching worked well for us as a co-teaching team because we ultimately had the same goal for the students as well as similar pedagogical beliefs (such as building relationships with students, maintaining high expectations, etc.). I foolishly thought I could replicate this level of relationship and like-mindedness in my other co-taught class. Unfortunately, that co-teacher and I did not reach the same level of understanding and collaboration. We had differing views of what a lesson should include and what roles we should each play. I learned quickly that team teaching was a model of co-teaching that was awkward and uncomfortable for us as a team. Therefore, we decided to try a different model of co-teaching to better meet our personal comfort level as well as meet the needs of our students.

Lesson Learned: Selecting Co-Teaching Models

To select co-teaching models, several factors should be considered and discussed among co-teachers, and there should be agreement among them concerning which models to try to incorporate into the co-taught classroom. If they discover that one model is not working in their class, the co-teachers should meet again and discuss possible models that they could utilize to meet the needs of their students. When expectations are set at the beginning of the school year (or prior to co-teaching), then all parties involved are aware and understand the way co-teaching will look in that classroom. The expectation should also be set that models could change from week to week based on student need and the benefits of a particular model for a specific lesson. For example, if the teachers wanted data on how students are performing during a lesson, then a one teach/one observe model may be best for that lesson. Setting expectations also allows both co-teachers to discern their position in the classroom and understand the best way to meet the needs of their ELs. Co-teaching routines also allow both teachers and students to have the same understanding of what will be happening when co-taught lessons occur. There should be no guesswork as to what each co-teacher will be doing when they are conducting a class together.

MISTAKE #4: UNDETERMINED ROLES AND RESPONSIBILITIES FOR EACH CO-TEACHER

After establishing the models of co-teaching that will be used in the classroom (what works best for the teachers and students), the expectation should be set that both teachers contribute to the successful achievement of all students in the co-taught class. This notion may sound like an obvious expectation, but it is important that both teachers understand their value and their role within the co-teaching team. For example, when the EL co-teacher comes into the classroom to co-teach, the classroom teacher should not leave or use that time to go make copies, cut out materials for other lessons, check emails, or merely become disengaged from the lesson. It should be established from the beginning that both teachers are valuable and each teacher should have a specific role (established based on the co-teaching model selected). Even if it is one teacher collecting data or providing individual support while the other teacher is providing a mini lesson or modeling an activity, those roles should be explicitly established and executed as planned. For example, in station teaching, both teachers should be responsible for a station and take an active role in planning and implementing the learning activities in those stations. There should also be an understanding that the specialist that comes into the class is not an assistant for the teacher. It is important as well that when a co-teacher contributes during the lesson—adds information, clarifies vocabulary, explores an alternative point of view, and so on—he or she proceeds in a respectful way as well as enriches instruction. When done appropriately, students may reach an "AHA" moment or gain a new insight into the current lesson. When done without regard to the lesson at hand, the contributions can become more like interruptions, distracting the students from what they are currently learning.

Consider the following scenario in which one co-teacher is leading a lesson, and the other co-teacher distracts students away from the lesson at hand:

> Once I was teaching a lesson in one of my co-taught classes. In the middle of the lesson, the classroom teacher interrupted and seemingly dismissed what I was teaching. The message to the students was essentially, "You don't need to worry about this. We're going to do something else instead." I was dumbfounded and found it difficult to continue with the lesson. I also realized the students were distracted from the lesson and inattentiveness increased. In this scenario, it seemed as if one co-teacher was trying to jeopardize the success of their students and the success of the lesson that had been planned.

Lesson Learned: Establishing Roles and Responsibilities

This scenario is another example of why co-planning and voicing opinions during co-planning sessions is important to the success of co-teaching. When both teachers are involved in the planning process, misconceptions and disagreements can be discussed ahead of time and not in front of students. A co-teacher should never distract away from the lesson plans that have been established and the instruction that the other co-teacher is trying to lead. Established roles and responsibilities and modeling for students how to collaborate effectively present a united co-teaching partnership creating a safe and productive working environment for students.

MISTAKE #5: THE EL TEACHER ONLY SHOULD TEACH THE EL STUDENTS

When co-teaching, both teachers should take responsibility for *all* student learning. It no longer is about *my* students and *your* students. Instead, it is about *our* students. When both co-teachers take responsibility for the learning of every student in the classroom, they understand the importance of both their roles, but also they create a community of learners. Teachers may be more likely to value their co-teacher and when they are both taking responsibility for student success as well as challenges. Teachers may better understand that their co-teaching partners may have strengths in areas that they struggle with, and they can benefit from and capitalize on each other's strengths in the classroom. Ideas may be shared more freely, and teachers will be more willing to speak up if they both understand it is both their responsibility to help all students succeed.

When strategies are implemented in the classroom (as opposed to a pullout setting), both teachers should be involved and both teachers should have a voice in determining best practices to meet the needs of all learners. In turn, all learners will receive effective strategies to meet their needs and become successful. When joint decision-making happens, we see achievement scores increase across the board. ELs become more confident and may begin to match the proficiency level of their peers.

Consider the following scenario:

> As an EL teacher, my entire career prior to co-teaching was based solely around which students were "mine" or ELs. So it was welcoming and eye-opening to me the level of shared responsibility that occurred when I started co-teaching. In one of my co-taught classes, all of the students saw me as their teacher in the same way they saw their classroom teacher. To the point that when EL testing started, students in the class were confused about why I was pulling certain students to test. My co-teacher made sure I was a part of the class, and students knew that we both were their teachers. In my other co-taught class, the teacher would still refer to the ELs as "my students" and specifically ask for support for them. Instead of seeking ways to discuss this with my co-teacher, I became frustrated, eventually feeling undervalued. I made the unfortunate decision to stop co-teaching in this class and start pulling EL students out instead. As a first year co-teacher, this was probably the biggest mistake I could make.

Lessons Learned: Co-Teaching Is Collaborative Teaching for All

One of the greatest benefits to co-teaching is that you are no longer alone. DuFour, DuFour, and Eaker (2018) state that teaching should no longer occur in isolation (planning by oneself, teaching by oneself, analyzing data by oneself). Instead, teaching should be a collaboration among teachers, sharing responsibility. This is especially true within co-teaching. All students have unique learning needs and those needs can be better met when there is more than one expert in the room. The old adage "two heads are better than one" can be illustrated through any collaborative model between teachers. Multiple teaching styles, varying perspectives, differing areas of expertise, and unique teaching strengths can more broadly meet the educational needs of students, as all students are unique individuals regardless of their language proficiency. Just within my first year co-teaching, I was able to analyze the difference in data between a class in which I felt safe to explore co-teaching and a class in which I foolishly abandoned co-teaching to return to my comfort zone of pullout teaching for only ELs.

STUDENT OUTCOMES

In Tables 5.1 and 5.2, you will see a comparison of two co-taught classes and their respective student data. Table 5.1, represents a class in which the co-teachers planned together, disagreed, rewrote their plans collaboratively, and then utilized multiple models of co-teaching in the classroom. Also both co-teachers understood that they were responsible for the success of all students in the classroom, and therefore worked together to use best strategies for all learners.

Table 5.2 represents a class where co-planning was done inconsistently and haphazardly. One co-teacher would alter lesson plans without the other knowing. This class also did not have two co-teachers that presented a united front; one co-teacher frequently dismissed the ideas of the other in front of students. Instead of working through different ways to become a better co-teaching team to meet the needs of learners, the EL specialist grew frustrated and decided to abandon the co-teaching model entirely. The specialist chose to revert back to a pullout model and serve the EL students separately from other students in the class.

When looking at both figures, you will notice that both sets of learners started around the same levels at the beginning of the school year and both classes had high needs, including EL students, also known as limited English proficient (LEP) as well as students receiving special education services (SpEd). However, you also will notice that in Table 5.1 all students

TABLE 5.1 Student Data for Class 1 With Consistent Co-Planning

Student Needs	Reading Level			Growth (in reading levels)	On Grade Level
	Beginning of Year	Middle of Year	End of Year		
Student 1	K	P	P	5 levels	Proficient
Student 2	L	O	R	7 levels	Proficient
Student 3	G	J	Q	10 levels	Proficient
Student 4	N	Q	R	4 levels	Proficient
Student 5	J	O	P	6 levels	Proficient
Student 6: LEP	H	J	M	5 levels	
Student 7: LEP	I	R	R	9 levels	Proficient
Student 8	J	O	P	6 levels	Proficient
Student 9: LEP & SpEd	E	E	G	2 levels	
Student 10: LEP & SpEd	E	E	G	2 levels	
Student 11: SpEd	F	G	J	4 levels	
Student 12: LEP	G	I	L	5 levels	
Student 13: LEP	H	R	S	11 levels	Proficient
Student 14: LEP	J	L	R	8 levels	Proficient
Student 15: LEP	I	J	M	5 levels	
Student 16: LEP	I	M	P	7 levels	Proficient
Student 17: LEP	L	N	S	7 levels	Proficient
Student 18	O	Q	P	1 level	Proficient
Student 19: LEP	L	M	O	3 levels	
Student 20	K	M	Q	6 levels	Proficient

Note: LEP: Limited English Proficient; SpEd: Special Education.

improved in their scores, many reaching grade-level proficiency whereas in Table 5.2 students continued to struggle and not reach grade-level proficiency in reading comprehension. As revealed in the data, the well-organized co-taught class was effective for all learners in the classroom and not just for the ELs whereas in the class where the teachers abandoned the co-teaching model, students were not as academically successful.

SUMMARY

Though many mistakes were made during my first year of co-teaching, several lessons were learned throughout the process:

1. Co-planning should include both teachers and their ideas even if the teachers disagree. When disagreements arise, teachers should

TABLE 5.2 Student Data for Class 2 With Inconsistent Co-Planning					
	Reading Level			**Growth (in reading levels)**	**On Grade Level**
Student Needs	**Beginning of Year**	**Middle of Year**	**End of Year**		
Student 1: LEP	I	J	J	1 level	
Student 2: LEP	I	H	K	2 levels	
Student 3: LEP	F	H	K	5 levels	
Student 4	J	L	O	5 levels	
Student 5	I	K	K	2 levels	
Student 6: LEP	F	G	J	4 levels	
Student 7: LEP	H	H	J	2 levels	
Student 8: LEP	H	I	L	4 levels	
Student 9: LEP	F	F	K	5 levels	
Student 10: LEP	I	J	M	4 levels	
Student 11: LEP	D	C	I	5 levels	
Student 12	K	J	S	8 levels	Proficient
Student 13: LEP	J	K	N	4 levels	
Student 14	I	J	N	5 levels	
Student 15	L	K	N	2 levels	

Note: LEP: Limited English Proficient; SpEd: Special Education.

   continue to voice their opinion and work through planning together so that each brings their area of expertise to the table. In doing so, they are ensuring that they are meeting the needs of all learners in their classroom.

2. Expectations for co-teaching should be set before students ever step foot in the classroom. Especially when both teachers are new to co-teaching, decisions should be made ahead of time so that they both have an understanding of what will be happening during instruction.

3. Co-teaching models should be discussed and then trial periods should last for several weeks to see which model is going to be most effective for a specific class. When one co-teaching model does not work, the specialist and classroom teacher should not simply give up. Instead, they should work together to discuss different co-teaching models that they could try in the classroom. If teachers find that they may not have enough time to plan together to do team teaching or parallel teaching, they may try to do station teaching or alternative teaching to meet the needs of those learners.

4. Co-teachers should always have a united front in front of the students in the classroom. Teachers should know the content that they

are teaching so that no discrepancies will occur during the lesson. Co-teachers should never talk down or speak negatively to their co-teacher in front of the class. They also should not try to distract from the lesson at hand to steer students in a different direction. Instead the co-teaching team should be respectful of one another, ensure that their plans align, and that they are both on the same page to safeguard the success of their students.

5. Both co-teachers should assume responsibility for all students in the classroom when they are both present. It should never be *my* students versus *your* students. When both teachers assume responsibility for all students in the classroom, the evidence revealed that all students improve in their learning. As part of this responsibility, co-teachers should identify their areas of expertise and their own personal challenges in the classroom. In doing so, they are able to capitalize on each other's strengths to ensure that students are receiving the best instruction possible.

Mistakes will be made, but it is vital to understand that co-teaching is beneficial for all students. So when co-teaching, learn from your mistakes, work collaboratively throughout the entire process, and co-teach in a way that best meets the needs of your individual learner.

REFERENCES

DuFour, R., DuFour, R., & Eaker, R. (2008). *Revisiting Professional Learning Communities at work: New insights for improving schools.* Bloomington, IN: Solution Tree.

Friend, M. P., & Cook, L. (2010). *Interactions: Collaboration skills for school professionals* (6th ed.). Boston, MA: Pearson Education.

CHAPTER 6

IS THERE MAGIC
IN CO-TEACHING?

Maria G. Dove
Molloy College

Andrea Honigsfeld
Molloy College

What constitutes effective programs for English learners (ELs)? If you had the opportunity to shadow an elementary school EL, you might have uncovered that her school day is fragmented by pullout English language development/English language learner (ELD/ELL) classes, reading help, academic intervention services, resource room, and so on, all created and prescribed to raise her level of academic and language fluency. For a secondary EL student, you may find him placed in classes that frequently segregate him from his English-speaking peers as well as content area teacher experts. In other situations, ELs may be included in general education classes, but they might receive little or no support for their academic success or linguistic development. These practices often provoke us to ask the following question: What are the barriers for ELs to have successful learning experiences in their general education classes?

Co-Teaching for English Learners, pages 61–78
Copyright © 2020 by Information Age Publishing
All rights of reproduction in any form reserved.

For more than two decades, we have investigated the complexities of co-teaching for English learners, defined as collaborative partnerships between general education and ELD/ELL teachers for integrated instruction of all students assigned to a class. One might characterize co-teaching for English learners as "a compromising balance of planning and delivery of instruction among teaching partners...[which includes] collaborative planning, delivery, assessment, and reflection...this balance and the interdependence of these components...bring about a successful co-taught class" (Dove & Honigsfeld, 2018, p. xi). We have uncovered various aspects of this practice, such as moving from isolation to collaboration (Calderón et al., 2019; Honigsfeld & Dove, 2010b), effective methods of preparation and implementation (Dove & Honigsfeld, 2014, 2018; Honigsfeld & Dove, 2012, 2015), instructional delivery strategies (Dove, 2009; Dove & Honigsfeld, 2018; Honigsfeld & Dove, 2017), and the documentation of student outcomes (Honigsfeld & Dove, 2019b). At first, our knowledge of co-teaching stemmed from our individual inquiries, reflections, and perspectives as practitioners in K–12 public education ELD/ELL programs. Later as a team, we directly examined the practice through more formal methods of research. In our investigations, we have held to the premise that the most influential factor of effective schools is the teachers who teach in them (Marzano, 2007; Rivkin, Hanushek, & Kain, 2005; Wright, Horn, & Sanders, 1997), and this premise has led us to more closely examine the workings of teacher teams who co-taught for the sake of ELs.

BACKGROUND

Co-teaching for the sake of students with disabilities has been well documented since it became an established practice in the 1990s (Friend & Cook, 2012; Murawski & Lochner, 2017; Villa, Thousand, & Nevin, 2013). In our past studies and publications, we have outlined the process of co-teaching implementation to determine how school communities initiate, establish, and employ inclusive or integrated program models for the sake of English learners (Dove, 2009; Dove & Honigsfeld, 2014, 2018; Honigsfeld & Dove, 2010a, 2012, 2019a). We have outlined what we call the collaborative instructional cycle—co-planning, co-teaching, co-assessment, and reflection—and have emphatically stated how co-teaching is only one part of the fundamental elements that make it an effective instructional delivery model.

Although we continue to investigate the entire instructional cycle, more recently we have been drawn to closely examining the co-teaching process—to investigate how teachers negotiate instructional delivery and document the impact of co-teaching with students. However, even narrowing our focus to instructional practices has its pitfalls in that research tends to reveal additional factors influencing the success of instructional programs from outside the class parameters. For example, Fullan (2016) cautioned, "The difficulty is that educational change is not a single entity, even if we keep the analysis at the simplest level of innovation in a classroom. Innovation is *multidimensional*" (p. 28).

In one of our case studies, we focused on how administrative and faculty support was generated for co-teaching for ELs in a suburban elementary school over the course of one school year including how professional development was established to build teacher capacity for the program change, and what barriers, if any, impeded the program's progress (Dove & Honigsfeld, 2014). We framed our study using Fullan's (2016) elements for successful change. The key findings of our research revealed that administrative leadership at the school building level was critical to the success of the collaborative, integrated program coupled with ongoing professional learning about co-teaching practices including full-day workshops, instructional coaching, and time for co-teachers to reflect on their own practices.

In this chapter, we document the outcomes of expanding our original case study limited to one school in the Northeast to include an investigation of co-teaching practices for the sake of ELs within public elementary and secondary schools throughout the United States over a 5-year period beginning in the Fall of 2013 and ending in the Spring of 2018. We explored the process of a cross-section of schools used to implement co-teaching as a program model and support system for integrated instruction to enhance ELs' access to grade-appropriate core content and opportunities for targeted English language and literacy development. We investigated the extent to which school-building administration and faculty were involved in the planning, implementation, and evaluation of this model, and what factors may have enhanced or impeded the process. In addition, we gathered data on the outcomes of the model's implementation including evidence of the model's effectiveness.

LITERATURE REVIEW

Much has been written about the cognitive, academic, and linguistic needs of English learners (see e.g., García & Kleifgen, 2018; Nieto & Bode, 2012). Numerous guidebooks and professional development materials have been produced on teacher collaboration and co-teaching for inclusive classrooms focusing on students with disabilities (Friend & Cook, 2012; Murawski & Lochner, 2017; Stein, 2016, 2017; Villa et al., 2013; Villa & Thousand, 2016). Much has been published about effective strategies general education teachers can use to offer more culturally and linguistically responsive instruction for ELs (Calderón & Slakk, 2018; Ferlazzo & Hull Sypnieski,

2018; Gibbons, 2015; Singer, 2018; Staehr Fenner & Snyder, 2017). However, very few resources are available to support general education teachers and ELD/ELL specialists collaborate effectively on all grade levels.

There is emerging research-based evidence (Dove & Honigsfeld, 2014; Greenberg Motamedi, Vazquez, Gandhi, & Holmgren, 2019; Honigsfeld & Dove, 2017; Peercy, Ditter, & Destefano, 2017), practitioner-documentation (Foltos, 2018; Norton, 2016), and state and local policy initiatives (NYSED, 2018; DESE, 2019) to substantiate the need for researching teacher collaboration and integrated services for ELs. The extant research may be described as focusing on several key themes:

- teacher learning and capacity building (such as the body of work developed by Martin-Beltrán & Madigan Peercy, 2014; and others);
- teacher relationship and trust building (Honigsfeld & Dove, 2017; Pawan & Ortloff, 2011);
- shifts in instructional practices and role definition due to collaborative and co-teaching approaches to serving ELs (Davison, 2006; Martin-Beltrán & Madigan Peercy, 2012; Peercy et al., 2017); and
- equity in education and culturally responsive teaching (Compton, 2018; Scanlan, Frattura, Schneider, & Capper, 2012; Theoharis & O'Toole, 2011).

While research on teacher collaboration and co-teaching is expanding (Kuusisaari, 2014), "the long-standing culture of teacher isolation and individualism, together with teachers' preference to preserve their individual autonomy, may hinder deep-level collaboration to occur" (Vangrieken, Dochy, Raes, & Kyndt, 2015, p. 36). Absent from the literature is the study of program implementation and the implications thereof on student learning outcomes. This study attempts to begin to address that gap.

THEORETICAL LENS

We were guided by Fullan's (2007) original model for successful change as a theoretical lens for our research as we had done so in our pilot study (Dove & Honigsfeld, 2014). Fullan asserted that "behaviors and emotions change before beliefs—we need to act in a new way before we get insights and feelings related to new beliefs and . . . shared vision or ownership (which is unquestionably necessary for success) is more an outcome of quality change than its precondition for success" (p. 41). These insights led Fullan to develop ten key elements of successful change:

1. Define closing the gap as the overarching goal.
2. Attend initially to the three basics.

3. Be driven by tapping into people's dignity and sense of respect.
4. Ensure that the best people are working on the problem.
5. Recognize that all successful strategies are socially based, and action oriented—change by doing rather than change by elaborate planning.
6. Assume that lack of capacity is the initial problem and work on it continuously.
7. Stay the course through continuity of good direction by leveraging leadership.
8. Build internal accountability linked to external accountability.
9. Establish conditions for the evolution of positive peer pressure.
10. Use the previous nine strategies to build public confidence. (p. 44).

In his revised work, Fullan (2016) emphasized six elements embedded in the change process including closing the achievement gap, using socially based strategies and action, assuming lack of capacity is the main issue, capitalizing leadership, establishing accountability, and cultivating peer pressure. We were drawn to Fullan's work for this study because he has successfully integrated multiple concepts that are inherent in educational change through collaborative actions. Additional theoretical frameworks and empirical research studies that have informed our research included seminal work by Capper and Frattura (2009), Collier and Thomas (2002); and Cummins (2001).

IN SEARCH OF CO-TEACHING
ACROSS THE UNITED STATES

Our exploratory investigation of co-teaching practices led us to first research possible locations where co-teaching for ELs was a documented program option. Some of these implementations were policy endorsed based on state or locally developed program design guidelines. Others exemplified local grassroots efforts to develop integrated instructional programs that were initiated by teachers and/or administrators predominately in response to (a) shifts in local demographics and (b) the introduction of rigorous state standards and accountability measures (DESE, 2019). We also were fortunate to be invited to various state conferences and school districts in places where co-teaching for ELs was being planned, piloted, and/or fully executed. Through these initial processes, we were introduced to institutions, administrators, teachers, and classes with appropriate programs to study co-teaching implementation and examine their outcomes.

Data Collection

For our data collection, we traveled to a number of schools in the following states that had initiated co-taught programs for English learners in place: Colorado, Georgia, Iowa, Massachusetts, Missouri, New York, North Carolina, South Carolina, Tennessee, Rhode Island, and Virginia. Most programs had been established for less than three years before the commencement of the study; a few programs had been established beyond three years. At each location we visited, we applied various methods to gather data to investigate co-teaching practices. The most common methods we used consisted of individual or paired interviews, focus group discussions, class observations, field notes, and document analysis. Some interviews were audio or video taped, and some class visits were photographed or video recorded. Different methods of data gathering were used at different sites, which was dependent upon the permission we received at each site. In all, 76 teachers and 23 administrators participated in the study, and we observed 18 co-taught classes.

Data Analysis

This study is a component of a larger scale investigation that has additional research foci and also involves case studies and survey research on principals' and teachers' experiences with collaborative practices to support ELs. Data aggregated for this study were analyzed both preliminarily and at the culmination of the research. Data collection yielded interview transcripts, field notes, and narrative descriptions of school visits, as well as artifact analyses. The different data sets initially were organized and coded separately. After coding was completed, the information from individual data sets was merged. Coding categories were closely related to the research questions. As Weber (1990) and Stemler (2001) suggested, revisions were made to the coding as deemed necessary, and the major categories were refined "to the point that maximizes mutual exclusivity and exhaustiveness" (Stemler, para 13). In addition, codes identified participant attitudes, beliefs, perceptions, and general ways of thinking about English learners and best instructional practices for them.

FINDINGS

We organized findings according to major themes and subthemes that emerged from the data analysis. Major themes included fidelity of model/program implementation, leadership, and teachers' professional learning and reflective practices. Subthemes consisted of the following: buy-in, commitment, local program variations and limitations; leadership challenges, roles, advocacy, student outcome data, and social-emotional learning. All subthemes are reported under their respective major themes.

Fidelity of Model Implementation

We examined co-teaching programs in 11 states and determined that there was little consensus about the way to initiate, develop, and implement a co-taught program for English learners. Some programs were initiated as a result of determined administrators who had a particular vision for equitable educational programs for English learners that included co-teaching. Other co-taught programs emerged through the advocacy of teacher teams who appealed to school leaders to establish such initiatives. A third group of co-taught programs were instituted due to some external school mechanism such as the respective state education department's regulations identifying co-teaching as a program requirement or option for ELs or a United States Department of Justice (USDOJ) settlement agreement with a school district to ensure equal educational opportunities for English learners. Some programs were developed on a small-scale basis; they were piloted by one or two teaching teams in the first year and expanded thereafter. There were entire schools that implemented co-teaching as one of several program models of instruction for ELs, whereas others mandated co-teaching as the only model of instruction.

Buy-In

Although our research uncovered that teachers' belief in the work of co-teaching was critical, it was not essential at the onset of co-taught programs. One principal shared the following about teacher buy-in:

> [Co-teaching] was really a very rough transition for our ELL teacher; she struggled with it greatly. On the exciting part of that though, now that we are starting to see some of our scores, some of our benchmarks, and how our students, you know, our ELL students are doing, we want to say that it's amazing, but really, it's not amazing because we've known all along that they've got what it takes; it's just a matter how we're going to teach them . . . And it's also very exciting because our full-time ELL teacher is really seeing that; and that's really validating her as well because I think she felt like she had been taken out of the decision and wasn't happy with that, and so I think that right now she's really excited to see the growth of her kids.

Initial buy-in for teachers did not seem to be fundamental to the success of co-taught programs where there were committed school leaders who initiated the practice. In these cases, initial teacher compliance with co-taught program directives led to gradual ownership of the program model, and over time, many of the same teachers became advocates for co-teaching ELs. However, lack of buy-in appeared to be more problematic when co-taught programs were the result of state regulations or USDOJ directives that had to be followed. Whole school initiation of these co-taught program mandates often had little if any buy-in from teachers or administrators who felt underprepared for the change. These program implementations sometimes resulted in strong opposition, passive support, or indifference by teachers and administrators alike. Nonetheless, there were several schools, in spite of such directives, that embraced co-teaching due to the fostered commitment of teacher teams and collaboration through dedicated and active school leadership.

Commitment

Co-taught programs for ELs that were most often successful with implementation and sustainability had teachers who were committed to (a) the overall welfare of their students, (b) instruction through co-teaching, and most of all (c) the practice of consistent collaboration. These teachers embraced the idea of gathering and examining assessment data to actively target particular areas of concern in students' development of language skills as well as content knowledge and application. They regularly reviewed group and individual student progress to make ongoing adjustments to instruction. Teaching teams frequently committed to small-group instruction, making time to develop materials for cooperative learning experiences and purposeful student-to-student interactions, thus giving ELs in particular more opportunities to practice their language skills.

Co-taught instruction was accomplished through creative class configurations that were fluidly executed. Most often, several class configurations were executed during one class period alternating between whole-class and small-group instruction. Productive co-taught classes had flexible teaching teams that embraced different co-teaching models, developed their own ways to configure classes for instruction, and had no problem regrouping students when needed. Effective teaching teams also committed to incorporating the systematic development of English language and literacy skills in conjunction with content.

Productive co-teaching teams made time to consistently collaborate with one another whether or not collaboration time was a part of their teaching schedules. Although we found that many outstanding co-taught programs had regularly scheduled collaborative planning periods for grade-level or content area teams as well as for co-teaching partnerships, we also noted that many teachers committed to working together outside of the school day whether or not they had common planning time.

Local Program Variations and Limitations

It can be challenging for teachers to balance the needs of all students at different levels of language proficiency and deliver English language development instruction within the framework of mandated program models that have specific guidelines for lesson delivery. Some programs required all instruction be delivered inside standard grade-level classes through co-teaching. In other districts, such as one in the state of Georgia, teachers and administrators interpreted state guidelines for instructional delivery to mean that ELD/ELL teachers should only work with English learners' in co-taught or push-in delivery model classes, and they supported their claims by highlighting the following from the Georgia Department of Education ESOL/Title III Resource Guide 2011–2012 for co-taught programs for English learners:

> In the ESOL Push-in model, the ESOL teacher and the content teacher are co-equals in the classroom, but each has a distinct role. The ESOL teacher is responsible for language support, while the content teacher is responsible for delivery of academic content. Research indicates that strong teaching partnerships occur when teachers know each other's curriculum, share responsibilities, plan together, share strategies, and share teaching equally. *When students break into groups, the ESOL teacher should work with ELs, while the content teacher focuses on mainstream students.* (p. 21)

One ELD/ELL teacher expressed to her principal that building foundational literacy skills with beginning level English learners in grades K–2 might warrant small-group instruction outside of the standard grade-level class. In turn, the building principal believed that piloting co-teaching with a limited number of teachers and maintaining much of the stand-alone classes for English language development as an approach to service delivery for English learners was preferable as compared with transitioning to an all co-taught program. "Ideally, wouldn't it be great to have everybody push in and flourish? And that would be wonderful, but I don't know how realistic that is."

Ultimately, these local variations did not affect the favorable outcomes of a co-taught delivery model of instruction for English learners. Yet, by examining co-taught programs and comparing them to each other, a specific pattern began to emerge. It appeared that although the programs we investigated varied in many ways, all successful co-teaching for ELs included regular collaboration between co-teachers as well as school leaders that were committed to the practice.

Leadership

Under leadership, three subthemes emerged from the data: (a) leadership challenges, (b) leadership roles in supporting collaborative EL program implementation, and (c) advocacy. Participants described various external and internal factors that contributed to how they encountered persuasive mental models among members of the immediate and broader school community regarding ELs. Some of the recurring challenges included lack of systemic or structural support for collaboration or lack of funding for securing additional teaching positions to ensure a more viable collaborative program model. Many leaders recounted incidents that involved ways they had to name, confront, and fearlessly pursue their vision for equity and inclusivity for all learners through teacher collaboration.

When defining the roles leaders assumed, the overarching theme that emerged from the study was advocacy. One administrator emphatically noted that English learners belong in general education classrooms: "They are not outsiders, they are not isolated, they are part of our community, they are valued." Another administrator discussed how she went about achieving a heightened level of understanding and responsiveness to ELs among her faculty: "You have to educate the staff...When we have a population of students whose needs are not being met in our system, our system needs to be changed to meet their needs." Finally, when we asked leaders to identify the major lessons learned and past and future goals set for themselves and their schools, several additional secondary themes emerged in the findings, including the need for greater community involvement and parent engagement, teachers' understanding, commitment to, and enactment of, students' funds of knowledge (Moll, Amanti, Neff, & Gonzalez, 1992), and enhanced opportunities for teacher collaboration, as articulated by one administrator: "I would really like to see that [...] we build a culture here that everyone is responsible for everyone's learning."

Teachers' Professional Learning and Reflection

School improvement policies and plans often focus on increasing teachers' professional learning in order to affect the delivery of instruction and increase student achievement, which "has led to a concentrated concern with professional development (PD) of teachers as one important way of achieving these goals" (Opfer & Pedder, 2011, p. 376). However, research on professional development has identified much of it as ineffective. Rucker (2018) cited several reasons why traditional PD is most often flawed including:

1. passive, surface learning instead of active, deep learning;
2. lack of ongoing support to address individual problems of practice;
3. no time for reflection; and
4. no measurable impact on student learning.

In accordance with Rucker (2018), we also determined that traditional PD—most often delivered in the form of the one-shot workshop—made limited impact on the professional learning of teachers charged with co-teaching ELs. In spite of the pressing demands to build the capacity of teaching partnerships, the traditional PD experienced by some co-teachers did not address the specific issues teachers were facing in their various co-taught classes, and some teachers expressed that they were left to "figure it out themselves."

To make the necessary adjustments in teaching practices required for co-taught programs, teachers reported that effective professional learning occurred when teaching teams engaged in ongoing instructional conversations with one another. These collaborations took place whether or not time was provided for them during the school day. In other words, even though some teaching teams did not have common planning time built into their schedules, they consulted with one another regularly. Teachers asserted that their knowledge and understanding of how to integrate content and English language development instruction improved significantly due to their collaborative efforts. We noted that teachers who met regularly described how they examined and reflected on their roles, responsibilities, instructional delivery, and assessment practices, which ultimately resulted in meaningful, sustained professional learning. Teachers also described how they adopted each other's content knowledge, instructional strategies, class management techniques, and formative assessment skills through the process of co-teaching together.

In addition to ongoing collaboration, teaching partnerships also benefited from instructional coaching. Teachers reported that coaching provided them with the personalized support they needed to answer questions about effective practices, review and develop strategies for individuals or groups of students, or problem solve issues that arose from day-to-day co-teaching. Some schools offered teaching teams opportunities to work with coaches from outside of the school, while other schools provided instructional peer coaches—teachers on special assignment or TOSAs—to offer support for planning, lesson delivery, curriculum writing, technology integration, and the development of assessments, materials, and resources. Coaching roles varied from school to school, and not all schools we investigated provided their co-teaching teams with instructional coaches. In any case, those teachers who had access to instructional coaches most often reported that the feedback they obtained through the coaching process enhanced their abilities to plan and execute lessons in co-taught classes.

Student Outcome Data

One aspect of teacher collaboration and reflection concerned the examination of student learning. Data-driven instruction was clearly the goal in many schools we visited; yet, using the data from annual testing did little in most cases to support the learning of ELs. For this reason, teachers often reflected on the outcomes of students from their formative assessments and periodic review of student writing. These measures were generally what guided teachers to reevaluate their teaching practices, alter their materials and resources, and rethink their grouping strategies.

Our efforts to collect achievement data to determine the general outcomes of co-taught programs were met with several roadblocks due to the limited availability of such data. Many of the co-taught programs were in the beginning stages of implementation and not enough time had passed to accumulate sufficient or accurate comparative data. Other programs had a low incidence of English learners and had few if any opportunities to compare the success of ELs across grade levels. Still others could not compare the progress of ELs because they may not have consistently been in co-taught programs. Therefore, much of the achievement success of co-taught programs was presented through the anecdotal reporting of teachers and administrators revealed in our interviews with them.

Some administrators were able to cite higher annual test scores for their English learners as compared with other local schools with similar demographics; they attributed the difference in achievement to teacher collaboration and/or their co-taught programs. Some teachers also shared their action research data, which were the results of test scores from both their co-taught and solo-taught classes; they determined that not only did ELs perform better in co-taught classes but all students achieved at a higher rate. Some school leaders identified an increase in graduation rates for English learners, and they attributed the rise in successful school completion to the inclusion of co-taught programs in their schools. One elementary school in particular became a turnaround school; it had strong systems in place for not only co-taught instruction but had regularly scheduled collaboration for grade-level teacher teams. All in all, the one outcome, consistently revealed in our interviews with teachers and administrators, was the value of ongoing, job-embedded, structured time for teacher collaboration and its positive impact on student learning.

Social Emotional Learning

When displaced from their home countries, family and friends, and the places where they felt safe, secure, and thrived in school, ELs are often challenged by the academic and social demands of schooling in the United States. As a result, ELs may not initially flourish in their new schools and communities when they first arrive, and their lack of safety, security, and stability may not be assuaged for several years. On this account, it is important for teachers to nurture the growth of ELs beyond academics so that they may "develop the social emotional knowledge, skills, attitudes, and behaviors needed for success in school and beyond" (U.S. Department of Education, 2017, p. 1).

Social-emotional learning was a subtheme that emerged as teachers and administrators reflected on the positive outcomes of co-taught classes. These conversations led to further discussions about the importance of ELs believing in their ability to achieve academically and how their self-efficacy was fostered in co-taught classes as they developed a sense of belonging because they *no longer had to leave to learn*. Co-teachers expressed how the support provided in co-taught classes increased ELs' positive self-efficacy resulting in a rise in students' motivation to take risks and more active participation in class.

Two administrators in particular described how, after 3 years, their high school co-taught program for ELs had increased graduation rates and decreased dropout rates because "the more connected kids feel with school, obviously, the more they will stay." One of the administrators reported, "We had students tell us they were going to drop out before they were in these [co-taught] classes and they decided to stay." The other administrator described how students felt in the following way:

> It's a big comfort for our students who come into the class and they realize they have a chance to pass this ELA Regents because they have these two teachers here, and they care so much…two educators in the classroom, I think it makes a big difference when they realize, "Wait, I'm not in this alone; I have people to help me, people to go to, and my parents to talk to also."

Even though evidence for academic success was limited in co-taught classes, data revealed that students' sense of belonging and perseverance to succeed was well-documented.

DISCUSSION

For the past decade, educators across the United States began to explore multiple, unique program designs to provide equitable educational experiences for ELs (Dove & Honigsfeld, 2018, 2019; López & Iribaren, 2014; Valentino & Reardon, 2014). One such program design choice is the integration of language and literacy development with the general education curriculum that is offered by two or more educators collaboratively delivering instruction for ELs and fluent English-speaking students within the shared learning environment of a co-taught class (Bell & Baecher, 2012; Honigsfeld & Dove, 2010a, 2012, 2015; Martin-Beltrán & Madigan Peercy, 2014; Russel, 2012). This study contributed to the understanding of what factors furthered successful implementation of collaborative, integrated approaches to supporting English learners.

The three major findings are well aligned to previous research on teacher collaboration related to English learners and students with disabilities (Honigsfeld & Dove, 2012; Scruggs, Mastropieri, & McDuffie, 2007). We further confirmed that fidelity of model/program implementation requires a careful design, consistent delivery, and systemic approach that does not shy away from teacher accountability. Similarly, our study substantiated that there needs to be a strong emphasis placed on the role of school district and building leaders as well as on the collaborating teachers' professional beliefs, reflective practices, and on-going professional growth. Of the many subthemes that emerged from the study, we need to emphasize some of the findings that may speak to limitations: Study participants reported (a) a range of local program variations, (b) limitations that may be well-anticipated considering the importance of local governance in the U.S. education system, as well as (c) leadership challenges and difficulties obtaining definitive data that consistently and objectively document positive student outcomes, be it academic, linguistic, or social-emotional.

CONCLUSION

Our study has confirmed that there is no magic in co-teaching although it can be quite magical. The magic is not in the act of co-delivering instruction, it is in the sustained, meaningful opportunities to collaborate and support students to develop their sense of belonging and efficacy to succeed. Our research suggests what happens outside the classroom has either equal or greater weight (effect) than what happens inside the classroom. Based on this multi-year, multi-state, comprehensive study, our recommendations are two-fold: We are making suggestions for future research as well as for program design and implementation.

Recommendations for Future Research

Future research in the area of teacher collaboration and co-teaching for the sake of English learners must be both broadened and narrowed. There is an urgent need for a comprehensive study that systemically examines ELD/ELL program design mandates across all 50 states and, more specifically, collaborative, integrated ELD/ELL program design implementation guidelines as well as actual implementation practices in the United States. In addition, there is a dire need for studies that closely follow ELs who participate in various ELD/ELL programs to document program efficacy and impact on student learning.

Recommendations for Co-teaching Program Design and Implementation

School districts that wish to establish a collaborative, integrated model of service for ELs with a key focus on co-teaching should consider the following:

1. Develop a shared understanding of (a) the student population in the district; (b) federal, state, and local guidelines of programming for ELs; and (c) comprehensive knowledge of culturally responsive and sustaining pedagogies as well as inclusive, integrated service options for ELs.
2. Establish an inclusive vision and mission that embraces a shared responsibility for all learners and ensures (a) a climate of belonging; (b) challenging, rigorous educational opportunities; and (c) a strong school–community partnership and parent engagement.
3. Design a pilot implementation plan for co-teaching that includes (a) intentional teacher team building, (b) strategic student placements, (c) ongoing professional development, (d) close monitoring and data collection, and (d) periodic review and revision.
4. Depending on the original pilot and the local context, scale up the implementation to include more classes, grade-levels, or school buildings and expand on all key features of implementation under Step 3.
5. Document successes and challenges and conduct periodic program reviews and evaluation.
6. Celebrate success and model change for others!

REFERENCES

Bell, A., & Baecher, L. (2012). Points on a continuum: ESL teachers reporting on collaboration. *TESOL Journal, 3*(3), 488–515.

Calderón, M. E., Dove, M. G., Staehr Fenner, D., Gottlieb, M., Honigsfeld, A., Singer, W. T., . . . Zacarian, D. (2019). *Breaking down the wall: Essential shifts for English learners' success.* Thousand Oaks, CA: Corwin.

Calderón, M. E., & Slakk, S. (2018). *Teaching reading to English learners, Grades 6–12* (2nd ed.). Thousand Oaks, CA: Corwin.

Capper, C. A., & Frattura, E. (2009). *Meeting the needs of students of ALL abilities: How leaders go beyond inclusion* (2nd ed.). Thousand Oaks, CA: Corwin.

Collier, V. P., & Thomas, W. P. (2002). Reforming education policies for English learners means better schools for all. *The State Education Standard, 3*(1), 30–36.

Compton, T. N. (2018). *Access to culturally responsive teaching for English language learners: Mainstream teacher perceptions and practice on inclusion* (Doctoral dissertation). Electronic Theses and Dissertations (Paper 2949). https://doi.org/10.18297/etd/2949

Cummins, J. (2001). *Negotiating identities: Education for empowerment for a diverse society*. Los Angeles: California Association for Bilingual Education.

Davison, C. (2006). Collaboration between ESL and content area teachers: How do we know when we are doing it right? *The International Journal of Bilingual Education and Bilingualism, 9*(4), 454–475.

DESE. (2019). *Collaboration tool*. Retrieved from http://www.doe.mass.edu/ele/instruction/

Dove, M. G. (2009). A grassroots approach to co-teaching for English language learners. In A. Honigsfeld & A. Cohan (Eds.), *Breaking the mold of school instruction and organization* (pp. 25–30). Lanham, MD: Rowman & Littlefield.

Dove, M. G., & Honigsfeld, A. (2014). Analysis of the implementation of an ESL co-teaching model in a suburban elementary school. *NYS TESOL Journal, 1*(1), 62–67.

Dove, M. G., & Honigsfeld, A. (2018). *Co-teaching for English learners: A guide to collaborative planning, instruction, assessment, and reflection*. Thousand Oaks, CA: Corwin.

Dove, M. G., & Honigsfeld, A. (2019). From isolation to collaboration. In M. E. Calderon, M. G. Dove, D. Staehr Fenner, M. Gottlieb, A. Honigsfeld, T. Ward Singer, . . . D. Zacarian (Eds.), Breaking down the wall: Essential shifts for English learners' success (pp. 73–88). Thousand Oaks, CA: Corwin.

Ferlazzo, L., & Hull Sypnieski, K. (2018). The ELL teacher's toolbox: Hundreds of practical ideas to support your students. San Francisco, CA: Jossey-Bass.

Foltos, L. (2018, January 29). *Teachers learn better together* [Blog post]. Retrieved from http://www.edutopia.org/article/teachers-learn-better-together

Friend, M., & Cook, L. (2012). *Interactions: Collaboration skills for school professionals* (7th ed.). Boston, MA: Allyn & Bacon.

Fullan, M. (2007). *The new meaning of educational change* (4th ed.). New York, NY: Teachers College Press.

Fullan, M. (2016). *The new meaning of educational change* (5th ed.). New York, NY: Teachers College Press.

García, O., & Kleifgen, J. A. (2018). *Educating emergent bilinguals: Policies, programs, and practices for English language learners*. New York, NY: Teachers College Press.

Gibbons, P. (2015). *Scaffolding language scaffolding learning: Teaching English language learners in the mainstream classroom*. Portsmouth, NH: Heinemann.

Greenberg Motamedi, J., Vazquez, M., Gandhi, E. V., & Holmgren, M. (2019). *Beaverton School District English language development minutes, models, and outcomes*. Portland, OR: Education Northwest.

Honigsfeld, A., & Dove, M. G. (2010a). *Collaboration and co-teaching: Strategies for English learners*. Thousand Oaks, CA: Corwin.

Honigsfeld, A., & Dove, M. (2010b). From isolation to partnership: ESL co-teaching leads to teacher leadership. *Teachers Teaching Teachers (T3), 5*(6), 1–4.

Honigsfeld, A., & Dove, M. G. (Eds.). (2012). *Co-teaching and other collaborative practices in the EFL/ESL classroom: Rationale, research, reflections, and recommendations*. Charlotte, NC: Information Age.

Honigsfeld, A., & Dove, M. G. (2015). *Collaboration and co-teaching for English learners: A leader's guide*. Thousand Oaks, CA: Corwin.

Honigsfeld, A., & Dove, M. G. (2017). The co-teaching flow inside the classroom. In M. Dantas-Whitney & S. Rilling (Eds.), *TESOL Voices: Insider accounts of classroom life, secondary education* (pp. 107–114). Alexandria, VA: TESOL International Association.

Honigsfeld, A., & Dove, M. G. (2019a). *Collaboration for English learners: A foundational guide to integrated practices* (2nd ed.). Thousand Oaks, CA: Corwin.

Honigsfeld, A., & Dove, M. G. (2019b). Evidence-based best practices in support of mainstream-ESOL teacher collaboration and co-teaching. In L. C. de Oliveira (Ed.), *The handbook of TESOL in K–12* (pp. 405–422). Hoboken, NJ: Wiley.

Kuusisaari, H. (2014). Teachers at the zone of proximal development—Collaboration promoting or hindering the development process. *Teaching and Teacher Education, 43*, 46–57.

López, F., & Iribaren, J. (2014). Creating and sustaining inclusive instructional settings for English language learners: Why, what, and how. *Theory Into Practice, 53*(2), 106–114. https://doi.org/10.1080/00405841.2014.885810

Martin-Beltrán, M., & Madigan Peercy, M. (2012). How can ESOL and mainstream teachers make the best of standards-based curriculum in order to collaborate? *TESOL Journal, 3*(3), 425–444. https://doi.org/10.1002/tesj.23

Martin-Beltrán, M., & Madigan Peercy, M. (2014). Collaboration to teach English language learners: Opportunities for shared teacher learning. *Teachers and Teaching, 20*(6), 721–737. https://doi.org/10.1080/13540602.2014.885704

Marzano, R. J. (2007). *The art and science of teaching: A comprehensive framework for effective instruction*. Alexandria, VA: ASCD.

Moll, L. C., Amanti, C., Neff, D., & Gonzalez, N. (1992). Funds of knowledge for teaching: Using a qualitative approach to connect homes and classrooms. *Theory Into Practice, 31*(2), 132–141.

Murawski, W. W., & Lochner, W. W. (2017). *Beyond co-teaching basics: A data-driven, no-fail model for continuous improvement*. Alexandria, VA: ASCD.

Nieto, S., & Bode, P. (2012). *Affirming diversity: The sociopolitical context of multicultural education* (6th ed.). New York, NY: Pearson.

Norton, J. (2016). *Successful coteaching: ESL teachers in the mainstream classroom*. Retrieved from http://newsmanager.commpartners.com/tesolc/issues/2016-10 -01/3.html

New York State Education Department. (2018). *Program options for English language learners/multilingual learners*. Retrieved from http://www.nysed.gov/ bilingual-ed/program-options-english-language-learnersmultilingual-learners

Opfer, V. D., & Pedder, D. (2011). Conceptualizing teacher learning. *Review of Educational Research, 81*(3), 376–407. Retrieved from https://journals.sagepub .com/doi/10.3102/0034654311413609

Pawan, F., & Ortloff, J. H. (2011). Sustaining collaboration: English-as-a-second-language, and content-area teachers. *Teaching and Teacher Education, 27*(2), 463–471.

Peercy, M. M., Ditter, M., & Destefano, M. (2017). "We need more consistency": Negotiating the division of labor in ESOL—Mainstream teacher collaboration. *TESOL Journal, 8*(1), 215–239. https://doi.org/10.1002/tesj.269

Rivkin, S. G., Hanushek, E. A., & Kain, J. F. (2005). Teachers, schools, and academic achievement. *Econometrica, 73*(2), 417–458.

Rucker, K. (2018). *The six flaws of "traditional" professional development.* Retrieved from https://www.gettingsmart.com/2018/02/the-six-flaws-of-traditional-professional-development/

Russell, F. A. (2012). A culture of collaboration: Meeting the instructional needs of adolescent English language learners. *TESOL Journal, 3*(3), 445–468. https://doi.org/10.1002/tesj.24

Scanlan, M., Frattura, E., Schneider, K., & Capper, C. (2012). Bilingual students within integrated comprehensive services: Collaborative strategies. In A. Honigsfeld & M. G. Dove (Eds.), *Coteaching and other collaborative practices in the EFL/ESL classroom: Rationale, research, reflections, and recommendations* (pp. 3–13). Charlotte, NC: Information Age.

Scruggs, T. E., Mastropieri, M. A., & McDuffie, K. A. (2007). Co-teaching in inclusive classrooms: A metasynthesis of qualitative research. *Exceptional Children, 73*(4), 392–416.

Singer, T. W. (2018). *EL excellence every day: The flip-to guide for differentiating academic literacy.* Thousand Oaks, CA: Corwin.

Staehr Fenner, D., & Snyder, S. (2017). *Unlocking English learners' potential: Strategies for making content accessible.* Thousand Oaks, CA: Corwin.

Stein, E. (2016). *Elevating co-teaching through UDL.* Wakefield, MA: CAST Professional.

Stein, E. (2017). *Two teachers in the room: Strategies for co-teaching success.* New York, NY: Routledge.

Stemler, S. (2001). An overview of content analysis. *Practical Assessment, Research & Evaluation, 7*(17). Retrieved from http://PAREonline.net/getvn.asp?v=7&n=17

Theoharis, G., & O'Toole, J. (2011). Leading inclusive ELL: Social justice leadership for English language learners. *Educational Administration Quarterly, 47*(4), 646–688. https://doi.org/10.1177/0013161X11401616

U.S. Department of Education. (2017). *Newcomer toolkit.* Retrieved from https://www2.ed.gov/about/offices/list/oela/newcomers-toolkit/ncomertoolkit.pdf

Valentino, R., & Reardon, S. (2014). Effectiveness of four instructional programs designed to serve English language learners: Variation by ethnicity and initial English proficiency. *Educational Evaluation and Policy Analysis, 37*(4), 612–637.

Vangrieken, K., Dochy, F., Raes, E., & Kyndt, E. (2015). Teacher collaboration: A systematic review. *Educational Research Review, 15,* 17–40.

Villa, R. A., & Thousand, J. S. (2016). *Leading an inclusive school: Access and success for all students.* Alexandria, VA: ASCD.

Villa, R., Thousand, J., & Nevin, A. (2013). *A guide to co-teaching: New lessons and strategies to facilitate student learning* (3rd ed.). Thousand Oaks, CA: Corwin.

Weber, R. P. (1990). *Basic content analysis* (2nd ed.). Newbury Park, CA: SAGE.

Wright, S. P., Horn, S. P., & Sanders, W. L. (1997). Teachers and classroom context effects on student achievement: Implications for teacher evaluation. *Journal of Personnel Evaluation in Education, 11*(1), 57–67.

PART II

SYSTEM-WIDE INITIATIVES: SCALING IT UP

CHAPTER 7

TWO BRAINS ARE BETTER THAN ONE!

State-Level Professional Development and Teachers' Descriptions of the Benefits of Co-Teaching

Joan R. Lachance
The University of North Carolina at Charlotte

Given the level of linguistic and cultural diversity within U.S schools, English learners' (ELs) academic success is a vital consideration in the scope of current K–12 education (U.S. Department of Education [USDE], 2015a). Federal legislation from the Every Student Succeeds Act (ESSA) related to ELs' academic success obliges states to give extensive considerations to students' academic outcomes as a direct result of informed, collaborative, and linguistically supportive instruction (USDE, 2015b). Yet, numerous practicing general education classroom teachers in some states continue to express their unpreparedness to work specifically with ELs, intensifying the need for practical recommendations related to professional development for co-teaching program design (Kolano, Davila, Lachance, & Coffey, 2014). This

Co-Teaching for English Learners, pages 81–93
Copyright © 2020 by Information Age Publishing
All rights of reproduction in any form reserved.

movement for collaborative transformation also calls for increased innovation from educator professional development programs. More than ever, state education agencies (SEAs) are giving increased focus to educators' development for shared practices resulting in student-centered co-teaching programs and collaborative teacher partnerships (Honigsfeld & Dove, 2015; Zwiers, O'Hara, & Pritchard, 2014).

Furthermore, the constructs of current professional development programs entail an increased emphasis on evidence-based co-teaching and collaboration practices to yield increased student outcomes that are mutually beneficial for ELs and native speakers of English (Echevarria, Vogt, & Short, 2016). As a direct result of research on the collaborative instructional cycle, various SEAs are implementing professional development initiatives to formally support collaborative techniques and instructional design approaches related to academic language development and co-teaching (Honigsfeld & Dove, 2010, 2015; Zwiers et al., 2014).

Following the national pattern of diverse student demographics, North Carolina's population of ELs has dramatically increased. In the 2015–2016 school year North Carolina reported that the EL population had surpassed 100,000, nearly six percent of the overall student population (North Carolina Department of Public Instruction [NCDPI], 2017). Between 2009 and 2013, the percentage of ELs identified as *immigrant*, born outside of the United States remained steady at 7.5% indicating a continuing enrollment of first-generation ELs. At the same time, nearly 75% of the current North Carolina elementary school students currently classified as ELs were born in the United States. The variation reflects the complex nature of designing and implementing effective teacher professional development services that are attentive to the broad scope of ELs in North Carolina classrooms (NCDPI, 2017).

Aiming to extend current literature and framed by relevant theory, this chapter showcases the findings of a mixed methods study of one southeastern state on the topic of K–12 teachers' descriptions of ELs' academic benefits as a result of co-teaching and collaborative practices. As part of a state-led professional development series, quantitative and qualitative data from approximately 70 educator participants, representing nearly 25 of the state's 100 county and 15 city school districts highlight descriptions about how co-teaching would specifically support their ELs' academic language development and school success. Additionally, participants predicted changed patterns of student growth as a direct result of implementing the co-teaching framework in their schools. Study findings and discussions include participants' views on the benefits of structured collaboration and co-teaching for improved student outcomes (Honigsfeld & Dove, 2010; WIDA, 2012; Wong-Fillmore, 2014). Emphasis was also given to participants' practical recommendations for programmatic logistics for successful co-teaching environments.

In direct response to North Carolina's focus on supporting K–12 classroom teachers in ways that promote increased EL student academic outcomes through co-teaching and collaboration, the purpose of this study was to examine teachers' predictions about the benefits of co-teaching and collaboration with their own students. The study's guiding research questions were:

1. How would you describe what the overall benefits of co-teaching and collaboration are with ELs?
2. What do you predict will happen with your EL student outcomes as a direct result of the co-teaching and collaboration training?
3. What recommendations would you make for successful co-teaching in your current classroom or program?

METHODS

The researcher conducted an explanatory mixed method design to combine quantitative and qualitative data collection and analysis (Creswell & Plano Clark, 2018). Characteristic to this type of research design, after interpreting quantitative data, attention was given to qualitative data analysis in order to gain clarity on teachers' descriptions and predictions about the benefits of co-teaching with their ELs. Furthermore, the study design granted participants with the opportunity to make recommendations for successful implementation of co-teaching and collaborative frameworks in the context of their current English as a second language (ESL) program services (Yin, 2014).

Context

The study was conducted with a specific format, with the intent of developing a specialized understanding of one group of practicing teachers' descriptions and predictions about the benefits of co-teaching and collaboration for their ELs. Specifically, the study examined the participants' predictions as a direct result of receiving formal co-teaching training. The study was relevant given that the participants' state has a conglomerate of formalized initiatives, fully implemented to further advance all teachers' competencies related to ELs' academic language development. One aspect of the state's larger set of initiatives includes a 3-day professional development course for the districts' K–12 classroom and ESL teachers. The participants for this particular study worked in K–12 general education and

ESL classrooms as well as some district-level personnel who lead curricular and pedagogical support to the ESL teachers and ESL program services.

Data Sources

The study's approach allowed for the exploration of the research questions in the authentic context of a formal, state-led teacher institute open to K–12 classroom and ESL teachers (Yin, 2014). The context allowed for a focus on representation of general education classroom and ESL teachers as well as other district-level ESL professionals, therefore representing a purposive sample of convenience (Miles, Huberman, & Saldaña, 2014). Data triangulation was achieved via multiple sources of evidence, all examined in the context where the data were collected during the teacher institute. The data sources from each of the participants were open-ended survey questions, in-person natural, emergent discussions, as well as artifacts and documents.

Survey

A survey was utilized with the 70 participating teachers, incorporating multiple item types. Seidman's (2013) research protocol shaped the open-ended questions and invited participants to self-report demographic data, such as professional roles, length of time working with ELs, areas of North Carolina teacher certification, and other general information. More specifically, for the purpose of this study, the participants were given a list of nine open-ended questions, organized around the topics of academic language, describing and predicting the benefits of co-teaching and collaboration for ELs, and articulating their viewpoints on the importance of the collaborative instructional cycle for academic language development (see Table 7.1). Finally, participants were asked to describe their recommendations for successful implementation within their own current school, district, and ESL program service parameters.

Natural Discussions

Another data source for the study included emergent, natural discussions with stratified sampling of the larger group (Gubrium, Holstein, Marvasti, & McKinney, 2012). The informal, natural discussions served the purpose of more in-depth and genuine dialogue about the concept of increased student success through co-teaching, its importance in helping ELs in school, and recommendations for successful implementation. The informal, natural discussions took place on-site at the 3-day teacher institute, in the context of the professional development environment, to capture participants' deeper, multidimensional understandings at the moment of

	Topic 1: Academic Language and Its Importance	Topic 2: Academic Language and Collaboration	Topic 3: Overall Benefits of Co-Teaching and Collaboration
Questions			
Questions 1, 4, and 7	How do you describe academic language?	How do you collaborate with other teachers of ELs in your school?	How would you describe the overall benefits of co-teaching and collaboration with ELs?
Questions 2, 5, and 8	How do you make decisions about the academic language you include in your plans to teach in your classroom?	How does this collaboration impact the ways you plan for, deliver, and assess instruction to develop academic language?	What do you predict the benefits of the co-teaching and collaboration training will be in for you and your students in your classroom?
Questions 3, 6, and 9	Describe your views on the importance of developing academic language with your students.	How do you see this collaboration impacting ELs development of academic language?	What do you predict will happen with your ELs' outcomes as a direct result of the co-teaching and collaboration training?

TABLE 7.1 Participant Questions by Topic

Note: The questions were disbursed over the 3-day training.

firsthand learning and new construction of meaning. Anecdotal notes and daily reflective logs summarizing the emergent, natural discussions were transcribed resulting in integrated, synthesized transcripts.

Artifacts and Documentation

Triangulated data sources included artifacts and documentation from the professional development teacher institute targeting the topic of co-teaching, collaboration, and its benefits for ELs. Artifacts and documentations such as small-group posters, 60-second video files as mock public service announcements, individual table-top note charts, model lesson plans, and daily tickets out were created by all the participants over the course of the 3-day professional development. Likewise, participants were invited to provide ancillary documents they used or intended to use post-training. The researcher examined archival curricular materials and participating teachers' professional development outcomes through the lens of described benefits of co-teaching and collaboration for ELs with connections to the research questions.

Participants

The professional development teacher institute enrollment totaled approximately 70 K–12 general education and ESL teachers as well as district-level EL coordinators. All were invited to participate in the study; 63 participants completed survey questions and participated in the 3-day course, yielding a 90% participation rate. Cross-curricular perspectives were considered as 78% of the participants were ESL teachers, 20% were general education teachers, and 2% represented district-level stakeholders.

Data Analysis

The researcher analyzed quantitative survey data to calculate demographic data to include percentages of participants' years of teaching, frequencies of current co-teaching and collaborative instructional cycle patterns, and areas of North Carolina teacher certification. The researcher also recursively analyzed qualitative data regarding academic language development with ELs, overall descriptions of the benefits of co-teaching with ELs in mind, and the participants' predictions about EL student outcomes as a direct result of the co-teaching and collaboration professional development. Themes were inductively examined within participants' descriptions to peg which aspects of co-teaching and collaboration were identified as beneficial and what recommendations were offered for successful implementation.

FINDINGS

The chapter showcases qualitative findings, highlighting authentic participant responses, which were categorized into two overarching themes (Saldaña, 2016) of (a) amplification of highly specialized pedagogies and (b) predicted student growth. These two larger themes, in connection with the research questions respectively, also revealed sub-thematic information regarding intensified support for both content concepts and academic language development, increased student engagement, students' sociocultural gains, and broadened access to curricular concepts in the context of school.

Amplification of Highly Specialized Pedagogies

Addressing one research question—"How would you describe what the overall benefits of co-teaching and collaboration are for ELs?"—the majority of the teachers described highly specialized pedagogies such as specialized teaching strategies and co-assessments designed with two teachers in mind. Furthermore, descriptions of specialized pedagogies emphasized both teachers' use of scaffolds for content concepts combined with scaffolds for academic language development throughout the co-instructional cycle. The need for collaborative approaches for students' content and academic language development was indicated, given the nature and complexity associated with ELs' learning content concepts while simultaneously acquiring academic English (Zweirs et al., 2014). The notion that having two teachers, each with an area of expertise, working collaboratively with students was resoundingly described as beneficial and supportive (Gibbons, 2015). One participant stated, "Co-teaching is like having the best of both worlds. Two teachers, focusing on content and language together with different [teaching] styles, is super-helpful for ELs." Another said, "Two teachers, each with an area of expertise, is ideal to help ELs! They [ELs] get double the focused support." Approximately 40% of the participants emphasized key points about students' benefiting from having both content and language experts in the same classroom, working with all students.

In conjunction with the point that co-teaching isn't an approach that only works with some learners, nearly 25% of the participants specifically referenced that co-teaching and collaboration would be beneficial for *all* students, not just ELs, to support academic language development. Participants' descriptions focused on students' need for specialized support in both content concepts and academic language development. Likewise, descriptions focused on pedagogical variations in content and language teaching methods, all of which were described as highly necessary and specialized for increased student outcomes. The emphasis on two teachers, each with an area of expertise, working collaboratively with students as an overall benefit of co-teaching was a recurring theme. Several teachers explicitly connected pedagogical variations within co-teaching as a highly specialized form of support. One participant wrote in the survey response:

> Two heads are always better than one. Co-teaching and collaboration encourages student motivation when they also see teachers working together for their benefit. The ELs would potentially be taught in a variety of ways and styles. This would allow them [the ELs] the opportunity to have these different styles, methods, and strategies to better understand the content area [concepts] and the academic language.

Another teacher shared perspective on the benefits of a collaborative approach. The participant responded in the survey by writing:

> I think co-teaching benefits ELs because the two teachers can work in such variation. It allows for more tailored instruction and specific attention to students' needs because content and language teachers are combining their expertise. This makes sure the ELs get to the content with support.

Repeatedly, teachers referenced combined, specialized teaching strategies, with some emphasizing content and others focused on academic language development. The need for collaborative approaches for students' content and academic language development were often intertwined in teachers' responses, demonstrating points about their thoughts on specialized pedagogies for both content and academic language development.

Predicted Student Growth

In connection with the research question—"What do you predict will happen with your ELs' outcomes as a direct result of this co-teaching and collaboration training?"—over 85% of the teachers recurrently expressed details regarding increased student academic growth. Of that 85%, nearly one fourth of the participants specifically referenced predicted improvements on high stakes grade-level assessments as well as English language development assessments, by name, used in North Carolina. One example of how a participant made an explicit connection to students' predicted growth on rigorous assessments as a result of co-teaching training was: "With co-teaching in place in my classroom, they [the ELs] will increase their language proficiency and have a better understand of language for the [names two assessments] tests." Whereas another noted that all students could be considered academic language learners who could potentially benefit from increased language skills as a result of co-teaching. The participant said: "With these new co-teaching practices, I believe the students' outcomes will be more targeted and specific for language and content. This is good for all kids!"

Another aspect of the participants' responses and predictions about the benefits of co-teaching for ELs was that nearly one third of the teachers made specific reference to students' growth in sociocultural ways. These details are significant given that student interaction and sociocultural elements have a direct relationship with successful academic outcomes (Gibbons, 2015; WIDA, 2012; Zwiers & Crawford, 2011). As one teacher participant amply stated, "With co-teaching in my classroom, the ELs will have a better chance of feeling less isolated. They [ELs] will feel more a part of something versus being pulled left and right. They can fully participate and own their own success." Another teacher participant said, "Not only will co-teaching help support their [ELs'] language learning, this [co-teaching] will help build students' confidence and comfort levels for more engagement."

Recommendations for Successful Co-Teaching

In connection to research question three—"What recommendations would you make for successful co-teaching in your current classroom or program?"—the participants' responses were sub-thematically categorized into three areas (Saldaña, 2016). The areas were: (a) time for co-planning, (b) the importance of administrator buy-in, and, (c) logistical challenges. While there were no participant responses indicating an absence of benefits of co-teaching for ELs, the details related to recommendations for successful co-teaching did reveal some areas of perceived challenge.

Nearly 75% of the participants indicated they would need greater clarity and significant support with regard to time. They expressed concerns for not having enough time to effectively co-plan given other required duties at school such as bus lot duty and after school tutoring. Parallel to this, participants' responses also gave heavy merit to co-planning as a foundational aspect of successful co-teaching. In relation to this, and furthering the participants' recommendation patterns, they also described the great need for school administration buy-in. Even when district directives might offer co-teaching as a valued approach to working with ELs, the participants indicated that schools' site administrators drive the process for any successful programmatic implementation plan. For further emphasis regarding administrative buy-in, the participants recommended having open, consistent, and creative conversations with their site administrators to see what could be done, both logistically and culturally, to support the use of co-teaching in their schools.

The topic of logistics and lack of time for co-planning, co-instruction, and co-assessment were described as challenging. Specifically, participants named varying programmatic parameters such as current pullout classes, ESL teachers who travel from school to school for service delivery, and different grade-level configurations as areas for logistical consideration. In order to successfully bring about effective implementation of co-teaching, said considerations would need to be addressed by both teachers and school administrators in new and creative ways.

Conclusively, the teacher participants revealed a unification within their responses that they believed co-teaching and collaboration as essentially beneficial for ELs' academic and sociocultural progress. Even with logistical challenges, the participants resoundingly expressed the need for co-teaching implementation in their schools. Ultimately, their descriptions and predictions were tightly aligned with research and literature supporting the importance of collaboration for engaged, successful language learning with ELs (Honigsfeld & Dove, 2015).

DISCUSSION

The open-ended survey directly connected to answering the research questions on describing the overall benefits of co-teaching, predicting student outcomes as a result of co-teaching professional development, and recommendations for successful implementation plans post-training. Findings suggested the majority of the participants see co-teaching as highly beneficial for ELs as well as *all* students. Participants' responses to the nine open-ended questions formulated descriptions about academic language, its importance, and its development via teacher collaboration. More importantly, participants' descriptions collectively confirmed their viewpoints that linked co-teaching with students' successful academic language and content area development. The participants' expressions about highly specialized pedagogies were also described as *amplified* within the co-instructional framework.

In discussion of research question two, findings indicated the participants resoundingly expressed the notion that ELs would undoubtedly have more opportunities for academic and sociocultural growth with co-teaching in place. Similarly, the participants' responses reported that they felt students' levels of confidence are lowered when ELs are pulled away from the general education classroom for pullout ESL services. The participants also reported that pullout services may create impressions of students' *flat* language development in isolation rather than a language-rich, all-inclusive, collaborative classroom. Finally, in connection with pullout ESL services, the participants indicated the perceived reduction in students' academic and social development, ultimately, reducing all students' levels of deeply engaged learning.

Additional discussion connected to research question three, findings from the open-ended survey questions, focus interview/discussions, and artifacts and documents demonstrated the participants' viewpoints on the essential considerations for successful co-teaching implementation. Even with significant logistical and time-related challenges noted, the participants unanimously expressed the aspiration to attempt implementing co-teaching in their schools. Only one participant indicated, "I'm not sure what to do" without further indicating a desire to share recommendations for implementation post-training.

Conversely, in further discussion on the study's findings, there were missing details from the participants about how to effectively monitor EL student progress once co-teaching frameworks were implemented. While they all predicted co-teaching would be highly beneficial in academic and social ways, they did not articulate how to ensure they measured students' growth patterns. Ultimately, noteworthy study details showed that participant teachers clearly believe co-teaching and the collaborative instructional cycle will have positive academic and sociocultural impacts on ELs' academic language development. Yet, they did not express details on how to measure student progress in their classrooms, which may indicate future directions for the state-led initiative on co-teaching training with regard to professional development for teachers, administrators, and other stakeholders.

IMPLICATIONS AND RECOMMENDATIONS
FOR FUTURE RESEARCH

The study intentionally included a large cross-section of EL and general education teachers. Participants represented different levels of educational backgrounds and work experience. Some participants were teaching in urban districts with large populations of ELs while others represented suburban and rural areas with fewer ELs. In total, the participants came from nearly 25 North Carolina school districts. It therefore stands to reason that teachers across the region, and possibly the nation, are likely to face similar challenges in how to best support EL student gains. The findings indicate that the majority of participating teachers have internalized the importance of co-teaching and could articulate details to describe ways they believe co-teaching better supports ELs' academic and sociocultural growth. The study's findings also revealed the participants were willing to embrace new challenges of teaching academic English and disciplinary literacy skills in collaboration with each other.

With these ideas and concepts in mind, some recommendations for future research might include the following:

1. Replicate the study in several other state-led professional development courses to compare the ways in which teachers describe overall benefits of co-teaching for ELs.
2. Encourage participants to disaggregate a particular aspect of pre- and post- training student data from each participating district to compare ways in which implemented co-teaching indicates students' growth.
3. Expand the study to include classroom visitations and observations to document how teachers actualize new knowledge about co-teaching to support collaborative academic language instruction.

CONCLUSION

The numbers of English learners indicate the shift in student demography is not a temporary phenomenon. Academic language development supported by co-teaching and collaborative practices, as indicated in this study's findings is a fundamental aspect of EL student success, both in ESL classrooms and content area classrooms. This study, and its corresponding findings and recommendations, address ways for ESL teachers and their colleagues to support ELs' academic and sociocultural development. The crucial relationships within the co-teaching and collaborative instructional cycle bridge together ESL instruction and content-based academic language development via highly specialized pedagogies. By examining the intersectionality of predicted benefits of co-teaching as described by ESL and general education classroom teachers, this study authentically responds to supporting English learners' overall academic and social gains in our schools.

REFERENCES

Creswell, J. W., & Plano Clark, V. L. (2018). *Designing and conducting mixed methods research* (3rd ed.). Thousand Oaks, CA: SAGE.

Echevarria, J., Vogt, M. E., & Short, D. L. (2016). *Making content comprehensible for English learners: The SIOP model* (5th ed.). Boston, MA: Pearson.

Gibbons, P. (2015). *Scaffolding language, scaffolding learning.* Portsmouth, NH: Heinemann.

Gubrium, J. F., Holstein, J. A., Marvasti, A. B., & McKinney, K. D. (Eds.). (2012). *The SAGE handbook of interview research: The complexities of the craft* (2nd ed.). Thousand Oaks, CA: SAGE.

Honigsfeld, A., & Dove, M. G. (2010). *Collaboration and co-teaching: Strategies for English learners.* Thousand Oaks, CA: Corwin Press.

Honigsfeld, A., & Dove, M. G. (2015). *Collaboration and co-teaching for English learners: A leader's guide.* Thousand Oaks, CA: Corwin Press.

Kolano, L., Davila, L., Lachance, J., & Coffey, H. (2014). Why North and South Carolina teachers say it matters in preparing them for English language learners. *The CATESOL Journal, 25*(1), 41–65.

Miles, M. B., Huberman, A. M., & Saldaña, J. (2014). *Qualitative data analysis* (3rd ed.). Thousand Oaks, CA: SAGE.

North Carolina Department of Public Instruction. (2017). *Language diversity in North Carolina.* Retrieved from https://sites.google.com/dpi.nc.gov/ncels/home/quick-links?authuser=0

Saldaña, J. (2016). *The coding manual for qualitative researchers* (3rd ed.). Thousand Oaks, CA: SAGE.

Seidman, I. (2013). *A guide for researchers in education and the social sciences* (4th ed.). New York, NY: Teachers College Press.

U.S. Department of Education. (2015a). *What you need to know: New guidance on ensuring English learners can participate meaningfully and equally in educational programs.* Retrieved from https://blog.ed.gov/2015/01/what-you-need-to-know-new-guidance-on-ensuring-english-learners-can-participate-meaningfully-and-equally-in-educational-programs/

U.S. Department of Education. (2015b). *Every Student Succeeds Act.* Retrieved from http://www.ed.gov/essa?src=rn

Wong-Fillmore, L. (2014). English language learners at the crossroads of education reform. *TESOL Quarterly, 48*(3), 624–632.

World-Class Instructional Design and Assessment. (2012). *The 2012 amplification of the English language development standards, kindergarten to grade 12.* Madison: Board of Regents of the University of Wisconsin on behalf of the WIDA Consortium.

Yin, R. K. (2014). *Case study research: Designs and methods* (5th ed.). Thousand Oaks, CA: SAGE.

Zwiers, J., & Crawford, M. (2011). *Academic conversations: Classroom talk that fosters critical thinking and content understandings.* Portland, ME: Stenhouse.

Zwiers, J., O'Hara, S., & Pritchard, R. H. (2014). *Common Core Standards in diverse classrooms: Essential practices for developing academic language and disciplinary literacy.* Portland, ME: Stenhouse.

CHAPTER 8

THE ST. LOUIS CO-TEACHING FOR ELs REGIONAL INITIATIVE

Debra Cole
Western Illinois University and Wheaton College

"They're coming to America—and then they're coming to St. Louis."
—Sarah Fenske (2016, para.1)

The St. Louis, Missouri metropolitan area became the new home of over 10,000 immigrants in 2015, and from 2014 to 2015, St. Louis experienced an increase of 8.9% foreign-born residents. That was the highest percent increase of the 20 largest metropolitan regions in the country (Fenske, 2016). In 2017, the St. Louis Regional Chamber noted an additional increase of foreign-born residents during 2016 (Tripp, 2017). Most recently, Axios reporter Kim Hart (2019) noted that for smaller cities like St. Louis, immigration could be making the difference between population loss and growth, as the native born population ages and immigrants of working age are needed to sustain economic growth and prosperity.

More than 12,000 refugees from over 40 different countries have settled in the state over the past ten years, with the highest number coming from Cuba, Somalia, Burma, Iraq, and Bhutan (Bouscaren, 2015). Before that,

Co-Teaching for English Learners, pages 95–104
Copyright © 2020 by Information Age Publishing

95

from 1995–2004, nearly 70,000 predominantly Muslim refugees became the settlers of *Little Bosnia*, bringing economic prosperity and community revitalization to South City (Rivero, 2015).

As the immigrant and refugee population has grown, so has the number and size of English for speakers of other languages (ESOL) programs in the school districts of St. Louis City, St. Louis County, and beyond. Though a majority (87%) of PreK–12 English learners (ELs) in the region speaks Spanish, there are 113 different home languages spoken by the rest (Mongabay, 2015). Missouri has reported teacher shortages for ELs for 15 of the last 20 years (Sanchez, 2017). While overall, only 7% of students in the region are ELs, six elementary schools in St. Louis Public Schools (SLPS) for example, enroll 15% to 38% ELs (Missouri Department of Elementary and Secondary Education, 2017).

Despite several decades of research, schools across the country continue to struggle to establish English language development (ELD) programs that effectively close the achievement gap for ELs within a reasonable amount of time (National Academies of Sciences, Engineering, and Medicine, 2017). To support districts in their efforts to improve opportunities for ELs to learn, the Missouri Department of Elementary and Secondary Education (MO-DESE) contracts with Regional Professional Development Centers (RPDC) to hire Missouri English Language Learning (MELL) instructional specialists. MELL instructional specialists provide professional development for both EL and classroom teachers in the form of training, coaching, and technical assistance.

When I started to work for MELL in 2012, I focused on supporting schools across the region to reorganize traditional pullout English as a second language (ESL) programs to be more collaborative and inclusive—getting EL and classroom teachers together to train, co-plan, and co-teach their ELs. I begin by presenting a brief documentary account of Marvin Elementary School in Ritenour School District in St. Louis County.

CO-TEACHING AT MARVIN ELEMENTARY (RITENOUR SCHOOL DISTRICT, ST. LOUIS COUNTY)

In October of 2012, ELs at Marvin were struggling. In addition to failing academically, some fifth grade students reported that they were reluctant to leave the pullout ESL class where they felt safe and accepted. Several schools in the area had begun training EL teachers to bring language development into the mainstream classroom through co-teaching. In particular, I had been part of piloting co-teaching in St. Louis Public Schools (SLPS) and found that it could be more effective than either pullout or push-in ESL. I suggested the idea to educators at Marvin and they agreed to give it a try.

It was a logistical challenge because ELs on each grade level were spread across several classrooms. One solution for 5th grade was for the EL teacher to collect the ELs to join one class for the science block every day. All 5th grade teachers agreed to teach science at the same time so students did not miss any instruction. The results were amazing! The co-teachers became skilled at team teaching whole group direct instruction and then dividing students into multiple groups to rotate through a variety of hands-on science stations. By end of the school year, these students outperformed all 5th graders in the district on the state science exam. Michael Smith, assistant principal when co-teaching began, commended the entire 5th grade team for their willingness to readjust schedules and to the co-teachers in particular. By putting student needs first and working together, ELs thrived.

Administrators, classroom and EL teachers at Marvin continue to work together by clustering students, co-planning, and co-teaching. Michael Smith, now the principal, notes that while there is high teacher turnover across the district, teachers working in the EL cluster classrooms tend to stay. He credits the high level of collaborative planning for creating the strong feelings of efficacy co-teachers develop when working with high-need students. Jared Martin, the current EL teacher for Grades 3, 4, and 5, tells how he manages to co-plan with six teachers each week:

> I generally get 15–20 minutes every Friday with each of the teachers. With Google Drive, I am able to see the major learning points coming up, so I am prepared to ask specific questions and make specific suggestions for supporting the ELs. I make a point to socialize with them outside of co-planning time, so the face-to-face time is extremely efficient.

When describing co-teaching benefits to students, Jared said, "They [students] see that they don't miss as much instructional time from the classroom. For the other kids, it's great too. It creates a special community with two teachers, where everyone shares the inside jokes." Teachers and students notice the benefits of working together as a whole class with teachers who understand and support the social, academic, and language development needs of each student. Collaborating teachers are not working in isolation. Instead, they work together to address the considerable challenge of working with high-needs students to achieve to their potential.

COMING TOGETHER

Across the districts I supported classroom teachers, EL teachers, and students in co-taught classrooms, reported having a less frenzied, less fragmented school day. EL students and teachers felt more fully included. As I observed the success ELs were having in one school, I shared with teachers in another school what was working. Soon teachers were asking to visit each other's classrooms. This growing interest spurred me to find a way to bring teams from across the region together for training and observing in each other's classrooms.

In the first year of the initiative, teams from fifteen schools representing six districts, came together with thirteen schools from St. Louis Public Schools (SLPS) and trained together throughout the 2015–2016 school year. In the second year of the regional initiative, 2016–2017, 96 teachers formed 51 teams in 32 different schools. In 2017–2018, when SLPS decided to train their schools internally, the regional initiative continued, bringing 59 teachers together to form 31 teams. These teams came from 18 schools representing 10 districts. In the third year, in 2018–2019, another 60 teachers from eight districts came together for the yearlong training.

During the Summer of 2015, Alla Gonzalez Del Castillo, director of ESOL and Elena Okanovic, ESOL instructional coordinator, both of SLPS, met with me to develop the basic structure that continues in SLPS and the regional initiative 4 years later. The training includes 4 full-day training sessions for each cohort spread out over the school year, an online book study, on-site consulting, and coordinated school visits.

Training Sessions

Teams attend all four sessions together. In some cases, EL teachers attend with two or more of their collaborating classroom teachers. The first 2 years we offered each session three times each, so teams could switch to attend on another date if needed. This also allowed more than one team per school to participate by reducing the number of substitutes needed for each day. This built-in flexibility resulted in 97% of the teams completing all four sessions.

Online Book Study

Between sessions, teams posted to a discussion board focused on one chapter each month of Honigsfeld and Dove's (2010) book, *Collaboration and Co-teaching: Strategies for English Learners.* We also uploaded the presentations and resources from the training sessions, allowing teachers a hybrid way to develop as co-teachers. This online connection became especially important during the annual English language proficiency testing window and inclement weather during January and February each year.

On-Site Consulting

In the first year, Elena Okanovic of SLPS and I collaborated to observe every SLPS team each semester. When I visited schools outside SLPS, the EL coordinator or building principal would often observe with me. This was key to building the capacity of school leaders to support effective co-teaching as they saw the importance of collaborative planning for maximizing the talents and training of both teachers. Following the observations, co-teachers debriefed the lesson with observers and completed the *Integrated Teaching for English Learners* (I-TELL; Honigsfeld & Dove, 2015) together. While these conversations typically only lasted 15–30 minutes, it was during these debrief meetings that the training, book study, and classroom visits came together.

Organized School Visits

When teams selected dates to attend training sessions, they also selected a second date when other teams could observe them. This worked especially well during Session 4 after teams had been practicing co-teaching for some time. Visiting teams debriefed the lesson together and completed one I-TELL (Honigsfeld & Dove, 2015) form that was also emailed to me and to the team they observed for further reflection.

Addressing Barriers

The most frequently reported barriers to co-teaching were a lack of co-planning time and having too many teachers to work with. To address these barriers in SLPS, Alla Gonzalez Del Castillo and I facilitated breakfast meetings for administrators, also giving each leader a copy of Honigsfeld and Dove's (2015) *Collaboration and Co-Teaching for English Learners: A Leader's Guide*. We hoped to convince them to cluster ELs and to help teachers schedule weekly co-planning time. I then worked with EL coordinators across the region to meet with as many building leaders as possible, sharing the same priorities.

KEEPING TOGETHER

After the first year, EL teachers reported pre- and post-English language proficiency scores for all ELs in the building, noting which students were in the co-taught classes. We also surveyed co-teachers, asking them to provide self-ratings on the I-TELL (Honigsfeld & Dove, 2015) at the beginning and

TABLE 8.1   Survey Questions About Building-Level Support for Co-Teaching for ELs
1. Rate the building leader support for co-teaching ELLs
1: We are frequently unable to co-plan or co-teach as scheduled due to conflicting responsibilities. 5: Our administrator holds us accountable to co-plan every week and protects our scheduled co-teaching time.
2. Rate the understanding of and support for clustering ELLs into fewer classrooms to allow for more effective co-planning and co-teaching.
1: There is no intentional placement of ELLs into the co-taught classroom.
5: Building leaders meet with each co-teaching team in the spring to work together to cluster students in the most effective way for language development, and carefully consider how to place ELLs who enroll after school starts.

end of the year. Two questions were added to evaluate building-level support (See Table 8.1).

We compared growth in English language proficiency (ELP) for ELs in co-taught classrooms to growth in ELP for those who were not placed in co-taught classes. We also compared growth in ELP for co-taught students whose teachers rated building leader support high to those whose teachers rated building leader support lower. We did not have the capacity to determine the reliability or validity of the I-TELL or the building support survey. However, we were able to identify trends showing that students in co-taught classrooms grew in ELP at the same rate or higher than those who were not. We also collected co-teacher reflections through the professional development discussion board. Ruth Juhlin and Abigail Cook, co-teachers at Busch Middle School in SLPS, put it this way,

> We wholeheartedly support the co-teaching model. As the enrollment number of ESOL students continues to increase at our school, co-teaching allows us to serve a larger number of students than pullout, without the stigma of pullout, and without students missing content.

Bolstered by these encouraging results, we started planning for and recruiting a new cohort of co-teachers for ELs. We invited experienced EL co-teachers to become regional trainers who met for a full day before the first day of each session to develop presentations, create training materials, and determine who would co-present each day. Several EL teachers repeated the training with a different classroom teacher. Experienced teams invited new teams to observe in their classrooms. Teams from new districts arranged to observe experienced teams in other districts. In this way, we have gradually built capacity to sustain and expand effective co-teaching for ELs. We also offered a *Co-teaching for ELLs Institute* in the second year

TABLE 8.2	Overview 2016–2017 Cohort Training Topics
Session #1:	1. Co-Teach ELL: 7 Approaches and Co-Teaching Partnership
	2. Mapping the CAN DOs/Student Portraits
Session #2:	1. A Closer Look at One Student Group Approaches
	2. Missouri English Language Development Standards
Co-Teach ELL Institute: *More Than Just Co-Teaching*	
Session #3:	1. A Closer Look at Two Student Groups & Multiple Groups Approaches
	2. Writing and Assessing Language Objectives
Session #4:	1. Field Trips
	2. Selecting the "Best Fit" Approach
	3. ELL Strategies
Ongoing:	Consulting/Coaching
	Online Book Discussions

to bring both cohorts together and invited others from around the state. See Table 8.2 for the learning activities designed for the 2016–2017 cohort.

Working Together

After the second year, regional trainers met to evaluate the program and to set goals for the following year. We looked at pre- and post-ratings on the I-TELL as well as survey questions about the frequency and intensity of co-planning and co-teaching. Teams that co-planned every week and co-taught a minimum of four lessons per week received the highest ratings on the I-TELL, leading us to recommend this as a baseline for establishing co-teaching for ELs.

Assessing Co-Teaching

When co-teachers rated the lessons they observed, they noted that it wasn't always easy to agree on what rating to give for each item, asking, "What makes this a 4, 3, 2, or 1?" After reviewing this feedback, Elena and I met in the Summer of 2016, to revise the I-TELL. We combined 13 items into six, and developed criteria for each rating for each item. Below is an excerpt for the second item unique to co-teaching for ELs because of the explicit focus on language development (See Table 8.3).

We also developed a form for evaluating the phases of co-planning described by Honigsfeld and Dove (2016), formatting the new rubrics into Google Forms for easier data collection. Elena in SLPS, and I in the other districts, evaluated co-planning sessions for each team in the fall. In the spring, both SLPS and the regional trainers used the *Observing Co-Teaching*

TABLE 8.3 Observing Co-Teaching for ELs, Feature 2, Rating of 4 Criteria
2. Language and Content Objectives are Addressed by Both Teachers—Both Language and Content are the "Main Thing"
4: Well Done
• Clear, specific, and measurable written language and content objectives are orally presented near the beginning, referred to during the class, and reviewed/revisited at the end. • Challenging language objectives are specific to the language needed for students to achieve the content objectives. • Language and content objectives are written in student friendly language. • Language objectives are modeled and practiced throughout the lesson.

form when observing and evaluating co-teaching. Teams on site visits also evaluated the lessons they observed using the new form.

CONCLUSION

We have continued to offer cohort-based professional learning around co-teaching for ELs every year for a total of 4 years now. The commitment of the regional trainers is evident in that even after I left the regional office to become the coordinator of EL and Immigrant Education in the Hazelwood School District, the 2018–2019 cohort had 58 teachers, forming 30 teams, from 19 schools, in 10 districts. From its inception in the 2015–2016 school year to the 2018–2019 school year, over 250 teachers, forming 170 teams, have come together through this unique collaboration impacting the educational experiences of so many English learners at the elementary, middle, and high school levels. At the end of the first week of school for 2019–2020, we are planning for two cohorts made up of at least 15 teams from Hazelwood, 20 teams from Mehlville, as well teams from more than five other school districts. For the first time ever, we will have teams at the preschool level too.

Co-teaching for us has become the pinnacle of teachers working together. John Hattie (2013) stated that "teachers, working together," have the highest impact on student learning of anything we do at school. We have found that teams that integrate specific, measurable language objectives with a special focus on oral language development have seen ELs grow in ELP, and *all* students make strides in content achievement. We have also found that explicit language instruction with ongoing formative language assessment does not have to be separate from the instruction of core content—rather it must be a complementary process for all students. The response below exemplifies why we work together in our classrooms, in our schools, in our districts, and across the region for the benefit of our ELs:

Co-teaching this year has been a blessing due to open honest conversations from planning to grading. Everyone benefits using this format. I am forced to think about things in a different way that makes my lesson plans more visual, interactive, and precise. My favorite part is when I am explaining a concept to the class, and my co-teacher jumps in or piggybacks with a different way of explaining it or uses a visual as I am talking. The extra examples are always great. As this is our first year together, she is learning more content and I am learning more about my delivery methods. WIN–WIN!

Parity is critical—not just in the relationship of the two teachers and in the status of ELs in the classroom, but also in the equal focus on language and content. When both language and content are the main thing we focus on, English learners—ALL learners thrive.

REFERENCES

Bouscaren, D. (2015, December 15). Who are the refugees in St. Louis? *St. Louis Public Radio.* Retrieved from http://news.stlpublicradio.org/post/who-are-refugees-st-louis#stream/0

Fenske, S. (2016, September 20). St. Louis shows biggest gain in foreign-born population of 20 largest metros. *Riverfront Times.* Retrieved from https://www.riverfronttimes.com/newsblog/2016/09/20/st-louis-shows-biggest-gain-in-foreign-born-population-of-20-largest-metros

Hart, K. (2019). *Exclusive: Immigrants are moving to smaller cities.* Retrieved from https://www.axios.com/exclusive-immigrants-are-moving-to-smaller-cities-1939abb9-c07d-4252-82ef-9f8edd8fcfc7.html

Hattie, J. (2013, November 22). *Why are so many of our teachers and schools so successful?* [Video]. Retrieved from https://www.youtube.com/watch?v=rzwJXUieD0U

Honigsfeld, A., & Dove, M. G. (2010). *Collaboration and co-teaching: Strategies for English learners.* Thousand Oaks, CA: Corwin Press.

Honigsfeld, A., & Dove, M. G. (2015). *Collaboration and co-teaching for English learners: A leader's guide.* Thousand Oaks, CA: Corwin Press.

Honigsfeld, A., & Dove, M. G. (2016). Co-teaching ELLs: Riding a tandem bike. *Educational Leadership, 73*(4), 56–60.

Missouri Department of Elementary and Secondary Education. (2017). *Missouri Comprehensive Data System.* Retrieved from https://apps.dese.mo.gov/MCDS/Home.aspx

Mongabay. (2015). *Languages spoken in St. Louis, MO.* Retrieved from https://names.mongabay.com/languages/cities/St._Louis_MO-IL.html

National Academies of Sciences, Engineering, and Medicine. (2017). *Promoting the educational success of children and youth learning English: Promising futures.* Retrieved from https://www.nap.edu/catalog/24677/promoting-the-educational-success-of-children-and-youth-learning-english

Rivero, D. (2015, November 25). This city let in tens of thousands of mostly Muslim refugees: Here's what happened. *Splinter*. Retrieved from http://fusion.net/story/238682/the-miracle-of-littlebosnia

Sanchez, C. (2017, February 23). English language learners: How your state is doing. *NPR*. Retrieved from https://www.npr.org/sections/ed/2017/02/23/512451228/5-million-english-language-learners-a-vast-pool-of-talent-at-risk

Tripp, B. (2017). Foreign-born population continues to grow in St. Louis. *St. Louis Regional Chamber* [blog post].

CHAPTER 9

CO-TEACHING PROGRAMMING FOR ENGLISH LEARNERS

From Exploration to Sustainability

Holly J. Porter
Cherry Creek School District #5

Co-teaching for the success of English learners is the norm in the Cherry Creek School District. It wasn't always that way, however. Focus, a drive to ensure fidelity to the program, and persistence in the face of setbacks, all contributed to the success of the program. The results of nearly a decade of intentional work around the components of a successful co-teaching model coupled with a laser-like focus on three tenets—language through content, meaningful access to grade-level content, and building the capacity of teachers—have resulted in high growth and achievement of English learners.

Many times schools question the success of co-teaching after just a few months of implementation. In reality, the issue does not lie in the validity of co-teaching itself, but is inherent in the difficult task of taking a program from exploration to sustainability. What makes it so difficult to bring

Co-Teaching for English Learners, pages 105–114
Copyright © 2020 by Information Age Publishing

any program from exploration to sustainability? This very question plagues those who implement anything new.

To address this question, Fixsen, Naoom, Blasé, Friedman, and Wallace (2005) outlined six stages of implementation: (a) exploration, (b) program installation, (c) initial implementation, (d) full operation, and then eventually (e) innovation and (f) sustainability. To move a program from exploration to sustainability requires that one clearly understands each stage, plans ahead, and is prepared for all of the nuances within each stage.

Our exploration stage started because our English learners were not performing well on any measures. The performance comparison of English learners and non-English learners in 2007 on our state reading assessment showed a 43% gap in the percentage of students at the proficient level as well as a 9% gap in the performance of our former (reclassified) English learners as compared with students who were never English learners. It was clearly evident that English learners were lagging behind their peers. In addition, the school days of our English learners were fragmented. In any given day, an English learner might have been in a grade-level class for about 25% of the day. The remainder of the day was spent in remedial classes, interventions, English as a second language (ESL) pullout, and specials or electives (Porter, 2009).

My colleagues and I researched how students perform nationwide in pullout programs, and we found that separate English language services are generally considered a remedial service for English learners, and students who transition out of these programs consistently demonstrate low levels of language proficiency and academic achievement (Frattura & Topinka, 2006). Thomas and Collier's (1997) research on language minority student achievement and program effectiveness also showed that students who transition out of pullout English learner programs generally only perform at about the 11th percentile by the time they graduate from high school. We saw the same results with our English learners. The desire to ensure that our students were getting the education they deserve, coupled with the eye-opening research, solidified our desire to do something different.

In an Office for Civil Rights (OCR) policy regarding the treatment of national origin minority students who are limited English proficient, Smith (1990) stated, "In providing educational services to language minority students, school districts may use any method or program that has proven successful, or may implement any sound educational program that promises to be successful" (para. 36).

The OCR policy supported our desire to try something new and novel. We asked, "What promising practices would work within the demographics and layout of our district?" We found a similar school district that was implementing co-teaching for English learners and decided to study its program model and its data based on information found online; we also spoke with the district's director of programming. We learned that like our district, this large suburban district also had multiple language groups represented, and its program for English learners was showing great success. We were intrigued and further examined what components would be necessary to implement a co-teaching model in our district.

Unintentionally, we had moved ourselves into the second stage of implementation, *program installation*. The question to ask at this stage of implementation is the following: "What tasks will help us get ready?" During this initial program installation stage "resources are being consumed in active preparation for actually doing this differently in keeping with the tenets of the evidence-based practice or program" (Fixsen et al., 2005, p. 16).

We knew that in order to have a successful co-teaching program, it would require a shift in thinking about how students are supported (Porter, 2009). A new co-teaching staffing ratio was introduced to ensure effectiveness of the program. Previously, a student-to-teacher ratio was utilized (i.e., total number of students per teacher). The ratio was shifted to be a teacher-to-teacher ratio (i.e., number of co-teachers the specialist would co-teach with). This shift ensured equitable distribution of staffing based on the needs of the co-teaching program, not the needs of pullout instruction. In the end, the ratio shift required less staffing than the previous ratio.

In addition, we developed a vision to guide our work as follows: "Our vision is to provide culturally and linguistically diverse learners with equitable access to cohesive learning opportunities that accelerate their social and academic English, provide meaningful access to grade-level content, and increase their overall achievement through collaboration and co-teaching." In alignment to the vision, we provided professional development to our co-teaching teams about setting up co-teaching. However, one of the things we quickly realized was that we also needed support for school administrators. In a conversation with one principal, he stated, "Co-teaching isn't working"; he wanted to try something different. When he was asked about the needed elements for co-teaching to work, it was evident that there were many components of co-teaching that were not in place; these missing elements could be the reason co-teaching was not successful. Due to this conversation and others like it, we developed a rubric to serve as the foundation for our program.

The rubric we developed is critical to ensure that everyone has the same information about the fundamental components of a successful co-teaching program. It includes both school level and instructional level components because focus and consistency from both the administrator level and the teacher level must go hand in hand. The school level components on the rubric include: classroom placement, time, resources, and professional learning. The instructional level components include: co-planning, co-teaching, assessment, reflection, and instruction (see Figure 9.1). All of

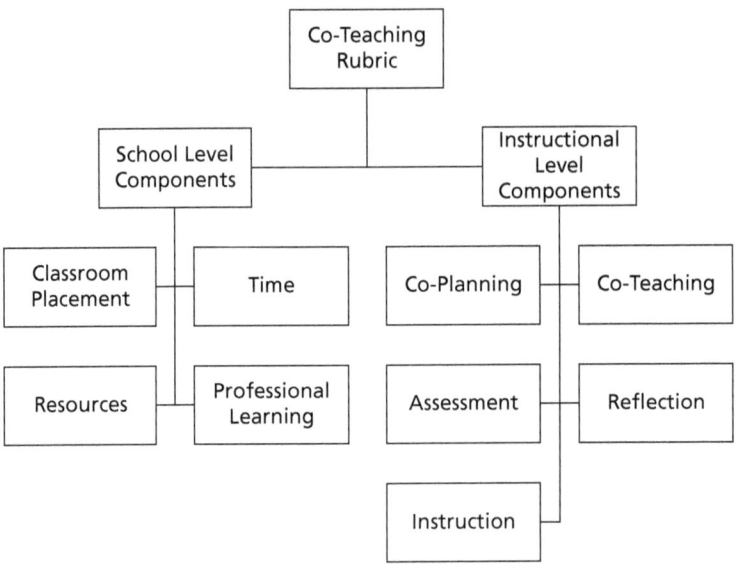

Figure 9.1 Co-teaching rubric components.

these components work together to ensure that co-teaching is done with fidelity. There are several indicators for each section of the rubric that delve deeper into the actual practices in place in a building (Porter, 2019).

Having a clear framework in place and resources devoted to the new model, we moved ourselves into the *initial implementation* stage. Joyce and Showers (2002) described this stage as an *initial awkward stage*, in which targeted support is necessary. The question that then arises in this stage is the following: "How do we navigate the initial awkward stage?" We had to ensure that we were prepared for the plethora of questions and ephemeral lack of efficacy that might result from our staff's feelings of uneasiness and uncertainty about how all of the components of co-teaching would work. "Implementation requires change. The change may be more or less dramatic, for an individual or an organization. In any case, change does not occur simultaneously or evenly in all parts of a practice or an organization" (Fixsen et al., 2005, p. 16).

Senge (2006) brought forth the insight of an unnamed organizational change consultant who stated, "People don't resist change. They resist being changed" (p. 144). This remark exemplifies how the difficulty in change isn't about the change itself; the difficulty is in the way in which change takes place or the fact that change takes place without a rationale or reason to do so. Ambrose (1987) discussed five elements necessary for managing complex change. Those elements include a common vision, knowledge and skills, incentives, resources, and an action plan. We had put several things in place related to these elements including a common vision, professional development to address knowledge and skills, celebrating small gains through incentives, a new staffing model to address resources, and most importantly a co-teaching rubric as the action plan.

To ensure we were not getting what Ambrose (1987) referred to as *false starts* in the absence of an action plan, we began to use the co-teaching rubric in a consistent and supportive manner with the expectation of a timeline for when co-teaching would be fully in place. The district-level program coordinators and director visited each school and walked through the co-teaching rubric with each co-teaching team. There is space on the rubric for teams to create goals for the year, which in turn, drove their specific, personalized professional development from the district-level coordinators. The rubric also provided insight for any full-scale professional development that was essential for all teachers based on those areas in which most schools had identified as needing support.

In the initial stage, we quickly realized we could get *stuck* if we didn't address some of the pitfalls that are common when implementing anything new. One of those pitfalls was believing the following: "This too shall pass." Many times in education, new ideas and innovative ways of instruction never reach full implementation because educators become accustomed to being able to *wait it out* until the next innovation comes along. This wait-and-see attitude became a common practice that we needed to overcome if we were to get traction with co-teaching. "During the initial stage of implementation, the compelling forces of fear of change, inertia and investment in the status quo combine with the inherently difficult and complex work of implementing something new. And, all of this occurs at a time when the program is struggling to begin and when confidence . . . is being tested" (Fixsen et al., 2005, p. 16).

True change can really only happen outside of one's comfort zone, and we encouraged people to take a risk outside of that zone and try something new without reverting to the old way of doing things. However, when people are challenged in new ways, they tend to attempt to subvert the risk of trying something new by adding new and different activities or attempting to fit what they are currently doing into the change to rationalize that nothing truly needs to change. To move past that point, there was urgency for an organizational change that would not allow the subversive actions of those attempting to return to the status quo. Kotter (2010) described the necessary action to move forward as an "urgent activity: action which is alert, fast moving, focused externally on important issues, relentless, and continuously purging irrelevant activities to provide time for the important and to prevent burnout" (p. 11). We used our vision as a filter through which we flowed all of our actions. When designing professional development, hiring staff, purchasing materials, and developing programming supports, we asked ourselves if the actions we were taking were focused on the three tenets of our vision: language through content, meaningful access to grade-level content, and building the capacity of teachers (Porter, 2019). If what we were proposing did not match with our tenets, it was purged to ensure that we focused on those things that would move us forward with co-teaching. One of the things that supported us in this endeavor was shifting our language and practice. Table 9.1 provides some examples of the ways in which we shifted language and practice in order to match our vision.

Because of our relentless focus on our vision and the alignment of all of our actions to support that vision, we persevered through questions such as: "Is this really working" and "What if we kept doing _____ in addition to co-teaching?" Maintaining a laser-like focus on what is important and what will get us to the point of full implementation was necessary. While it was tempting to start altering the co-teaching program model in its infancy, we were careful not to make any changes to the foundational aspects of the model before it reached full implementation.

Full implementation of our program was only realized after several years of focused effort. The question we asked in this stage was the following: "How do we maintain the program as accepted practice?" Our co-teaching program is now accepted practice in the district, and it is the "way we do things" for English learners, but it did not happen quickly or without effort. "A high level of involvement by program developers on a continuing basis is a feature of many successful implementation programs" (Fixsen et al., 2005, p. 21). For this reason, we continued to utilize our co-teaching rubric to meet with principals and teachers on an annual basis to gauge our co-teaching implementation and what supports we needed. This check in process was necessary as the needs of each school ebbs and flows given changes in staff, the English learner population, state standards, and many other factors. Once a program is *in place*, it only stays in place with support and follow through focused on the vision.

TABLE 9.1 Shifts in Language and Practice

Kids need to be *serviced.*	Kids need to be *supported*
Teachers of ELA are *interventionists.*	Teachers of ELA are *specialists.*
English language acquisition requires an *intervention.*	English language acquisition is a *process.*
"I am going to *push-in* to the classroom and service *my* kids (touch them)."	"I am going to *co-teach* in the classroom and support all of *our* kids."
Kids are safe in my *pull out* group.	Kids should be safe in the *classroom*
Language is learned in a *traditional grammatical* way, separate from content.	Language is learned in a *functional* way, through the content.

Fixsen et al. (2005) also provided that "most evaluations of attempted program implementations occur during the initial implementation stage, not the full operational stage. Thus, evaluations of newly implemented programs may result in poor results, not because the program at an implementation site is ineffective, but because results at the implementation site were assessed before the program was completely implemented and fully operational" (p. 18). While we certainly looked at the performance of our students throughout the initial implementation stage, we did not evaluate the program success until we reached full implementation.

For a district of 55,000 students, full implementation at all levels has taken us almost a decade. Nevertheless, the results of our programming shift are measurable and remarkable. We have seen the growth and performance of our English learners among the highest in the state as evidenced by receiving the state English Language Proficiency Act Excellence Award for all 4 years it has been awarded (Colorado Department of Education, n.d.). An example of the median growth percentile comparison of our English learners to their native English-speaking peers is shown in Figure 9.2. These growth comparisons are similar in reading and writing as well. As our state has recently shifted to a new assessment, we are currently developing new comparative data.

We have also seen a dramatic decrease in the numbers of long-term English learners. Based on an internal data analysis in 2017, we determined that 94% of our English learners were reclassified to a monitor status within 5 years, and their performance was at or above their non-English learner peers based on our requirements for reclassification. The data on the percentage of long-term English learners based on the number of years they remained in the program is found in Table 9.2.

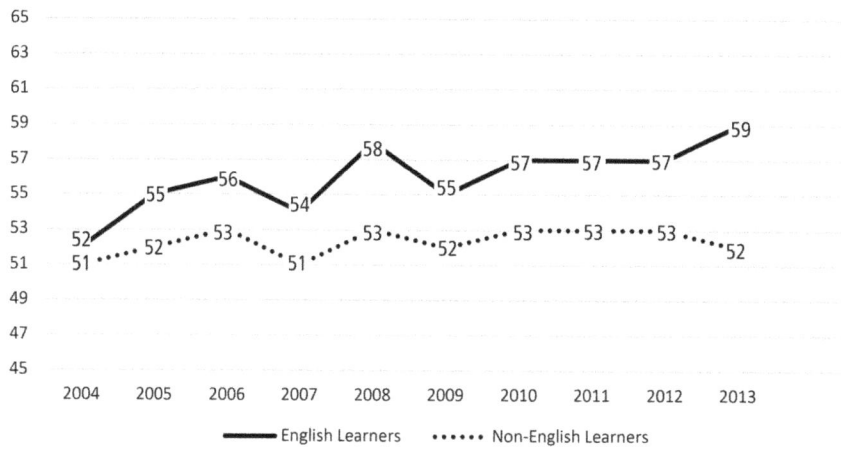

Figure 9.2 Median growth percentiles on the Colorado State Assessment Program.

TABLE 9.2 2017 Reclassification of English Learners	
Percent of English learners in program after 3 years	15.29%[a]
Percent of English learners in program after 4 years	9.45%[a]
Percent of English learners in program after 5 years	5.94%[a]
Percent of students reclassified within 3 years	84.71%
Percent of students reclassified within 5 years	94.06%

[a] Some of these students may also be dually identified with disabilities

An example of the high performance of English learners once they are reclassified is shown in Figure 9.3. These data show that the gap between the performance of former English learners and students who have never been English learners has reversed—the English learners outperformed their peers. Figure 9.4 demonstrates a similar trend on our most recent state adopted assessment, Colorado Measures of Academic Success (CMAS), developed by the Partnership for Assessment of Readiness for College and Careers (PARCC).

Beyond simple focus and perseverance to reach full implementation, it is also necessary to provide time to allow for *innovation* in the program. The question to ask at this level is the following: "What needs to be 'tweaked' to improve the implementation of the program?" With our co-teaching program in full implementation, we began to have the opportunity to see which parts of our rubric and the program itself could be tweaked to allow for ever greater success for our English learners. "Each attempted implementation

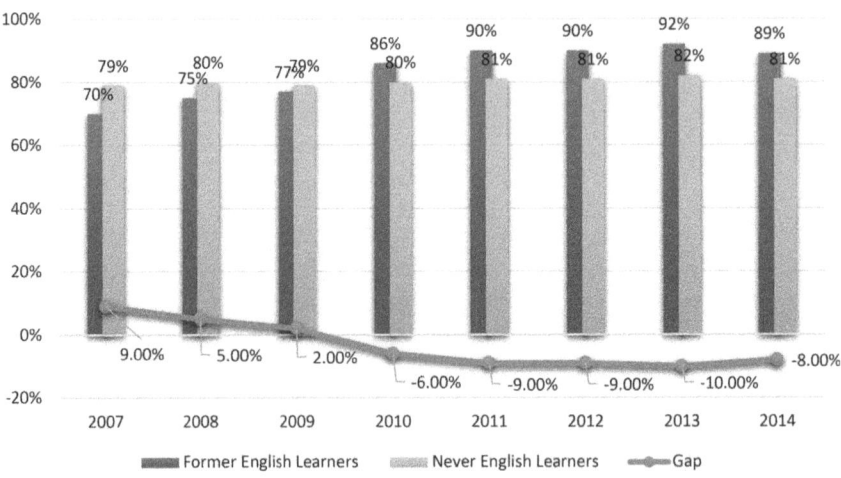

Figure 9.3   Performance of elementary former English learners compared to never English learners 2007–2014.

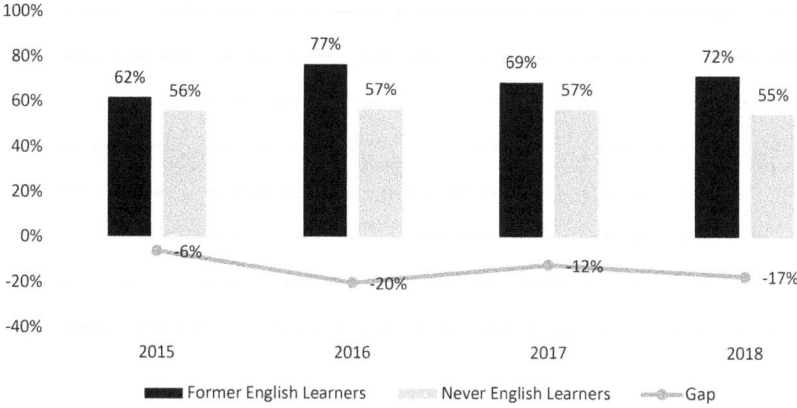

Figure 9.4   Performance of elementary former English learners compared to never English learners 2015–2018.

of evidence-based practices and programs presents an opportunity to learn more about the program itself and the conditions under which it can be used with fidelity and good effect" (Fixsen et al., 2005, p. 17). The additions we since have made to our rubric have clarified and emphasized those things that ensure alignment with our vision. Most importantly, our focus has been solidified and enhanced by our intentional inclusion of the importance of using a functional language approach and integrating language and content in co-planning, co-assessment, and co-instruction.

Our perseverance and belief in continuous improvement has led us to the level of *sustainability*. The question to ask regarding this stage is the following: "How do we keep a good thing going?" "The goal during this stage is the long-term survival and continued effectiveness of the implementation site in the context of a changing world" (Fixsen et al., 2005, p. 17). For us, this means that we continue our laser-like focus. We continue to use our rubric and filter our actions through our three tenets: language through content, meaningful access to grade-level content, and building the capacity of teachers. We continue to look for those things we can tweak to achieve continual success in a changing educational landscape. In the words of Bob Dylan, a person should always "be careful never really to arrive at a place where he thinks he's *at* somewhere. You always have to realize that you're constantly in a state of becoming" (Scorsese et al., 2005).

REFERENCES

Ambrose, D. (1987). *Managing complex change*. Pittsburgh, PA: The Enterprise Group.

Colorado Department of Education. (n.d.). *ELPA excellence award*. Retrieved from https://www.cde.state.co.us/cde_english/elpaexcellenceaward

Fixsen, D. L., Naoom, S. F., Blase, K. A., Friedman, R. M., & Wallace, F. (2005). *Implementation research: A synthesis of the literature* (FMHI Publication #231). Tampa: University of South Florida, Louis de la Parte Florida Mental Health Institute, The National Implementation Research Network.

Frattura, E. M., & Topinka, C. (2016). Theoretical underpinnings of separate educational programs. *Education and Urban Society, 38*(3), 327–344.

Joyce, B. R., & Showers, B. (2002). *Student achievement through staff development*. Alexandria, VA: ASCD.

Kotter, J. P. (2010). *A sense of urgency*. Boston, MA: Harvard Business Press.

Porter, H. J. (2009). *The elementary principal and academic achievement of English language learners: A case study* (Unpublished doctoral dissertation). University of Northern Colorado, Greeley, CO.

Porter, H. J. (2019). *Co-teaching content and language: Key components for success*. Manuscript in preparation.

Scorsese, M. (Director & Producer), Tedeschi, D., Rosen, J., Lacy, S., Sinclair, N., & Wall, A. (Producers). (2005). *No direction home* [Documentary]. Australia: Paramount Pictures.

Senge, P. M. (2006). *The fifth discipline*. London, England: Random House Business.

Smith, W. L. (1990, April 6). *Policy regarding the treatment of national origin minority students who are limited English proficient* [Letter to Office for Civil Rights Senior Staff]. Washington, DC: United States Department of Education.

Thomas, W., & Collier, V. (1997). *Language minority student achievement and program effectiveness*. Washington DC: National Clearinghouse for Bilingual Education.

CHAPTER 10

THE IMPACT OF A SUSTAINED PROFESSIONAL LEARNING COMMUNITY AROUND CO-TEACHING FOR ELLs

Lucia Perez-Medina
New York City Department of Education

Professional learning can be frustrating if it is not meaningful, transparent, collaborative, engaging, and strategic. With key changes to policy concerning a shift from pullout or stand-alone instruction for English language development to an integrated model of content and language instruction for English language learners (ELLs), many schools are still faced with understanding the essential components of co-teaching for ELLs in general education classes. In the field, many teachers expressed various challenges with implementing integrated co-teaching practices, and support is needed for these practices to be sustained. Yet, DuFour and Reeves (2015) cautioned that a professional learning community (PLC) is much more than a meeting. It requires ongoing collaboration that builds upon recursive cycles of collective inquiry and action research. Similarly, Fullan (2014) stated,

Co-Teaching for English Learners, pages 115–122
Copyright © 2020 by Information Age Publishing
All rights of reproduction in any form reserved.

"When the school is organized to focus on a small number of shared goals, and when professional learning is targeted to those goals and is a collective enterprise, the evidence is overwhelming that teachers can do dramatically better by way of student achievement" (p. 79). As a result, my school district strategically implemented a sustained PLC around co-teaching for ELLs. Although practical challenges still exist in our system around planning, instructing, and assessing ELLs collaboratively, I hope to shed light on how one district addressed some of these challenges and present the impact collaborative learning had on various stakeholders.

There is a clear distinction between being compliant and being committed. Oftentimes when a new policy or mandate is implemented, some schools rush to implement the change. When you ask for the rationale behind the change, the most common response is "because we have to" rather than "because it's important to support student outcomes." Knowing the challenges teachers had expressed, awareness of integrated practices was not enough. As the district's ELL administrator, my goal was not only to make school leaders and teachers aware of the mandates but to provide professional learning that enhanced teacher practice and supported student outcomes.

The journey began 2 years ago. We launched a PLC that included all the schools in the district. Each school committed to sending one co-teaching team to participate in a total of 15 hours of professional development (PD) with the ultimate goal of each team to create a lab site at their individual schools that would build capacity via a train-the-trainer model. Each PD session built on the previous one and included a bridge to practice where co-teaching partners planned, implemented a series of lessons, measured student progress, and reflected on their practice. All participants received a copy of the book *Collaboration and Co-Teaching: Strategies for English Learners* (Honigsfeld & Dove, 2010). As part of the PLC, teachers explored evidence-based collaborative practices and co-teaching models of instruction that exemplified an integrated service delivery for ELLs.

PROFESSIONAL LEARNING AT A GLANCE

During the professional learning series developed for the PLC, participants explored the challenges teachers faced with the shift in the New York State Commissioner's Regulations Part 154 (2015) for teaching ELLs. It was important to establish a clear and specific rationale for co-teaching for ELLs and ensure that the district had a common definition of co-teaching. A session was provided in which teachers briefly explored solutions to common questions concerning integrated services including curriculum, co-planning, scheduling, co-instruction, roles, responsibilities, and strategies for ELLs at different proficiency levels. What I realized was that one session was not enough to address all the concerns co-teachers were confronting.

In response to the district's needs, we had established a districtwide professional learning community to support co-teaching practices. Yet, in order to maximize the professional learning opportunity for our school communities, school leaders and teachers were interviewed to highlight current practices, strengths, challenges, and potential barriers to implementing co-teaching with fidelity. We gathered all the feedback from the field. It was clear that there were inconsistencies regarding collaborative school culture, different views around collaborative practices to support all learners, and a vague knowledge of what co-teaching models for ELLs should be. In addition, most teachers expressed minimal to no co-planning time. It was important to include professional learning sessions that addressed practical recommendations for strengthening instructional and program decisions based on student outcomes. As a result, the PLC focused on creating a systemic, collaborative process geared towards a schoolwide success model for ELLs that directly impacts teacher practice and student outcomes. The information gathered from the feedback from the field informed the professional learning plan (see Figure 10.1).

During the first PLC session, all participants engaged in a co-teaching quick write. They responded to the following questions in four squares: "What is your definition of co-teaching?"; "What do you see your role in co-teaching?"; "What does co-teaching look like?"; and "What does co-teaching not look like?" This warm-up activity helped create a common understanding of what co-teaching is and what it is not. Each partnership completed the co-teaching self-evaluation checklist individually and then compared their responses to their partners. Co-teaching teams also completed a commitment survey. During the initial session of the PLC, learning opportunities included exploring various co-teaching models and watching video clips of the selected models in action. At the end of the first session, participants selected a planning tool to support their collaborative planning. Teachers were expected to be prepared to share their experience of co-planning and the impact it had on student outcomes.

Participants shared creative ways to support planning. Some of the planning techniques included keeping curricular plans on a Google Drive or sustaining an articulation log, where each teacher wrote what they had worked on. Part of the session went into sharing collaboration strategies and planning how each team was going to promote shared accountability and responsibility for student learning. Honigsfeld and Dove's *Features of a Collaborative School Culture* and *Formal Collaborative Practices* were also explored in depth (Honigsfeld & Dove, 2010):

PLC Overarching Goals:

School teams will:
- Understand key changes to CR part 154 around an integrated model of instruction.
- Distinguish the difference between push-in/pull-out model and stand-alone/integrated co-teaching.
- Explore evidence-based collaborative practices and co-teaching models of instruction that exemplify an integrated service delivery for ELLs.
- Discuss the implementation of various co-teaching models to enhance differentiation of instruction for ELLs.
- Evaluate and adapt select tools for collaborations (co-teaching, co-assessing, and reflection).
- Reflect on practices and identify adjustments that can be made to support English Language Learners.

PLC 1—What are the essential components of an integrated, collaborative ENL program? 9:00 a.m.–2:30 p.m.	PLC 2—Why is collaboration needed? How do teachers plan, instruct, and assess ELLs collaboratively? 9:00 a.m.–2:30 p.m.	PLC 3—Which planning tools are more effective for co-teaching and why? How can we build capacity within our school communities? 9:00 a.m.–2:30 p.m.
Objectives: *Participants will be able to:* • Define integrated ENL and co-teaching. • Explore the rationale behind the integrated ENL service delivery. • Explore the integrated ENL service delivery framework: The four components of the collaborative instructional cycle: Co-planning, co-teaching, co-assessing, and reflection. • Explore 4 co-teaching models. • Watch and analyze co-teaching video clips. • Develop an action plan based on new learning leading to actionable next steps within their school communities. Prepared by: Lucia Perez Medina	**Objectives:** *Participants will be able to:* • Recap and reflect from last session. • Explore 3 co-teaching models. • Watch and analyze co-teaching video clips. • Share successes and challenges with the co-teaching models. • Uncover solutions to common questions concerning integrated ENL including curriculum, co-planning scheduling, co-instruction, roles and responsibilities, and strategies for ELLs at different proficiency levels. • Explore ways to plan, instruct and assess ELLs collaboratively. • Plan an upcoming unit together using various co-teaching models.	**Objectives:** *Participants will be able to:* • Recap and reflect from last session. • Share new successes and potential challenges with various co-teaching models explored. • Share strategies/techniques tried for planning, instructing and assessing ELLs collaboratively. • Evaluate and adapt select tools for collaboration (co-planning, co-assessing, and reflection) • Share portraits of collaboration and potential lab sites. • Develop an action plan based on new learning to build capacity within their school communities.

Figure 10.1 Brooklyn South field support center ELL team professional learning community (PLC)/study group arc 2015–2016.

Features of a Collaborative School Culture

- Shared vision and mission: Clearly agreed-upon desired outcomes, shared values, and goals that focus on all students characterize the vision.
- Curriculum alignment: Through curriculum mapping and coordinated curriculum development programs, coherence is established.
- Shared instructional practices: Planning, implementation, and assessment practices are coordinated among all faculty.
- Ongoing, shared professional development: Individual teacher learning is integrated into collaborative efforts to enhance all teachers' practice.
- Student-centered approach: Instructional focus is on the needs of the learner; students develop their own understanding through active learning techniques.

Formal Collaborative Practices

- Joint planning
- Curriculum mapping and alignment
- Parallel teaching
- Co-developing instructional material
- Collaborative assessment of student work
- Co-teaching as a framework for sustained collaboration

To my surprise, co-teaching partners began volunteering to be recorded using various co-teaching models. The district was able to capture these lessons, and a video library was created. This voluntary action led teachers to have autonomy with and ownership of their work. It empowered them to go back to their schools and advocate for time to turnkey the information they learned as well as share the impact of co-teaching on student learning. School leaders began reaching out for assistance on how to facilitate time for co-teaching partnerships to meet. During our final session together, co-teachers had to create an action plan to facilitate learning in their school communities to build capacity.

IMPACT ON TEACHER PRACTICE

After the districtwide PLC concluded, job-embedded professional learning continued at the school level. Lab sites at each school were established, visited by faculty, and feedback was shared. The lab sites opened for inter-visitation by faculty across the district as well. Additionally, teachers reflected on the impact the sustained professional learning had on their practice by identifying what stage they had reached (Stage 1: Survival; Stage 2: Capability; Stage 3: Mastery; Stage 4: Innovation) and how to move their practice along.

At the beginning, 60% of the teachers who participated in the PLC reported being at the survival stage, where they were still figuring out their collaborative teaching style; they disclosed that they were not completely sure how to collaborate, but they were trying their best. Only 1% reported being at the innovation stage where their co-teaching partnerships appeared to progress naturally and both teachers could facilitate learning experiences for all students; the collaborative practices these teachers forged became models for others embarking on co-teaching. At the end of the PLC, only 5% reported that they remained at the survival stage; 50% reported being capable, 25% reported reaching mastery, and 20% reaching innovation. Capitalizing on the success of those teachers who reported reaching innovation, they were selected to present at various forums on the impact learning about integrated practices had on their own practice and how the strategies they incorporated into their practice strengthened their school culture.

TAKEAWAYS

Most of the district's teachers embraced collaborative practices, but the supports for teachers were minimal, and the biggest challenge was creating buy-in. Throughout the series, participants had to turnkey the strategies they learned in the PLC with the other co-teaching partners in their school communities. We ended our series with a celebration, sharing our growth and our personal reflections. We also shared strategies participants explored to promote buy-in.

Teachers' reflections illustrated that they saw the value and importance of strengthening school cultures and embracing collaborative practices. All teachers appreciated that both content and English as a new language (ENL) teachers participated in professional learning together around co-teaching to support ELLs and articulated the benefits of collaborative planning. They saw the value these practices had in terms of coherent structures, common strategies, continuity, and clarity of learning, communication, and transparency. Some teachers' reflections included their observations of student growth via students' writing samples and reading levels.

Most ENL teachers that co-teach in various classes explained how they previously would take their resources, particularly anchor charts, with them from class to class because they didn't feel comfortable leaving them behind. However, since the development of more collaborative school cultures, ENL teachers felt more connected to each classroom community, which motivated them to create anchor charts and other resources that could remain in the classrooms where they co-taught. The biggest shift was their mindsets. Teachers went from saying *my* classroom and *my* students or group to *our* students and *our* class. Once teachers saw the value in the work and learned how the collaborative instructional cycle—collaborative planning, instructional delivery, collaborative assessment of student learning, and reflection on action and in action—came to life, they were able to share the impact it has had on their practice with their school communities. Teachers shared that their administrators saw how the co-teaching partnerships strengthened and began facilitating more planning time for them and other partnerships. As a result, school leaders anticipate more co-teaching partnerships flourishing.

If schools are grappling with how to strengthen their co-teaching practices, here are some recommendations for budding co-teachers:

- Start exploring planning tools with a partner who is willing to work together with you.
- Use co-assessment and reflection results to yield improvements in both instruction and student outcomes.
- Share how you overcame challenges collaboratively.
- Document the process and outcomes of your collaborative practices.
- Take time to celebrate your successes with others.

All teachers should have the opportunity to participate in professional learning around co-teaching practices for ELLs. One way is to start with a cohort or a vertical teacher team and engage them in book study to explore authors such as Honigsfeld and Dove and other researchers in the field of co-teaching. Coordinating instruction using common language and common practices is important. Create a plan to provide teams opportunities to explore tools collaboratively among teachers who share the responsibility of teaching the same ELLs. This practice is crucial to promote buy-in and sustain collaborative practices in a school community.

REFERENCES

Honigsfeld, A., & Dove, M. G. (2010). *Collaboration and co-teaching: Strategies for English learners.* Thousand Oaks, CA: Corwin.

DuFour, R., & Reeves, D. (2015, October 2). Professional Learning Communities still work (If done right). *Education Week.* Retrieved from https://www.edweek.org/tm/articles/2015/10/02/professional-learning-communities-still-work-if-done.html

Fullan, M. (2014). *The principal: Three keys to maximizing impact.* Thousand Oaks, CA: Corwin Press.

New York State Commissioner's Regulations Part 154. (2015). Retrieved from http://www.nysed.gov/bilingual-ed/regulations-concerning-english -language-learnersmultilingual-learners

PART III

COLLABORATIVE PLANNING
AND CO-TEACHING PRACTICES

COLLABORATIVE MEANING MAKING OF STUDENT DATA TO GUIDE INSTRUCTION FOR ENGLISH LEARNERS

Amy Frederick
University of Wisconsin–River Falls

Anne C. Ittner
Western Oregon University

Have you visited schools in which the English language (EL) teachers support a variety of grade levels and subject areas back-to-back throughout the day without a moment to meet or plan with their mainstream co-teachers? A typical school day for one of these teachers might resemble the following: The EL teacher comes to a class just as the lesson is beginning. The lesson is delivered by the general education (GE) teacher while the EL teacher sits on the side of the room or crouches by one EL student whispering helpful words to them while trying not to disturb the rest of the class. If feeling bold, the EL teacher may interject, "Can I show the students a picture of that?"

Co-Teaching for English Learners, pages 125–133
Copyright © 2020 by Information Age Publishing

or "So what you're saying is . . ." while the GE teacher waits to jump back in to continue the lesson. At student work time, the EL teacher walks around the room assisting students. One or two of the EL students who need help most receive support. The lesson closes, and the EL teacher waves goodbye to the GE teacher and the students and scoots off to another classroom just in time to catch the beginning of another lesson. To say that the English learners in such classrooms are receiving the support services they need and are entitled to would be a stretch—many ELs getting only a few moments of the EL teacher's support and instruction or none at all. With this framework for EL instruction, the EL teacher's status is diminished to that of a teacher's aide rather than a language expert. In essence, co-teaching without co-planning doesn't work well.

Across the United States, co-teaching is becoming a prominent practice for teaching students who are adding English as a new language. Co-teaching holds promise as a way to facilitate the implementation of instructional modifications that help ELs achieve at levels more comparable to those of their English-speaking peers by building vocabulary, using students' primary languages as support, and promoting productive interaction among ELs and English speakers (Goldenberg, 2010). An ideal collaboration between EL and GE teachers facilitates the integration of content-based English language teaching and EL-accessible content teaching (Davison, 2006). Though challenging, making time to assess, plan, and reflect collaboratively is an integral part of co-teaching (Honigsfeld & Dove, 2019). Assessing, planning, and reflecting happen outside of class in many different configurations, such as team meetings, informal discussions between co-teachers, and professional learning communities. Here, we will refer to these as *co-planning sessions*. In this chapter, we share two cases from research we conducted within two schools. We investigated how EL teachers worked with colleagues in general education settings. The teachers we studied dedicated time to plan together, used an inquiry approach to examine student data, and shared their expertise to make instructional plans for teaching content and language.

THINKING TOGETHER

When teachers come together to talk about their teaching in co-planning sessions, what often occurs is much more than conversations about a teacher guide or choosing an instructional method. Instead, these co-planning sessions become sites of negotiated meaning and knowledge construction as teachers solve problems, share experiences, make sense of data, and reflect on their own teaching and learning (Frederick, 2013). Sociocultural theories help us understand that learning is social—the result of dialogic mediation happens through interacting with others and the environment (Vygotsky, 1978). In collaborative planning sessions, individuals contribute ideas and solutions while at the same time provide support for each other's learning as a form of apprenticeship. The thinking and learning that happens in these spaces influences how teachers enact their teaching in complex ways. Teachers do not passively acquire the knowledge they need to teach. They are agents of transformation—constructing knowledge themselves within their instructional and professional contexts (Borg, 2003). Therefore, the outcomes of these meetings include both the instructional plans derived from collaborative knowledge construction as well as enhanced pedagogical knowledge.

In the two schools we spotlight in this chapter, EL and GE co-teachers, as well as other school specialists, regularly participated in co-planning sessions. In these meetings, they examined and interpreted student data to hypothesize about the student needs in order to develop appropriate classroom approaches and improve outcomes for students. The teachers used multiple student data sources, such as large-scale and classroom assessment scores, student writing samples, and observational notes, to guide their inquiry (Love, Stiles, Mundry, & DiRanna, 2008; García & DeNicolo, 2016). There is growing evidence that inquiry groups such as these can produce measurable achievement growth (Gallimore, Ermeling, Saunders, & Goldenberg, 2009).

MAKING A SPACE FOR LEARNING ABOUT ELs

For the past decade, teachers at Bloom Park Elementary (pseudonym) have been using a co-teaching model to deliver English learner services. The school is set in a working class neighborhood in a large, midwestern urban school district where 66% of the students are designated as English learners. I (Amy) met with the first-grade team for several months in order to better understand what the practices of collaboration appeared to be there. The team consisted of three GE teachers, the EL teacher, and two special education teachers. The EL teacher spent his day co-teaching in classes with the three GE teachers and working with the English learners, who were mostly refugee newcomers. In addition to teaching together, the school and the team prioritized regular collaborative time to examine student assessment data, plan instruction, and reflect on their co-teaching. On Mondays and Tuesdays, they met during their preparation time for an hour as a professional learning community (PLC) with their instructional coach to focus on math and reading instruction. On Thursdays they met again during their common preparation period to plan literacy lessons. The members of the team also met informally and "on-the-fly" in different configurations as part of their regular planning practice. These meetings were before school drop-ins, hallway conversations, or in-class pre-briefings before a lesson. Their total weekly collaborative planning time was often between 3–4 hours!

As I observed their meetings, I came to understand that a variety of collaborative learning and planning processes were involved. Embedded in these practices was the notion that thinking together was more effective than thinking alone. Yet, coming together in a common space—just a meeting—does not ensure a beneficial outcome. Rather, it is in the interaction of the people within that space where cognition, and thus action, can be affected. This first-grade team shared their own learning, engaged in collaborative inquiry, reflected on their teaching, and discussed successful practices based in research and experience. Within this space, the teachers addressed issues and learning strategies specific to language learners. Because the EL teacher was present in the meetings and was seen as an equal participant, there were many conversations around EL-related issues (that may not have occurred without him). He often asked questions about the role of language in content areas and shared his experiences with language learning and culture.

During one of the first PLC meetings of the year, the first-grade teachers compared student writing samples to end of the year benchmarks and made observations about the student writing. One student, who was an English learner, had written, "I go fishing with my mom dad and my sisters [sic]" and had sketched three people with fishing poles. While the GE teachers noticed the complete sentence, nice handwriting, and that the words matched the pictures, the EL teacher noted that the student had written in the present tense rather than past and had correctly used –*ing* and plural -*s*. These observations led him to ask further questions:

> It looks very perfect and so my wondering was, because all the sounds are represented and the sight words are correct and everything is perfect, if the writing was done from memory? There are no invented spelling or other strategies used. I would want to know more about this student—if she's willing to take a risk or if she's being safe with staying around the known.

These comments led the team to discuss the writing from a new perspective and consider the role that the student's oral language played on her writing, and more importantly, what this meant for future instruction.

In another meeting, the instructional coach shared a summary of first grade scores on an oral language test that had been administered as part of a series of formative classroom assessments. After analyzing the data, the teachers in the PLC came to the conclusion that they wanted to raise the scores of students in the "intensive need" category, but they worried that they didn't have the strategies to support their students with lower English language proficiency. With the help of the EL teacher, they brainstormed a list of strategies that included:

- increasing student talk time,
- modeling and chorally reading shorter chunks of text,
- retelling stories, and
- asking children to listen and repeat what is said by others.

After that, they set student outcome goals, put strategies into practice, and monitored student growth over time.

In both of these meetings, the EL teacher shared important under-standings of language development with his colleagues that benefited the group. If the EL teacher had not been a part of these meetings, it is unlikely that the focus would have turned to ELs. Through the collaborative plan-ning process, the teachers gained the strategies they needed to improve their instructional practice for ELs.

WHY ARE ALL OF OUR ENGLISH LEARNERS IN READING INTERVENTION? A CASE FOR THINKING TOGETHER

To begin the process of identifying students for reading intervention, teach-ers at Weston Elementary (pseudonym) reviewed their students' most re-cent screening data on phonics, fluency, and comprehension assessments. As they looked carefully at the screening data, they noticed a trend: Despite the fact that many of the English learners had reached grade-level bench-marks in reading fluency measures, they lagged behind in comprehension. Weston was a rural school in which less than 20% of the students were Eng-lish learners; many of them were identified as needing reading interven-tion. This data sparked an important conversation, were teachers doing enough to meet the needs of English learners in reading intervention?

With the screening data in mind, the principal at Weston convened a multi-perspective team including a reading interventionist, an EL teacher, and three primary GE teachers. The goal of the multi-perspective team was to plan and study a specific reading intervention with a focus on language development. The hope was by increasing language support during the reading intervention the students would simultaneously develop language and reading skills, and improve their comprehension of text. The teachers on the team decided that phonics interventions would be a good place to start, since many English learners in the school were receiving interven-tions in this area.

Over the course of 10 weeks, the team engaged in a series of purpose-ful, co-planning sessions (Table 11.1) and used guiding questions to draw

TABLE 11.1 Co-Planning for Instructional Improvements

Session Topics	Purpose	Guiding Questions
Week One: Current Realities	• Analyze most recent data from a variety of formative and summative assessments • Determine instructional strategy to improve	What is the most current data in language and other content areas? Where do we want our students to be? What instructional strategy could we improve to benefit ELs?
Week Two: Sharing our Knowledge	• Share evidence based-practices • Develop common understandings	According to our own expertise, what do we see as valuable approaches to teach a specific content area? What are evidence-based practices in this area? In what area could we use more expertise in order to reach our goal?
Week Three: Proposing Strategies	• Propose strategies to improve a specific instructional goal	Based on what we discussed, what are strategies that we propose trying?
Weeks Four–Nine:	Implement Instruction	
Week Ten: Next Steps	• Discuss success and obstacles of instructional improvements	What worked? What data tells us that it worked? How should we move forward from here?

on the diverse perspectives of the members of the group. Ultimately, they hoped to build an intervention that utilized evidence-based practices from language and reading instruction.

In the first session, *Current Realities*, the reading interventionist shared reading levels, correct words per minute measures, and decoding inventories for a few English learners who had recently been in reading intervention. For the same students, the EL teacher shared language proficiency levels in reading, writing, speaking and listening and data from a listening task. Sharing reading and language data proved to be an important step for two reasons:

1. The reading interventionist and the EL teacher were able to explain how they translated the data into usable information; and
2. Some of the GE teachers were unaware of their own students' language proficiency levels.

Finally, the group concluded the meeting with an agreement to focus on embedding language support into the phonics interventions.

A week later, teachers met again in a session, *Sharing Our Knowledge*. The purpose of this meeting was to identify evidence-based practices used in reading intervention and language development. The teachers discussed practices such as:

- providing explicit and systematic instruction,
- using a students' primary language to clarify concepts in English,
- noticing cognates, and
- pointing out similarities and differences in languages.

They found commonalities in their practices, asked questions, and began to build consensus on strategies that they could eventually implement during the reading intervention.

In the next session, *Proposing Strategies*, they reviewed the collection of practices compiled in the previous meeting, and proposed how the phonics interventions could be modified with language support. For example, the EL teacher suggested that students could use their primary language to clarify words they were learning how to decode. They also agreed to give students opportunities to use a graphic organizer to draw, write, and talk about the words they were learning.

Following the meeting, teachers implemented the phonics intervention with language support in their classrooms for 6 weeks. During this time, they took notes, made observations, and continued to collect reading and language data to determine the effectiveness of the intervention. In a final session, *Next Steps*, teachers analyzed the student data. They noted patterns and reflected on gains. All students who received the intervention with language support showed progress in both reading and language measures. Teachers agreed that the intervention had been effective. Students weren't the only ones who grew in the process. They also learned that giving students a chance to talk about what they were reading was essential. Teachers were able to expand their approaches to analyzing reading and language data and implementing interventions to meet the needs of all their students.

IMPLICATIONS AND RECOMMENDATIONS

There are many ingredients to effective co-planning sessions. It takes coordination, communication, and commitment to make them work. We make four recommendations based on our experiences working with teachers to implement evidence-based instruction for ELs:

1. *Commit consistent time to planning.* While teachers at Weston and Bloom met on the fly frequently to collaborate, they were also committed to regular weekly co-planning sessions. Administrators not only supported the planning but made it clear that it was an expectation for all teachers. Meeting time was held *sacred* and not traded for other school initiatives.

2. *Use a variety of data sources to inform instructional decisions.* Reviewing data provides teachers an entry point for discussion about improvement. At both schools, teachers examined both literacy and language assessments as they started their co-planning cycle. Teachers at Bloom reviewed end-of-year writing benchmarks and oral language data to make sense of students' writing samples. Teachers at Weston used screening measures and language proficiency levels to plan a reading intervention.

3. *Engage in systematic approaches to planning and implementation.* Plan for sessions with pre-determined purposes and use guiding questions (Leseaux & Marietta, 2012) to help facilitate the process. Two of those questions are: (a) "Do our student assessment data show that most ELs are making good progress?" and (b) "Are we collecting the appropriate data to measure progress?"

4. *Share expertise in language and content areas.* Teachers at Bloom Elementary recognized that they would not have taken into consideration the connection between language and literacy if the EL teacher had not been present. While they reviewed student work samples, the EL teacher provided a further look into how English language development may be influencing student writing. GE teachers felt more confident in their teaching of ELs as a result of co-planning with the EL teacher, who gained an equal voice in planning and elevated status in the classroom.

When teachers put their heads together to examine student learning and share pedagogical expertise, the results can be powerful. Co-planning sessions can become a source of support and learning for teachers which may lead to classroom innovations. The culmination of the interaction among teachers results in a sharing of ideas, explaining perspectives in teaching, building opportunities for future learning from each other, and ultimately working towards improving school success for ELs.

REFERENCES

Borg, S. (2003). Teacher cognition in language teaching: A review of research on what language teachers think, know, believe, and do. *Language Teaching, 36*(2), 81–109.

Davison, C. (2006). Collaboration between ESL and content teachers: How do we know when we are doing it right? *The International Journal of Bilingual Education and Bilingualism 9*(4), 454–475.

Frederick, A. (2013). *A case study of a first-grade teacher team collaboratively planning literacy instruction for English learners* (Doctoral dissertation). Retrieved from ProQuest Dissertations Database. (1429502370)

Gallimore, R., Ermeling, B., Saunders, W., & Goldenberg, C. (2009). Moving the learning of teaching closer to practice: Teacher education implications of school-based inquiry teams. *The Elementary School Journal, 109*(5), 537–553.

García, G. E., & DeNicolo, C. P. (2016). Improving the language and literacy assessment of emergent bilinguals. In L. Helman (Ed.), *Literacy development with English learners: Research-based instruction in grades K–6* (2nd ed.; pp. 64–86). New York, NY: The Guilford Press.

Goldenberg, C. (2010). Improving achievement for English learners: Conclusions from recent reviews and emerging research. In G. Li & P. A. Edwards (Eds.), *Best practices in ELL instruction* (pp. 15–43). New York, NY: The Guilford Press.

Honigsfeld, A., & Dove, M. G. (2019). *Collaboration for English learners: A foundational guide to integrated practices* (2nd ed.). Thousand Oaks, CA: Corwin Press.

Lesaux, N. K., & Marietta, S. H. (2012). *Making assessment matter: Using test results to differentiate reading instruction.* New York, NY: Guilford Press.

Love, N., Stiles, K. E., Mundry, S., & DiRanna, K. (2008). *A data coach's guide to improving learning for all students: Unleashing the power of collaborative inquiry.* Thousand Oaks, CA: Corwin Press.

Vygotsky, L. S. (1978). *Mind and society: The development of higher mental processes.* Cambridge, MA: Harvard University Press.

CHAPTER 12

DIVERGENT PATHS
OF UNDERSTANDING

Teacher and Leader Perceptions
of Co-Teaching for English Learners

Felice Atesoglu Russell
Central Connecticut State University

I think sometimes you have to settle for not the way you think it should be,
but the reality of how we're going to get through the day.
—ESOL Teacher, Sycamore Elementary School

NAVIGATING UNFAMILIAR TERRAIN: THE CHALLENGE
OF IMPLEMENTING CO-TEACHING

The number of English learner (EL) students[1] in K–12 schools continues to rise (McGill, 2012). As this student population increases, states and school districts are responding by implementing new models of instruction to meet the needs of these students. In order to meet the dual demand of learning both language and content simultaneously (Bunch, 2013), many

Co-Teaching for English Learners, pages 135–145
Copyright © 2020 by Information Age Publishing

states and districts are implementing co-teaching models of instruction where the English to speakers of other languages (ESOL) and mainstream teachers work collaboratively. In these models, the ESOL and mainstream teacher are asked to co-plan, co-teach, and co-assess as they instruct ELs within a mainstream classroom context.

As practice moves ahead, the research has not yet caught up with how effective such co-teaching models are for meeting the instructional needs of ELs. In particular, in many cases teachers are unprepared to co-teach and struggle as they attempt to develop routines and share the division of labor (Peercy, Ditter, & Destefano, 2016). At the same time, we know that in some instances opportunities to co-teach have resulted in the development of teacher leadership and enhanced student learning (Dove & Honigsfeld, 2010). The particular case presented in this chapter, adds to this growing body of literature related to the challenges and opportunities of co-teaching and the supports that can positively impact these collaborative relationships (Martin-Beltran, Peercy, & Selvi, 2012; Peercy, Martin-Beltran, Yazan, & DeStefano, 2017).

This case study examines the perceptions of teachers and leaders involved in implementing new models of instruction involving co-teaching between ESOL and third grade teaching pairs. In particular, the analysis presented in this chapter focuses on the following research questions:

1. How do teachers perceive the purpose and implementation of new models of co-teaching?
2. How do leaders perceive the purpose and implementation of new models of co-teaching?

THEORETICAL FRAMEWORK

This analysis draws on collective sensemaking and sociocultural learning theory as lenses to understand how collaborating teachers made sense of their new relationships and work within the context of implementing new collaborative models of instruction for ELs. Collective sensemaking (Coburn, 2001; Horn, 2018; Spillane, Reiser, & Reimer, 2006) refers to both the formal and informal relationships and networks among teachers and leaders and how these shape sensemaking—in this case, teacher and leader sensemaking of the new collaborative models of instruction for EL students. This sensemaking is embedded within the context of teachers' and leaders' work, their schools, districts, and communities. This theory helps to unpack how individuals make different sense of similar messages (e.g., This year you will be co-teaching with a new ESOL teacher). Who teachers and leaders interact with both in their formal and informal networks can further play a role in how teachers and leaders make sense of the same messages. For example, teachers new to the building may not have any other teachers with whom they can confide in related to their uncertainties connected to the new co-teaching models; whereas, a veteran teacher that has been in the building for many years will likely be able to use their informal networks to make sense of new policies related to co-teaching in different ways.

I draw on collective sensemaking theory to understand the phenomenon of leadership practice and teachers' collaborative work and relationships to highlight their understanding of implementing new models of instruction for ELs. Specifically, sensemaking helps to shed light on teacher and leader learning and collaboration as a dynamic process that engages educators as they make sense of instruction, their roles, and the contextual constraints (Horn, 2018). As new instructional policies are implemented, sensemaking is used as teachers and leaders enact their understandings of the educational process (Spillane et al., 2006). Furthermore, I rely on sociocultural learning theory to illuminate teacher professional learning and collaboration as a dynamic process that occurs within and across individuals as they interact with various tools in their specific contexts (Lave & Wenger, 1991). Using sociocultural learning theory, I am able to highlight teacher and leader learning as a social process that is embedded in the interaction between relationships and context. In particular, this analysis seeks to understand how collaborative efforts focused on meeting the needs of ELs in this setting were navigated given the challenges associated with implementing new models of co-teaching.

Current theories of motivation suggest that in order to improve teacher practice, teacher evaluation policies should not reduce teacher autonomy or trust (Firestone, 2014). As schools implement new models of collaboration and co-teaching among ESOL and mainstream teachers, co-teaching pairs are often assigned to work with one another with little input from the teachers themselves. Teachers may perceive such teaching assignments to be at odds with their sense of autonomy as professionals and result in indifference between teachers that are assigned to work with one another. It is important to recognize that limiting teacher opinion, thus teacher autonomy, when it comes to co-teaching arrangements can potentially impede teacher trust. This type of arrangement, set-up for teachers without their feedback, can lead to *contrived collegiality* (Hargreaves, 1994) and can lead to deleterious effects and unintended outcomes.

Recently, scholars have noted that collaborative school cultures can lead to improved academic outcomes for ELs because these environments encourage the ongoing interaction between ESOL teachers and mainstream content teachers (Russell, 2012). This collaborative work can be supported or constrained by the leadership of the school. The culture and norms that principals establish in a school, such as articulating a vision to support ELs or implementing common literacy instructional strategies across grade levels and content areas, can greatly influence the ability of teacher leaders to impact instructional practice in classrooms. In this way, principals can act as a supporting context for instructional leadership work with teachers (Mangin, 2007; Taylor, 2008).

BACKGROUND AND CO-TEACHING CONTEXT

This qualitative case study examined ESOL and third-grade co-teaching pairs engaged in a school–university partnership over the course of one school year drawing on observation, survey, interview, and document analysis as data sources. The school–university partnership was an endeavor between a college of education and a large, county school district with a growing EL student population. This partnership supported the involvement of one university-based teacher educator with a partner elementary school to serve as a facilitator of professional learning for school visits, observations, and coaching activities over one academic school year.

Sycamore Elementary is located in a large, metropolitan area in the southeastern United States. At the time of data collection, 1,188 students attended the school with 91% of the students eligible for free and reduced lunch and 63% of the students classified as EL students. The school was in the first year of implementing new models for serving EL students. These included the following models:

30+ Technology Model

In the 30+ technology model, ESOL teachers provided 30 minutes of direct instruction per day to all levels of English language proficiency inside the mainstream classroom. In addition, students received 15 minutes or more of ESOL support using an interactive technology program within the mainstream classroom.

Balanced Plus Model

In the balanced plus model, ESOL teachers provided a minimum of 45–50 minutes of support per day to all levels of English language proficiency in the mainstream setting in small groups alongside the mainstream teacher. The ESOL teacher could present English language arts content to the whole class or use small-group and individual instruction with ELs.

There were eight focal teachers involved in this study: four ESOL teachers and four third-grade classroom teachers. Thus, between the eight focal teachers, there were a total of four co-teaching pairs. Among the eight focal teachers, the four ESOL teachers all had been at the school for many years and were veteran teachers. Out of the four third-grade teachers, one was a new teacher, two had been teaching for a few years each, and one was an experienced teacher; however, this was her first year at Sycamore Elementary. While all of the teachers had experience collaborating across ESOL and mainstream (e.g., using the ESOL push-in model), this was the first time any of the teachers were officially engaged in co-teaching. One co-teaching pair was using the 30+ technology model and the other three co-teaching pairs were engaged with the balanced plus model. The models were approved by the state and selected based on a needs analysis conducted by school and district leaders. Occasions for learning that engaged the university-based teacher educator and teachers included: a needs assessment survey, instructional coaching cycles, classroom observations, lunchtime brown bags, a book study focused on academic language, exit surveys, and interviews.

DIVERGENT PERSPECTIVES ON THE LIMITATIONS AND POSSIBILITIES OF CO-TEACHING

Several findings that emerged from the data included (a) leaders struggled with the best way to support co-teaching at the district and school levels, (b) teachers and leaders had disparate views about the role and purpose of co-teaching, and (c) teachers did not always buy-in to what co-teaching was "supposed" to look like or be even when given time and resources.

Struggle to Support Co-Teaching at District and School Levels

The district ESOL coordinator struggled to figure out how to meet the professional learning needs of co-teaching pairs in a large district with a high level of need. When asked about the implementation of co-teaching at Sycamore Elementary School, the district ESOL coordinator lamented that there was a lack of district-level support staff. She noted that the district employed just one elementary support staff to cover 94 schools. As a result, it was impossible for her and the other support staff to get out and individually provide support. While the school–university partnership was meant to support teacher collaboration, due to the fact that the university-based teacher educator was not supervisory and new to the school, developing relationships and trust took time, and teacher engagement was fairly passive as there was minimal accountability. Furthermore, the district ESOL coordinator noted that most of the teachers had not been involved in classroom-level instructional coaching; as a result, the process of developing trust and sharing their classrooms and practice with an outsider was further complicated.

Interviews revealed that it was often the ESOL teachers that had received professional development at the school and/or district levels. However, it was clear that providing professional development for ESOL teachers but not the mainstream teachers was problematic. The ESOL coordinator described the phenomenon of ESOL teachers receiving training on a particular topic (e.g., collaboration) and then finding it difficult to go to the mainstream teacher and propose changes or suggest implementing new ideas. By providing professional development for ESOL teachers but not their mainstream co-teacher, the ESOL teachers were positioned as the ones responsible for collaboration instead of a collaborative process. One ESOL teacher noted her frustration with providing professional development and resources for half of the co-teaching pair. For example, ESOL teachers were provided with a resource book on collaboration; however, mainstream teachers did not receive the same resource.

Furthermore, support was not provided in time for teachers to implement the new instructional models in the intended manner. The ESOL coordinator noted that as the school year got underway, teachers did not have all of the necessary information. For instance, she noted that while teachers were expected to implement new collaborative models (e.g., balanced plus), she did not think that most of them were told about the model they would be using or how they should use it at the beginning of the school year.

Disparate Views About the Role and Purpose of Co-Teaching

The data revealed that teachers and leaders had disparate views about the role and purpose of co-teaching. The Sycamore principal described her perception of teachers' responses to co-teaching as using as much small-group instruction as possible. So, when the additional teacher was co-teaching, the default was to use small-group work and rotations. As a result, she noted that planning could be a bit looser than if there was more whole-group instruction with both co-teachers vested in planning together. So in this sense, it seemed that teachers considered the ESOL teacher as a support teacher and not a colleague with whom they could or should co-plan, co-teach, and co-asses student learning. The intention with the new co-teaching model was for the ESOL and mainstream teacher to have opportunities to work with the whole class. The ESOL teacher would be responsible for the consideration of language demands and scaffolding language development and the mainstream teacher would consider content standards and objectives.

Overall, communication about the role and purpose of co-teaching was limited. Teachers—both ESOL and mainstream—did not have a solid sense of what the collaborative work was supposed to look like. Teachers ended up creating their own systems and routines to enact the work of co-teaching; however, this was often at odds with the vision that district and school leaders had for this collaborative type of instruction. Ultimately, while the goal was co-teaching, what emerged in certain instances was both the ESOL and mainstream teachers parallel teaching—each teacher planning, teaching, and assessing on their own but in the same classroom space. As a result of these divergent views, EL students were not always receiving instruction through a cohesive and integrated co-teaching plan. Students ended up with piecemeal efforts that served to reify the separation and *siloing* of content and English language instruction.

Buying-In to Co-Teaching

Teachers did not always *buy-in* to the district and school's model of co-teaching, despite being given time and/or resources to implement the model. The principal noted, "[Some of them] have common planning time, and then I still hear people saying, uh, but I never, ever met with her." This was frustrating for the principal to hear, but it was also true that not all co-teaching pairs had common planning time, as she also went on to say that she would have to think about finding ways to provide all of the teachers with more time to meet. Observation and interview data indicated that there were missed opportunities for co-teachers to engage and that not all teachers had the same level of investment in the new instructional models of co-teaching. Additionally, some ESOL teachers that wanted to engage felt left out of the planning process with the mainstream teachers. The principal described one ESOL teacher's self-reported perceptions of not being included in the planning process or as involved in the mainstream classroom as she would have liked. This was often a two-way street as the ESOL coordinator noted that in co-teaching situations the ESOL teacher was not always present and engaged in helping to plan and get set-up in the mainstream classrooms. She reflected on feedback she received from mainstream teachers who reported that they had set-up their classrooms, routines, and lesson plans on their own at the start of the school year. Then, a month into the school year, their ESOL co-teacher was assigned and ready to co-teach. At this point, they were expected to recalibrate and incorporate co-teaching, which was challenging for many of them to do.

Meanwhile, district and school leaders had certain expectations for co-teaching, but it was not always clear how these expectations were communicated to teachers. The ESOL chair at Sycamore Elementary noted some of the growing pains associated with figuring out co-teaching. She stated, "Teachers should have plans by Thursday for the next week; but they don't, so the ESOL teachers have a hard time planning ahead." She went on to describe how this could complicate planning and instruction for ESOL teachers. It seemed that many of the mainstream teachers considered their level of importance as more significant than that of the ESOL teacher. This is a problematic phenomenon that has been identified in research (Creese, 2002) and played out in this particular co-teaching context. As a result, if mainstream teachers decided to change their lesson plans at the last minute, they did not consider it a big deal; however, this would often leave the ESOL teacher scrambling to figure out their lessons for the day.

Resultantly, ESOL teachers felt as though mainstream teachers did not always respect their contributions. One veteran ESOL teacher described it this way, "One of the stigmas that we tend to have in our ESOL group is, there are some general ed. teachers that think we don't do our share of the planning." Indeed, there was a perceptible lack of buy-in by the mainstream teachers. They were not sure of the role and responsibilities of their collaborating ESOL co-teachers. As a result, co-teaching pairs were not always working well with one another or in the most effective ways. Ultimately, over the course of the study year, co-teaching pairs fell into manageable routines that did not always align with the vision of school and district leaders.

The goal for co-teaching was for increased opportunities to co-plan, co-teach, and co-assess. Ideally, ESOL and mainstream teachers would be working together to consider the content and language objectives for their lessons and assessments. The ESOL teacher would be available to provide language scaffolds and supports while supporting the mainstream teacher in implementing high quality, rigorous instruction. In reality, the principal described from her perspective how teachers had ultimately gotten to the point of figuring out what would work best with each teacher and had developed their own ways of co-teaching. It seemed that much of what co-teachers were doing on a daily basis did not align with the original goals and intentions of the co-teaching model. Specifically, teachers' *manageable routines* did not always support the original goals and intent of co-teaching. Teachers, in some ways, reverted back to old work patterns and roles despite the new co-teaching instructional model.

Ultimately, given the goal of co-teaching to support EL student's language development within the context of content instruction, the fact that co-teaching pairs were not implementing the model in the ways intended represented a missed opportunity for EL student learning. It was not uncommon to find an ESOL teacher observing whole-group instruction during a portion of their 45–50 minutes of ESOL support or when released to small-group instruction, to find an ESOL teacher delivering a lesson disconnected from the mainstream teacher's lesson. At the same time, there were instances of co-teaching in action. One successful co-teaching pair could be found planning on the same day and time each week, capitalizing on one another's strengths, and sharing the planning and delivery of whole-group instruction. Another co-teaching pair engaged in a pattern of the ESOL teacher providing small-group enrichment and follow-up lessons based on instruction from the week before to provide additional support, scaffolding, and reinforcement of material that students were exposed to in the prior week. The teachers reported that this approach was having a positive impact on their EL students and their learning. While not always implemented in intended ways, it seemed that teachers were experimenting with a variety of "co-teaching" strategies in ways that made sense to them and their students, at least in that moment.

NARROWING THE GAP BETWEEN INTENTION AND REALITY OF CO-TEACHING: RECOMMENDATIONS FOR PRACTICE

As more schools implement such models, illustrative case studies such as this are important for both research and practice. Given research in this area is limited, this study contributes to what we know about perceptions about implementing co-teaching in linguistically diverse contexts. A key objective of this research was to develop a deeper understanding of how teachers and leaders engaged in collective sensemaking (Coburn, 2001) related to implementing co-teaching.

Given the inherent challenges and opportunities of ESOL and mainstream co-teaching models, this research suggests the following recommendations for practice:

1. Develop and implement sustainable, innovative professional development models that support teachers as they implement co-teaching.
2. Provide work-embedded professional development opportunities for both ESOL and mainstream teachers together.
3. Offer ample guidance and support for co-teaching pairs at the beginning of the school year.
4. Cultivate school leaders' expertise in setting the vision and support for the ongoing work of co-teaching as an integral part of the school's professional development plan.

CONCLUSION

Supporting sustainable, innovative professional development models that are focused on meeting increased academic demands for ELs (Hakuta, 2011) through co-teaching, could mitigate the disparate views between teachers and leaders about the role and purpose of co-teaching. Furthermore, such intentional professional learning opportunities could lead to increased ESOL and mainstream teacher buy-in to the co-teaching model. The implementation of co-teaching, when undergirded by a strong leadership vision and targeted support, has the potential to positively impact the content learning and language development needs of EL students that the model was initially designed to address.

NOTE

1. I refer to English learner (EL) students in this chapter as students that are receiving English language services based on their formally assessed English proficiency levels. I recognize that these students are emergent bilingual or multilingual learners and bring linguistic and cultural resources.

REFERENCES

Bunch, G. C. (2013). Pedagogical language knowledge: Preparing mainstream teachers for English learners in the new standards era. *Review of Research in Education, 37*(1), 298–341.

Coburn, C. E. (2001). Collective sensemaking about reading: How teachers mediate reading policy in their professional communities. *Educational Evaluation and Policy Analysis, 23*(2), 145–170. https://doi.org/10.3102/01623737023002145

Creese, A. (2002). The discursive construction of power in teacher partnerships: Language and subject specialists in mainstream schools. *TESOL Quarterly, 36*(4), 597–616.

Dove, M. G., & Honigsfeld, A. (2010). ESL coteaching and collaboration: Opportunities to develop teacher leadership and enhance student learning. *TESOL Journal, 1*(1), 3–22.

Firestone, W. (2014). Teacher evaluation policy and conflicting theories of motivation. *Educational Researcher, 43*(2), 100–107.

Hakuta, K. (2011). Educating language minority students and affirming their equal rights: Research and practical perspectives. *Educational Researcher, 40*(4), 163–174.

Hargreaves, A. (1994). *Changing teachers, changing times: Teachers' work and culture in the postmodern age.* New York, NY: Teachers College Press.

Horn, I. S. (2018). Accountability as a design for teacher learning: Sensemaking about mathematics and equity in the NCLB era. *Urban Education, 53*(3), 382–408.

Lave, J., & Wenger, E. (1991). *Situated learning: Legitimate peripheral participation.* Cambridge, England: Cambridge University Press.

Mangin, M. M. (2007). Facilitating elementary principals' support for instructional teacher leadership. *Educational Administration Quarterly, 43*(3), 319–357.

Martin-Beltran, M., Peercy, M. M., & Selvi, A. F. (2012). Collaboration to teach elementary English language learners: ESOL and mainstream teachers confronting challenges through shared tools and vision. In A. Honigsfeld & M. G. Dove (Eds.), *Coteaching and other collaborative practices in the EFL/ESL classroom: Rationale, research, reflections, and recommendations* (pp. 111–120). Charlotte, NC: Information Age.

McGill, B. (2012). *Mapping language: Limited English proficiency in America.* Retrieved from https://www.nationaljournal.com/s/106868/mapping-language-limited-english-proficiency-america

Peercy, M. M., Ditter, M., & Destefano, M. (2016). "We need more consistency": Negotiating the division of labor in ESOL-mainstream teacher collaboration. *TESOL Journal, 8*(1), 215–239. https://doi.org/10.1002/tesj.269

Peercy, M. M., Martin-Beltrán, M., Yazan, B., & DeStefano, M. (2017). "Jump in any time": How teacher struggle with curricular reform generates opportunities for teacher learning. *Action in Teacher Education, 39*(2), 1–15. https://doi.org/10.1080/01626620.2016.1248302

Russell, F. A. (2012). A culture of collaboration: Meeting the instructional needs of adolescent English language learners. *TESOL Journal, 3*(3), 445–468. https://doi.org/10.1002/tesj.24

Spillane, J. P., Reiser, B. J., & Reimer, T. (2006). Policy implementation and cognition: Reframing and Refocusing implementation research. *Review of Research in Education, 72*(3), 387–431.

Taylor, J. E. (2008). Instructional coaching: The state of the art. In M. M. Mangin & S. R. Stoelinga (Eds.), *Effective teacher leadership: Using research to inform and reform* (pp. 10–35). New York, NY: Teachers College Press.

CHAPTER 13

SHARED SPACES

Systems At Work in English as a New Language Co-Teaching Classrooms

Beth Clark-Gareca
SUNY New Paltz

David Mumper
The Hudson Valley Regional Bilingual Education Resource Network

I think it's good to have more teachers for extra help. Ms. Strong, she's nice. Yeah, I like her for our teacher! Ms. Fermier helps me a lot to help me to get back on track if I get lost. Ms. Dobsen helps me a lot on spelling, incorrections [sic], and directions . . . and Ms. Hanson, she tells me about good English. She helps me a lot with helping me getting better with English and speaking. She helps me to say better words.

—Daniel, 6th grade

Recent legislation in New York has spurred increased implementation of co-teaching models of instruction between content teachers and English as a new language (ENL) teachers (NYSED, 2015). In response to increasing numbers of multilingual learners (MLLs) in New York schools, new legislation has been introduced to ensure that the specific learning needs and

Co-Teaching for English Learners, pages 147–158

appropriate instruction for this growing population of students are being met (NYSED, 2014, 2015). Co-teaching partnerships have great potential to deliver high levels of accessible, academic instruction for MLLs. Though co-teaching for MLLs can take many different forms (Dove & Honigsfeld, 2010; Honigsfeld & Dove, 2012), its overarching promise is that students will benefit from the expertise of two or more teachers in one class while maximizing opportunities to use the target language in authentic settings (Graziano & Navarrete, 2012). In model co-teaching partnerships, each teacher works to his/her strengths, learns from the partner teacher, and negotiates and collaborates toward the mutual goal of a cohesive curriculum that is both linguistically and academically sound. This is the conception with which co-teaching was implemented in New York, in hopes that it would reduce the instructional transitions for MLLs caused by pullout instruction, that is, when students are withdrawn from class for small-group instruction, and allow students greater access to core content in general education classes.

Shared space is a defining feature of co-teaching partnerships. Stemming from work by Lefebvre (1974/1991), classroom spaces in recent years have been re-conceptualized to support more dynamic and flexible teaching models, with physical and emotional space being two identified facets within this classroom ecology (Stevens, 2016). In collaborative classrooms, teachers need to negotiate the physical space between the four walls of their classrooms, as well as the figurative instructional space within their curriculum for collaboration and compromise. These aspects of space account for some of the negotiation that needs to take place when more than one teacher has a role in and responsibility for the education of children; they were also an important lens through which we considered various classroom systems.

FOCUS OF THE STUDY

In this descriptive case study, we documented what co-teaching looks like in action in two classrooms in two school districts in the Hudson Valley region of New York. The research questions that guided this study are as follows:

1. What are some of the systems of co-teaching currently in place in the Hudson Valley?
2. How do stakeholders understand the goals of co-teaching, and how do the current systems meet these goals?
3. How does the use of space affect the ways that students and teachers interact through co-teaching?

Thinking about co-teaching as a flexible, multi-faceted model, we decided to focus on the systems of how teachers and students shared the physical classroom space. We considered especially teacher positionality within the observed classes, in terms of their roles, location, participation, and language use. This piece draws on the work of Cook and Friend (1995) and their identification of six co-teaching models (one teach, one observe; one teach, one assist; parallel teaching; station teaching; alternative teaching; team teaching) from the field of special education. More recent contributions by Scruggs and Mastropieri (2017) identify six lacking areas in co-teaching, including common planning, content knowledge by the special education teacher, communication, control or *turf issues*, differences in teaching philosophy, and disagreements about discipline and behavior time, which can impact its efficacy. This chapter also relies on Honigsfeld and Dove's (2010, 2012) seven-model framework, which defines multiple configurations of co-teaching and collaborative partnerships in ENL classrooms. Cook and Friend's (1995) publication is considered the seminal work on co-teaching stemming from the field of special education. Dove and Honigsfeld's (2010, 2018) work has described the co-teaching model further with a particular focus on ELLs. These three frameworks guided the development of our observation, interview protocols, and our thinking of the ways systems of co-teaching had been constructed in the observed classrooms.

DATA COLLECTION

Data for this study were collected in two schools in two districts in the mid-Hudson region of New York. Classroom selections were the result of convenience sampling, based upon administrator and teacher willingness to permit data collection in classrooms. Observations of classroom co-teaching were conducted in each of the identified classrooms for approximately 40 minutes. Observation protocols attended to student groupings, adults in the room, languages and modalities used, and lesson structure. Given our focus on the shared physical classroom space, particular attention was given to the seating structures and the movement of adults and students within shared spaces in the classroom.

After the observations, interviews were conducted with co-teachers and students to learn more about their participant perspectives on the affordances and weaknesses of co-teaching models. The interviews were transcribed, and the observation protocols and interview transcripts were normed, and eventually evaluated and coded separately by the researchers. The data were then thematically coded, based on structural aspects of the classroom, teacher turn taking, academic language, co-planning, and co-assessment. All children were invited to participate, and ultimately, five students, two MLLs and three non-MLLs from Classroom 2 took part in an interview. Daniel and Jaden, both MLLs at the expanding level of proficiency, had been receiving ENL services for 7 years and had recently been identified as long-term English language learners (LTELs). Both boys also had individualized education programs (IEPs). Carlos, Maria Rosana, and Annie[2] were not MLLs and did not have IEPs.

Classroom Profiles

Classroom 1 was a 9th grade science class in McAllister Regional High School. Three adults co-taught in the room—one science/special education teacher, Ms. Luna, one ESOL teacher, Ms. Geller, and one teaching assistant (TA), Ms. Brown. There were 17 MLLs ranging from beginning to advanced proficiency. Students were sitting in pods of 5–6 desks, and at each pod sat an adult to guide students' progress, translate, and answer questions when necessary. The groups, which were taught by the science teacher and the TA were conducted exclusively in English, while the group facilitated by the ESOL teacher was characterized by strategic use of both English and Spanish. The students in this group were identified to have the lowest English proficiency level, and they were placed in this group intentionally so as to receive translation support from the ENL teacher.

Classroom 2 was a 6th grade class in Forest Plains Regional Middle School. During the observed period of instruction, five adults with professional roles were available to support the learning of the children: Ms. Strong, the general education teacher, Ms. Fermier, the special education teacher, Ms. Banner, the student teacher, Ms. Lloyd, the TA, and Ms. Hanson, the ENL teacher. There were 19 students in this class, of whom six were MLLs. Students were grouped at tables of four to six students according to their reading levels, and for most of the duration of the ~20-minute minilesson, each adult was sitting with a group, with the exception of the special education teacher, who circulated with a clipboard in hand.

FINDINGS

Upon analyzing our data, a complex picture of co-teaching emerged. Findings related to the research questions have been grouped in categories which address teacher understandings of co-teaching systems, the realities of having multiple adults in classrooms, the roles of content and ENL teachers, and the identified benefits of working in the same classroom space. The last section presents feedback from the students as to their impressions of co-teaching systems and the shared spaces that their teachers inhabited.

Teacher Understandings of Co-Teaching Systems

Teachers whom we interviewed demonstrated a range of understandings regarding co-teaching practices, though they all appeared to have a working compass and an awareness of the broad contours of effective co-teaching systems. Some teachers did, for example, speak about and cite examples of research-based models in their own classrooms. For example, Ms. Luna described her own context:

> Pretty much we do a mix of the parallel teaching, and then we do a mix of one teach, one assist. When we are going through notes and worksheets, we'll do one teach, one assist, and then when we are doing labs or more intensive activities, we usually do the parallel teaching and break them into groups and make the groups small and be able to help the kids a little bit more.

Perhaps more important, in addition to these kinds of statements, we observed teacher teams in action using a range of purposeful, effective co-teaching strategies to address the learning needs of their students, including MLLs. For example, teachers worked together in a number of different configurations, some more fluid than others, but all demonstrated the intention of active collaboration for the students' benefit. These specific strategies are explored below.

More Than Just Pairs

The norm in the districts that we visited for this study was not co-teaching pairs, but rather teams of three or more adults (five, in one case), teaching in an integrated co-taught setting. These larger teams meant that teachers had more roles to negotiate, both with the students and with their colleagues. Yet, there were many more opportunities for teachers to work with small, focused groups of students. For the most part, the teachers reported that having more adults in the room was helpful because each teacher could assist and work with any student who required it. As Ms. Luna stated, "They are all of ours." TAs were an integral part of the co-teaching teams and had consistent contact with the children in class, though they did add to the instructional complexity within the classrooms. Ms. Strong, as the content teacher tasked with determining classroom roles, laughed explaining, "It can be very stressful. I am not trained in managing adults!"

When looking at the models that guided our analysis, we also found that the integrated frameworks from special education (Cook & Friend, 1995; Scruggs & Mastropieri, 2017) described the particular contexts that we saw more aptly than did the productive, cohesive co-teaching ENL models from Honigsfeld and Dove (2010, 2012). Newer work by Dove and Honigsfeld

(2018) provides more detail as to how co-teaching models can be constructed in classrooms; yet, our findings suggest that establishing norms and addressing barriers to coordinated teaching in some ENL classrooms is still a
work in progress.

Content Teachers: Supported Roles

Feedback from the content teachers in the classrooms we observed regarding the efficacy of co-teaching was positive. Both content teachers highlighted the increased capacity of two teachers to respond to divergent student learning needs. Ms. Luna said, "It's just way more interventions; you
have a whole lot more interventions." Content teachers recognized that co-
teaching is particularly helpful for students in the early stages of language
acquisition; Ms. Geller shared, "This year...we gave most of the support
at the lower level, which is where they need it most." Ms. Strong focused
on Ms. Hanson's role, "She [Ms. Hanson] was kind of free to float around
and help all of the ESL students also, and it was good that she was able to
hit those language needs as well." Prior to the recent implementation of
co-teaching in New York, MLLs were far less likely to have an ENL teacher present in their content classes, and it appears that, in the classrooms
we visited, co-teaching has indeed improved access to the curriculum for
MLLs, especially those in the early stages of language acquisition.

ENL Teachers: Uncertain Roles

Similar to the content teachers, the ENL teachers we interviewed expressed that co-teaching systems in their schools offered students the opportunity to grow academically. Ms. Hanson stated,

> I think it has great potential because I will tell you what I do see. The ex-
> panding level students, I see where...they truly are bombarded with the writ-
> ing...I do think it really helps them. And even the lower level [student], I
> think the transitioning kids, too; they grow in ways that they don't grow if they
> didn't have that [co-taught] experience.

However, they seemed to feel there is currently more potential than actual
benefit for co-teaching to meet the broader needs of MLLs. The structures
of the ENL teachers' schedules and the implicit loss of autonomy were
troublesome. Ms. Hanson explained, "This [the whole co-teaching system]
is very ineffective...You have to be aware that the quality of instruction suf-
fers because of being spread across [many different classes]...I would go
home every day feeling like I wasn't doing my job." Though Ms. Geller was

more optimistic about her current co-teaching situation, both ENL teachers insisted that teaching with multiple teachers in different content areas was a significant barrier to realizing the goals of co-teaching.

Benefits of Sharing the Classroom Space

Our class observations indicated that even without consistent, structured lesson planning, teachers had developed working routines and systems to effectively share the classroom space. With few exceptions, teachers appeared to speak, move around the classroom, and engage learners in ways that did not distract and allowed students to focus on one thing at a time. Carlos explained, "Class is usually well-flowing," and that teachers, "usually don't interrupt each other." Students in both classes we observed sat in groups of four to six, and in each case, teacher talk was used effectively to (a) address the entire class, (b) lead small-group discussion in two or more groups, or (c) speak with a single student. Teachers in both classrooms effectively used the physical and sonic space in the room without any apparent distractions to each other or students. Additionally, any stigma that students may have felt being pulled from class sessions or receiving specialized instruction was mitigated through co-teaching. Said Ms. Strong, "I think the ESL kids know what Ms. Hanson's role is, but I don't think the other kids quite know." Content teachers also spoke to the benefits of smaller teacher-student ratios to address students' academic needs. "Now, it [student–teacher ratio] is pretty much 1 to 15 instead of 1 to 30," said Ms. Luna. Ms. Strong highlighted how the shared space and smaller ratio allows the ENL teacher to observe and intervene more effectively: "I'm just worried about just getting the curriculum to them; she's kind of with the kids in the class watching and saying, 'Listen, so and so wasn't able to get that'; and she can pick up on things."

Though we observed no obviously problematic or dysfunctional use of the classroom space, teachers feel that there is considerable room for improvement. Ms. Hanson said,

> I notice that the co-teaching between the regular ed. and the special ed. teachers, they share the room. The room belongs to both of them. So that doesn't happen in our experience. I think that could work, but you have to have that kind of consistency and that kind of relationship with the other teacher.

The classrooms we observed reflected Ms. Hanson's impression that the space, though shared, primarily belonged to one teacher. The ENL teacher's role and movement in the classroom space was characterized by three more specific parameters: (a) by *place*, for example, during group work, a teacher was likely to stay at one table rather than occupy the entire room;

(b) by *objective*, as with Ms. Hanson's working with students to help them in "zeroing in on the skills"; or (c) by *student group*, for example, moving to a particular group of struggling MLL students. Of note is that it was rare for any teacher to simultaneously occupy the same general zone of the classroom as another teacher. Teachers tended to allow their colleagues physical as well as instructional space during the observed lessons.

Student Feedback

The children described the co-teaching teams in their classrooms with great enthusiasm, citing its primary benefit to be an abundance of help toward answering questions. When asked about the differences between having multiple teachers rather than just one, like Daniel in the opening vignette, most of the children expressed their preference for having more interactions with adults in their classrooms. Maria Rosana explained, "Ms. Strong, she has so many people to take care of, [so] if she was alone, I don't know if she'd be able to answer all our questions." Jaden agreed, saying, "When you have multiple teachers, you raise your hand, and they come to you. You don't have to wait that long." In contrast, though, Annie warned that sometimes

> [The] teacher would be right there waiting for you . . . you won't be trying to think it out; they'll just be running to you as you are just putting your hand up. I like the single teacher . . . because I don't have everybody just at my begging [sic] call and when I'm sitting there . . . I just have to do all the thinking to myself.

This student's concerns are important; with too many supports and scaffolds, teachers run the risk of impeding development beyond the *zone of proximal development* (Vygotsky, 1978), and in so doing undermine students' ability to solve problems and become self-directed learners. We saw evidence of this happening in one of our classroom observations, when one teacher posed questions to a group of students in order to steer them towards a solution. After many low-level, incremental questions and answers were exchanged in quick succession, it was clear that students were not developing the critical thinking necessary to solve the problem. Described as "learned helplessness," Ms. Hanson lamented the role that she and other teachers played in kids believing that "they couldn't do anything on their own." Evaluating her co-teaching context critically, she continued, "There are way too many adults in that classroom."

IMPLICATIONS

Considering that empirical research related to ENL co-teaching is in its infancy, this study has definite implications for practice and professional development. Factors such as the inconsistency of co-teaching systems and deficiencies in co-planning and co-assessment were focused on as important areas to address to improve instruction in schools where co-teaching has been implemented.

Inconsistent Systems

It has been difficult to establish consistent co-teaching systems in regions such as the mid-Hudson, where we conducted this research for at least two reasons:

1. Co-teaching in content classes with MLLs is a new approach, and districts are still experimenting with staffing, scheduling, and other systems.
2. Districts' MLLs typically number in the tens or hundreds, rather than thousands, and therefore districts have often decided to shift teachers' assignments to account for year-to-year fluctuations in enrollment, staffing, and scheduling.

Consequently, ENL teachers feel that they have been shuffled from class to class, have struggled to learn new content, and have feared that they "can be thrown into any content at any time." Ms. Geller explained that in her biology class "... last year it was heavily content, very wordy, and it was just very difficult. But it was harder for me to modify because it was my first year, so I didn't know what content was important and what wasn't." She contrasted this with her co-taught high school government class, where the content was more familiar to her, and

> it's more equal, and we go back and forth with the content. So if the teacher didn't know how to clarify something or explain something, then I could just easily jump in and say, "Oh remember that time," and we kind of know where we're both thinking or trying to clarify.

The changes in assignments from one year to the next are illustrative. Last year, Ms. Geller co-taught one class (biology), and this year she co-teaches in four classes (two ELA sections with the same co-teacher, a section of government, and a section of biology, each with a different co-teacher). Over the past 3 years, Ms. Hanson co-taught the first year with three teachers, the second year with four teachers, and this current year with five teachers. She shared that "the more it increases, the harder it gets. I can't keep up with all the different things they are doing." She felt that only *one* of her classes reflected true co-teaching, where planning, instruction and "everything was a shared effort." None of the other classes, in her view, could be considered co-teaching. When describing her current teaching arrangement, she told us that this year, "to alleviate the stress for me, I said I'm not going to use that term *co-teaching* anymore. I'll use *support*, I'll use *push-in*, but I realized this summer that that term was stressing me out to no end because it was not happening."

Like many other co-teachers, Ms. Hanson wanted to be a successful co-teacher through collaborating effectively with her co-teaching partners. She understood what the model required theoretically; however in practice, she recognized that the natural constraints associated with working with multiple co-teaching partners were incompatible with her understanding of what co-teaching should be. Feeling disingenuous in her role, she looked for other, more marginal words to describe the work that she was doing.

Planning and Assessment Deficiencies

Our analysis of current co-teaching systems brought a significant, additional challenge into focus: in both case studies, co-teaching implementation was missing one or more of its key features. Co-planning and co-assessing, which are generally recognized as crucial components for success (Dove & Honigsfeld, 2018; Honigsfeld & Dove, 2010), were conspicuously absent or when they were present, were conducted as an afterthought or on the fly. Some of the contributing factors were clear, such as the complexity of coordinating with three, four, or five different co-teachers in different content areas, and schedule changes from year to year, which made it nearly impossible to develop plans for long-term routines and systems. ENL teachers, as expert teachers in their own right, need to have the opportunity to design and develop appropriate lessons and assessments. With long-term investment in collaborative planning, both teachers would eventually save a great deal of time and have the opportunity to implement more effective and impactful lessons. Ms. Hanson explained,

> What has happened many times is I'll go home, and I'll create all these different things, and I'll go in the next day, and they've changed the lesson. And that is the problem of being with five teachers. If it was only one teacher, she would say, "Oh, you know, let's change this for tomorrow," and I wouldn't go home and do 2 hours of [work]. So that's frustrating. It's very frustrating.

Though our study does not attempt to determine whether these concerns are statewide, it is worth noting that in this sample, administrators and teachers echoed that co-planning is difficult or not occurring in their schools. Without a coordinated effort toward integrating content through planning, the motivation for ENL teachers to continue their work with professionalism and dedication will likely decline over time.

CONCLUSIONS

In classrooms where content teachers, ENL teachers, and others are working side-by-side, the negotiation of classroom and instructional space among teachers is critical to the system working cohesively and productively. We know that students can reap multiple instructional benefits from having consistent access to a knowledgeable adult. We also know that teachers can learn from their peers and grow as educators through collaboration. Despite its challenges, the implementation of co-teaching in New York's schools continues to hold the promise of providing multiple advantages for all participants involved. However, for its true potential to be realized and sustained, teams of teachers and administrators must determine (a) how many different co-teaching partnerships each teacher can successfully negotiate; (b) ways to sustain these partnerships from year to year; and (c) how to allocate scheduled time for teacher partners to plan lessons, problem-solve, and communicate their shared curricular goals. With careful, deliberate mapping of co-teachers' varied roles and responsibilities, spaces such as the classrooms studied here can easily evolve into optimal learning systems that enhance educational access for MLLs.

REFERENCES

Cook, L., & Friend, M. (1995). Co-teaching: Guidelines for creating effective practices. *Focus on Exceptional Children, 28*(3), 1–16.

Dove, M. G., & Honigsfeld, A. (2010). ESL co-teaching and collaboration: Opportunities to develop teacher leadership and enhance student learning. *TESOL Journal, 1*(1), 3–22.

Dove, M. G., & Honigsfeld, A. (2018). *Co-teaching for English learners: A guide to collaborative planning, instruction, assessment, and reflection.* Thousand Oaks, CA: Corwin Press.

Graziano, K., & Navarrete, L. (2012). Coteaching in a teacher education classroom: Collaboration, compromise, and creativity. *Issues in Teacher Education, 21*(1), 109–126.

Honigsfeld, A., & Dove, M. G. (2010). *Collaboration and co-teaching: Strategies for English learners.* Thousand Oaks, CA: Corwin.

Honigsfeld, A., & Dove, M. G. (Eds.). (2012). *Coteaching and other collaborative practices in the EFL/ESL classroom: Rationale, research, reflections, and recommendations.* Charlotte, NC: Information Age.

Lefebvre, H. (1991). *The production of space* (D. Nicholson-Smith, Trans.). Oxford, England: Blackwell. (Original work published 1974)

NYSED. (2014). *SED releases "Blueprint for English Language Learner Success."* Retrieved from http://www.nysed.gov/news/2015/sed-releases-blueprint-english-language-learners-success

NYSED. (2015). *CR Part 154-2 (9-12) English as New Language (ENL) units of study and staffing requirements.* Retrieved from http://www.nysed.gov/common/nysed/files/programs/bilingual-ed/enl-9-12-units-of-study-table-5-6-15.pdf

Scruggs, T., & Mastropieri, M. (2017). Making inclusion work with co-teaching. *Teaching Exceptional Children, 49*(4), 284–293.

Stevens, M. (2016). Space for all: Middle level students in blended learning environments. *Voices from the Middle, 24*(2), 50–55.

Vygotsky, L. S. (1978). *Mind in society: Development of higher psychological processes.* Cambridge, MA: Harvard University Press.

CHAPTER 14

THE MEANING OF "CO" IN CO-TEACHING

Resolving Co-Teaching Challenges

Karrie S. Woodruff
Oregon State University

Classrooms are like teachers' own ships. Teachers are the decision makers of their domains, and the responsibilities of each classroom fall solely on their shoulders. But when there are two teachers, who is the captain? Figuring out a meaningful role is important for a teacher's sense of self-efficacy, and one's confidence in his or her ability to succeed, which is important in how an individual approaches goals, tasks, and challenges. Both classroom teachers and specialists negotiate and often re-negotiate teaching partnerships, and no two co-teaching relationships are alike. In a partnership, teachers must consider the logistics and effects of their co-teaching. What happens when two teachers share a classroom? How are decisions made? How much thought goes into this negotiation? How do teachers resolve issues when they arise? How do co-teachers know when their instruction is effective? How does effective co-teaching impact students?

Co-Teaching for English Learners, pages 159–170
Copyright © 2020 by Information Age Publishing
All rights of reproduction in any form reserved.

This qualitative study uncovers the process of becoming more effective co-teachers, and how teachers negotiate professional agreements in terms of planning, instruction, and class management. The objective of this study is to provide readers with information that can help them to develop strategies for improving their own co-teacher relationships for optimal student learning.

In co-teaching, two teachers collaborate to deliver specialized instruction (Friend, Cook, Hurley-Chamberlain, & Shamberger, 2010) or English language development (ELD; Honigsfeld & Dove, 2010, 2019) within the general education classroom. Educators and researchers in the ELD field in the last 20 years have drawn from established co-teaching models in special education to explore options for pairing ELD specialists and content teachers.

Researchers of ELD co-teaching often refer to a continuum framework for effective collaboration between an ELD and mainstream teacher put forward by Davison (2006): pseudo-compliance, compliance, accommodation, convergence, and creative co-construction. Peercy and Martin-Beltran (2012) concluded that co-teacher effectiveness—originally defined by Davison (2006)—emerged from the team's positive attitude and willingness to engage in productive struggle regarding instruction and collaboration. Teachers who reported successful collaboration in Bell and Baecher's (2012) study explained that they valued each other's expertise and shared ideas, resources, and responsibilities.

Power dynamics between ELD and content area teachers is a consistent theme in ELD co-teaching research. Studies reveal that teachers understand their division of roles and responsibilities. However, ELD teachers are perceived as having lower status, and therefore they often play a supportive and/or service role. Language development remains on the periphery of the classroom agenda, and the ELD teachers feel frustrated (Creese, 2002, 2004, 2005, 2006; Peercy, Ditter, & Destefano, 2017). This dynamic is a main reason why many ELD teachers prefer the pullout model of service (Bell & Baecher, 2012). On the other hand, Russell (2012, 2014) described a relationship between a content teacher and an ELD teacher/facilitator, in which the ELD teacher/facilitator co-teaches with the content teacher and coaches them, as well. In this case, the fact that the ELD teacher holds a dual role, including an administrator-like role of facilitator, elevates her from a supportive role to which many ELD teachers are relegated and equalizes her co-teaching relationship with the content teacher. Also, the co-teacher relationship described by Gardner (2006) is equalized by the ELD teacher's seniority over the novice content teacher. There are scenarios such as these that offset the typical power dynamic. The goal, of course, is to achieve Davison's optimal level of "creative co-construction" (p. 466) in a co-teaching partnership.

Another theme among studies relates to teacher perception, communication, and aligned vision as factors influencing team trust and efficacy. Peercy and Martin-Beltran (2012) reported that when teachers perceived that their partner teacher had previous experience either as a mainstream or ELD teacher, trust increased. In contrast, when teachers perceived that their counterpart had limited expertise, trust decreased, and teachers had difficulty working together. Sense of trust and willingness to work together improved in teacher teams where expectations and routines were aligned and communicated. In a similar vein, the most effective teams were those that were willing to address conflict (Peercy & Martin-Beltran, 2012) and openly shared ideas and perspectives (York-Barr, Ghere, & Sommerness, 2007). Throughout this study, I examine themes of division of roles and responsibilities; power dynamics between ELD and classroom teachers; and co-teacher perception, communication and vision alignment, and how these all result in effectiveness of collaboration.

CONTEXT AND METHODOLOGY OF THE STUDY

As an ELD teacher within the embedded ELD model, I explore the successes and challenges of co-teaching within a Spanish–English dual immersion elementary school that is in its third year of implementation of the co-teaching model at every grade level (K–5). Embedded ELD refers to English language development that takes place in the mainstream classroom and is contextualized within content material. This chapter is based on the experiences of nine elementary co-teachers at this school, including three ELD teachers and six classroom teachers, both new and seasoned. In half-hour semi-structured interviews over the course of a month, I reflected individually with each teacher on co-teaching practices, roles and responsibilities, decision-making processes, success, tension, and communication, and then I analyzed the interviews looking for common themes.

The study took place in a Spanish–English dual immersion elementary school in the Pacific Northwest. The student population is approximately 450 students comprised of 50% Spanish speakers, 45% English speakers, and the remaining percentage other minoritized groups. Among the teacher participants, eight out of nine were women, and all were White. The school, which became dual-language in the early 2000s, has five teachers who are English only and paired with a Spanish only partner. The students, then, have two teachers—one for English and one for Spanish, and alternate between languages weekly. (These language pairs are considered a *team*; the term *co-teachers* refers to a classroom teacher and an ELD teacher who teach in the same classroom.) There are eight teachers who teach their classes in both English and Spanish. I am one of four ELD teachers. ELD teachers are assigned to a grade-level team: one grade level for part-time teachers and two grade levels for full-time. Therefore, ELD teachers work with several different classroom teachers during the day. With very few exceptions,

TABLE 14.1 Language Specialist Teacher Co-Teaching Assignments

ELD Teacher/FTE	Jackie (0.7)	Molly (1.0)	Josh (1.0)	Laura (0.5)
Grade Level(s)	K	1 & 4	2 & 3	5
# of Classroom Teachers	3	6	5	2
Language Support	English	Bilingual	English	Bilingual
Time Per Day in Each Classroom	75–105 min.	30–45 min.	60–75 min.	60–120 min.
Subjects Co-Taught	AM Calendar, Literacy, Reading Groups, Writing, Math	AM Calendar, Literacy, Reading Groups, Writing, Science	Literacy, Reading Groups, Writing	Literacy, Reading Groups, Writing, Science

Note: Schedules vary from day to day and week to week depending on language schedules (e.g., English/Spanish rotation), teacher needs, student needs, and specific skill set of the specialist teacher.

co-teaching partners have shifted every year for the last 3 years due to staffing changes. (See Table 14.1 for details on co-teacher assignments.)

Until 3 years ago, all English learners in K–5 were pulled out of their grade-level classes for special English lessons throughout the district. While standardized test results demonstrated growth in ELD, standardized test scores in academic content indicated that language skills were not transferring. As a result, district and building administration made the decision to move to a co-teaching model that provides language development along with academic content in schools with high numbers of English learners. This decision was met with varying degrees of teacher support and buy-in, and there was little guidance in terms of expectations. The building principal emphasized that this strategy was intended for teachers to discover their own approach to co-teaching. While much growth has occurred in co-teaching, it has been challenging to discover a path to *effective* co-teaching, and teachers acknowledged that there is more to learn and develop in the embedded ELD model.

FINDINGS

There were four main themes that emerged from the teacher interviews. They included (a) the role of experience in the co-teaching power dynamic; (b) how roles and responsibilities are decided between the classroom and ELD teachers; (c) the importance of maintaining a student-oriented focus while allowing for each teacher's strengths, style, and ideas; and (d) the importance of proactive, direct, and compassionate communication in a partnership.

Initial Negotiations of the Relationship:
Experience Matters

Participants reflected that in co-teaching, the more experienced teacher tended to take the lead. This leadership took the form of implementing discipline and procedures, curriculum planning, and/or leading class activities. Correspondingly, less experienced teachers were more open to co-teaching: the sharing of tasks and decision-making in order to create a learning experience. Generally, classroom teachers were assumed to be the lead teacher, *unless* the ELD teacher had more teaching experience than the classroom teacher, particularly within that grade or subject matter. A classroom teacher who had less experience than the ELD teacher was more likely to invite the ELD teacher to have more input in class discipline and procedures, curriculum planning, and leading whole-group lessons, which tended to create a more equal working relationship. Tensions arose, however, when the *newer* teacher desired autonomy, and the more experienced teacher was still leading. Because of the newness of the co-teaching model and the recent reconfiguration of teams and co-teaching partners, statements about the sense of co-teaching efficacy pertained more to *relative* experience and personal confidence.

Seasoned classroom teachers working with less-experienced ELD teachers noted that *trust* was an issue in co-teaching. Experienced classroom teachers found that they were hesitant to permit whole-group instruction by the ELD teacher because class time was too precious to take away from the lesson. Experienced classroom teacher Debbie said,

> [Giving up control] depends on the person who's coming in to co-teach with you. Are they effective? Because if they're not effective, I'm not going to have my kids be their guinea pigs. If they are not effective, we'd have to work something out. Like model, and watch.

This perspective was common. All classroom teachers in the study who had more experience than their co-teacher expressed that they were somewhat hesitant to relinquish class time because of their uncertainty about whether the ELD teacher could manage the class as effectively as they could. Conversely, those classroom teachers with equal or less teaching experience than their partner indicated that they were more willing to share class time.

Decisively Divide and Conquer

Although co-teaching experts suggest that the relationship and the sharing of responsibilities should be equal or equitable (Friend et al., 2010; Leatherman, 2009; Pratt, 2014; Pratt, Imbody, Wolf, & Patterson, 2017; Scruggs, Mastropieri, & McDuffie, 2007; Tannock, 2009; Sileo, 2011), they are often *un*equal. Co-teachers recognize that their teaching responsibilities are not and cannot be exactly 50/50, but that each teacher brings a focus and skill set to the classroom. ELD and classroom teachers report that students seem to consider the classroom teacher to be their *main teacher,* since she is with her students all day long, while various assistants, specialty teachers, and volunteers come and go. ELD teachers appear at a particular time, and specialize in language-learning pedagogies like Guided Language Acquisition Device (G.L.A.D.; Brechtel, 2001), Sheltered Instruction Observation Protocol (SIOP; Echevarría, Vogt, & Short, 2016), Academic Conversations (Zwiers & Crawford, 2011), and Culturally Responsive Teaching (Gay, 2000). These strategies benefit all students; however, they are essential for language learners. In our school, ELD teachers have combinations of strategies that they offer to classroom teachers that are sometimes beyond the regular repertoire of class activities, bringing a language or culture focus to the lesson. Classroom teachers are generally open to the ELD teachers' agenda, as most classroom teachers have an ESOL endorsement, and the culture of language learning is reinforced by our unofficial school mantra: "Everyone is a language learner."

Josh, an ELD teacher who works with five classroom teachers in two grades, shared his perspective regarding his role. He views his role as supportive, and he follows each classroom teacher's lead:

> For the most part, I'm trying to follow what each classroom teacher is doing, as they have a big idea in mind. They have an overall perspective of what they want their students to do...I have to be flexible, and that means being able to follow and find ways to help and support rather than lead the curriculum. If the responsibility were officially on me, I know I would step right up and do that. But as it isn't, anytime that I push too hard in trying to do things, that's where the tension comes. There's no tension as long as I recognize that the classroom teacher has a plan, and I try to make it better rather than to substitute my own.

Debbie, one of Josh's co-teachers, says of their relationship, "He has been so open about, 'How can I help you? I want to take something off your shoulders.' And that has made it easy. That's why we work together so well."

Over 3 years in the co-teaching model, our school has refined the ELD teacher's job to, primarily, bring focus to the needs of English language learners, who are legally entitled to language development services (U.S. Department of Education, 2015). Exactly what ELD teachers do with their classroom teachers varies from pair to pair because the shared skill set and dynamic are so different. ELD teacher Molly takes the lead in one of her co-teaching relationships, because she has more experience with the grade level than the classroom teacher. She is skilled in the management (effective discipline and procedures) of that grade level, and she is more familiar with the curriculum.

In another classroom, she does only small reading groups—she acknowledges that she is less experienced with that grade level, planning time is scarce, and her schedule with six classroom teachers limits her ability to be in the classroom during literacy, which is the usual time for co-teaching.

All teachers in our school concur that there is not enough co-teacher planning time. It is mostly done "on the fly," during lunch or recess, or passing in the hallway. Co-teachers often default to having the classroom teacher share the lesson plan in advance, and then the ELD teacher proposes ways to make it more language-oriented through the use of visuals and charts, providing background information, vocabulary-building activities, scaffolding, multicultural perspectives, and so on. Co-teachers develop a method for working together. Even if it is not well planned, the ELD teachers can involve themselves in the lesson by asking clarifying questions, highlighting pertinent vocabulary, creating impromptu visuals, or working with a small group of students. One classroom teacher talked about the nonverbal cues that she refined with her ELD co-teacher: In the midst of her lesson, she looks at her co-teacher and says, "As I'm reading my book, can you ...?" Without finishing her sentence, the ELD teacher jumps in with a language activity. Sometimes, the cue is just a look.

Participating teachers report that one way an ELD teacher can support numerous classroom teachers most efficiently is by preparing materials and corresponding strategies that teach content and language simultaneously. Most ELD teachers reported taking on the task of "behind the scenes" work: making visuals, graphic organizers and other scaffolds to aid in language learning, which is a great support to teachers and ELD students. ELD teachers also have functioned as peer coaches, modeling language-focused learning activities. This exchange of teaching strategies has equalized the power dynamic, giving each professional a sense of value. As classroom teachers share ELD co-teachers, and these assignments are prone to change yearly, the use of these common strategies creates a more cohesive school culture.

A Good Working Relationship: Give and Take

Molly, an ELD teacher who switched from the classroom teacher role, recalled an especially good co-teaching relationship she had a few years ago:

> My co-teacher and I had a similar vision and goals for the students because it was student focused. When we're focused on the students' needs and the students' data rather than our own ideas and opinions, it's easier to make decisions together. When we knew where the students needed to go, that made the planning easier because it was focused on the kids. That also makes the decision-making quick since we don't have time each week to plan together.

She noted that she and her co-teacher had similar teaching styles and a positive personal relationship, and those further helped their co-teaching dynamic. Molly described the co-teaching experience as "magical" and "awesome." While most participants reported having a positive co-teaching relationship at some time, they also talked about having to work at the relationship.

Co-teaching expert, Friend (2008) noted the importance of addressing small issues before they become big problems, such as student discipline, teaching strategies, or classroom logistics. Reaching a compromise is easier if it is accomplished before either person becomes frustrated. It is important to debrief related roles and responsibilities, even amidst a busy day, so that co-teachers can reflect on and refine their practices, and it is also important that both educators are active participants (Friend, 2008). Several teacher participants in this study reported experiencing instances of co-teaching challenges (and perhaps incompatibility) in terms of style, or even philosophy of education. Some teachers talked about some areas of discontentment with their co-teaching arrangement, but had not offered any reconciliation in regards to the issues. One pair had left their concerns unaddressed for so long that they reached a point of frustration, contention and uncertainty of whether or not the relationship could be repaired.

One of the greatest challenges of co-teaching is striking the balance of contributing in a meaningful way, while not dominating the relationship. One experienced classroom teacher said, "The challenge lies in our willingness to give up a little bit because we're so used to being in control of everything." She added that *because* she is an experienced teacher, she felt comfortable giving up some control and inviting her co-teacher to contribute substantially in ways that are appropriate to his role, which they had clearly defined. One of the most difficult aspects of the job for ELD teachers was the struggle with the lack of autonomy. In our school, one ELD teacher took the autonomous role of the *writing teacher,* for example, and led whole group writing lessons regularly. This was an acceptable solution for the teacher who desired autonomy and had a special interest, and for co-teachers with irreconcilable teaching styles.

One belief that is part of our education philosophy is that all students have strengths, and this philosophy extends to teachers as well. Tension resulted when strengths went unacknowledged. When ideas of one teacher were consistently over-ruled by *better* ideas of another, it led to feelings of inadequacy and powerlessness. Functional co-teaching is built on mutual respect, and cultivation of shared ideas. Several of the participants said, "More heads together is better." The acceptance of an idea affirms self-efficacy; *building* on ideas affirms team-efficacy and the value of co-teaching. A positive co-teaching relationship is student-oriented, and allows for each teacher's strengths, style and ideas.

Communication Is Key

Nearly all teachers interviewed said that open communication would help them work more effectively as a team, but very few teachers had been able to communicate about tension they felt with a co-teacher. Some of them said that they had not felt it was bad enough to warrant "confrontation." Several admitted that they found it very difficult to bring up concerns, even if they caused significant tension. Yet, many of them stated that they wanted clear communication from their partner.

Because time together outside of class was limited, direct communication (balanced with respect and compassion, of course) was most efficient. To avoid misunderstandings that sometimes cause irreversible damage, it makes sense to be cognizant of and then verbalize teaching philosophies, experiences, strengths and areas in need of growth. It saves time, whereas observing and discovering these things happenstance will take months, or possibly go undiscovered completely. One classroom teacher, Michelle, confessed that she had felt some tension in her co-teaching relationships, was working on identifying her true feelings, and then advocating for herself in an appropriate and professional way. She joked that she needed a therapist for co-teaching relationships. Another teacher, Kelly, who had been both ELD and classroom teacher, reflected that she had wondered what her co-teachers were thinking. Whether she guessed too positively or too negatively, neither guess was likely accurate or helpful without a guided conversation with her co-teachers.

Based on interviews, tensions seemed to arise from three basic issues: differing philosophies, the need for control or autonomy, and communication. These challenges hindered a co-teaching partnership that would result in optimal student learning. While this study did not look at the specific quantitative aspect of co-teaching, this is what classroom and ELD teachers had to say about its benefits overall:

> It's powerful for kids to see people teach together. If you come at it where you both know where your strengths are in that topic, and do that together, it's so much better for kids. And it's better for you. But it takes experience, it takes time . . . It takes time learning how to work with them, their habits and their strengths, where to push and where to pull back, and what to expect. (Jane, classroom teacher)

> What has helped is when there's a mindset of language . . . To have the specialist helps bring an awareness of that part. It's another person at each grade level to talk about best practice, or what we could be doing different. (Michelle, classroom teacher)

> It's much better for kids. I really like that kids aren't being segregated, literally brought away from the classroom, missing instruction . . . I think instruction needs to happen with everyone, so that everyone's voice has value, and we

can encourage English language learners to have that agency and confidence in their own voice, and that can't happen when we take them away. I've seen [co-teaching] work at our school, I've felt that it's been successful . . . The data really grows and there's huge successes, and that gives me hope . . . We could show huge student growth based on our collaboration . . . A team of people is stronger than one. I'm glad we do this model, and I like having this role that is kind of like a coach in some ways, and someone who gets to focus on language. (Molly, ELD teacher)

In spite of the growth pains and challenges in co-teaching, all teachers expressed a willingness to work at the co-teaching relationship. Most indicated that they had experienced some success in this model, and they observed co-teaching to have a positive impact on English learners.

CONCLUSIONS AND IMPLICATIONS

Trust is essential in the co-teaching relationship, and is developed from ongoing opportunities for collaborative conversations around goal setting, shared decision-making, joint risk taking, having high expectations of each other, relying on each other, and overcoming one's professional insecurities (Honigsfeld & Dove, 2015). This study affirms that it is important for teacher partners to proactively discuss their co-teaching vision, including their agreed upon roles and responsibilities based on their personal and professional skill set. It is critical for co-teachers to listen to and learn from each other; teachers must offer ideas according to their expertise *and* acknowledge their partner's ideas. And teachers need to reflect on and talk with each other about their co-teaching practice, before issues arise. Co-teachers need to return to this conversation regularly because communication reduces tension between partners. Effective collaboration does not come from merely getting along and shying away from conflict. The goal for the best, most authentic co-teaching is to *engage* in open dialog about teaching practices and have confidence that the relationship can endure such challenges. A structured or guided dialogue at the beginning, middle, and end of the co-teaching year would facilitate reflection and communication for co-teachers.

When teachers trust each other, they no longer need to focus on the uncertainties of their relationship and can focus on the students (Honigsfeld & Dove, 2015). The next step is examining how we can guide teachers to be more reflective and critical of their own practice, and then to communicate honestly and earnestly with their co-teachers for greater efficacy and effectiveness for student learning.

REFERENCES

Bell, A., & Baecher, L. (2012). Points on a continuum: ESL teachers reporting on collaboration. *TESOL Journal, 3*(3), 488–515.

Brechtel, M. (2001). *Bringing it all together: Language and literacy in the multilingual classroom* (Rev. ed.). Carlsbad, CA: Dominie Press.

Creese, A. (2002). The discourse construction of power in teacher partnerships: Language and subject specialists in mainstream schools. *TESOL Quarterly, 36*(4), 597–616.

Creese, A. (2004). Bilingual teachers in mainstream secondary classes: Using Turkish to learn curriculum. In J. Brutt-Griffler & M. M. Varghese (Eds.), *Bilingualism and language pedagogy* (pp. 97–111). London, England: Multilingual Matters.

Creese, A. (2005). *Teacher collaboration and talk in multilingual classes.* London, England: Multilingual Matters.

Creese, A. (2006). Supporting talk? Partnership teachers in classroom interaction. *International Journal of Bilingual Education and Bilingualism, 9*(4), 434–453.

Davison, C. (2006). Collaboration between ESL and content teachers: How do we know when we are doing it right? *International Journal of Bilingual Education and Bilingualism,9*(4), 454–475.

Echevarría, J., Vogt, M. E., & Short, D. (2016). *Making content comprehensible for English language learners: The SIOP model* (5th ed.) Boston, MA: Allyn & Bacon.

Friend, M. (2008). Co-teaching: A simple solution that isn't so simple after all. *Journal of Curriculum and Instruction, 2*(2), 9–19.

Friend, M., Cook, L., Hurley-Chamberlain, D., & Shamberger, C. (2010). Co-teaching: An illustration of the complexity of collaboration in special education. *Journal of Educational and Psychological Consultation, 20*(1), 9–27.

Gardner, S. (2006). Centre-stage in the instructional register: Partnership talk in primary EAL. *International Journal of Bilingual Education and Bilingualism, 9*(4), 476–494.

Gay, G. (2000). *Culturally responsive teaching: Theory, research, and practice.* New York, NY: Teachers College Press.

Honigsfeld, A., & Dove, M. G. (2010). *Collaboration and co-teaching: Strategies for English learners.* Thousand Oaks, CA: Corwin Press.

Honigsfeld, A., & Dove, M. G. (2015). Co-teaching ELLs: Riding a tandem bike. *Educational Leadership, 73*(4), 56–60.

Honigsfeld, A., & Dove, M. G. (2019). *Collaborating for English learners: A foundational guide to integrated practices* (2nd ed.). Thousand Oaks, CA: Corwin Press.

Leatherman, J. (2009). Teachers' voices concerning collaborative teams within an inclusive elementary school. *Teaching Education, 20*(2), 189–202.

Peercy, M. M., Ditter, M., & Destefano, M. (2017). "We need more consistency": Negotiating the division of labor in ESOL—Mainstream teacher collaboration. *TESOL Journal, 8*(1), 215–239.

Peercy, M. M., & Martin-Beltran, M. (2012). Envisioning collaboration: including ESOL students *and* teachers in the mainstream classroom. *International Journal of Inclusive Education, 16*(7–8), 657–673.

Pratt, S. M. (2014). Achieving symbiosis: Working through challenges found in co-teaching to achieve effective co-teaching relationships. *Teaching and Teacher Education, 41*, 1–12.

Pratt, S. M., Imbody, S. M., Wolf, L. D., & Patterson, A. L. (2017). Co-planning in co-teaching: A practical solution. *Intervention in School and Clinic, 52*(4), 243–249.

Russell, F. (2012). A culture of collaboration: Meeting the instructional needs of adolescent English language learners. *TESOL Journal, 3*(3), 445–468.

Russell, F. (2014). Collaborative literacy work in a high school: Enhancing teacher capacity for English learner instruction in the mainstream. *International Journal of Inclusive Education, 18*(11), 1189–1207.

Scruggs, T. E., Mastropieri, M. A., & McDuffie, K. A. (2007). Co-teaching in inclusive classrooms: A metasynthesis of qualitative research. *Exceptional Children, 73*(4), 392–416.

Sileo, J. M. (2011). Co-teaching: Getting to know your partner. *TEACHING Exceptional Children, 43*(5), 32–38.

Tannock, M. T. (2009). Tangible and intangible elements of collaborative teaching. *Intervention in School and Clinic, 44*(3), 173–178.

U.S. Department of Education. (2015). *Schools' civil rights obligations to English learner students and limited English proficient parents.* Retrieved from https://www2.ed.gov/about/offices/list/ocr/ellresources.html

York-Barr, J., Ghere, G. S., & Sommerness, J. (2007). Collaborative teaching to increase ELL student learning. *Journal of Education for Students Placed at Risk, 12*(3), 301–335.

Zwiers, J., & Crawford, M. (2011). *Academic conversations: Classroom talk that fosters critical thinking and content understandings.* Portland, ME: Stenhouse.

PART IV

CO-TEACHING TO ENHANCE INSTRUCTIONAL PRACTICE

CHAPTER 15

POSITIVE OUTCOMES FOR ELs IN AN INTEGRATED SOCIAL STUDIES CLASS

Carrie McDermott
Molloy College

Andrea Honigsfeld
Molloy College

The bell rings; it is 9:28 a.m., and the freshmen and sophomores at an east coast suburban high school pile into the class. They are chatting as they head for their desks situated in triads and quartets. The student make-up is varied and includes English learners (ELs), students with exceptionality, and the general population. There are students from diverse backgrounds including Hondurans, Salvadorans, Chinese, and South Korean. Two teachers—one social studies and one English as a new language (ENL)—are situated on opposite sides of the classroom, welcoming students as they enter the room.

As the class begins, the two teachers present students with an intriguing task, to analyze the following quote accompanied by an image projected on the board, "In order for a country to be great, she must show her influence throughout the world and carry everywhere she can her language,

Co-Teaching for English Learners, pages 173–183
Copyright © 2020 by Information Age Publishing
All rights of reproduction in any form reserved.

her customs, her flag, her arms, and her genius" (Jules Ferry, French Prime Minister 1880). As a warm-up activity, students work in pairs to analyze the quote to help them focus on the topic of the upcoming lesson: The New Age of Imperialism. The song, *Missionary* by Operation Ivy, is quietly playing in the background. Its lyrics are meant to help students understand the topic:

I start it, I end it, I kill and words will defend it,
Got big plans, blood stained hands
Wanna see my name on the map.
On my way to save the world...
Got a brand-new set of words, the going rate is cheap,
Unconditional devotion, unquestioning belief.
Words carved in stone, chiseled in with sharpened bones...

As students finish their analysis, they are given the lyrics and listen to the song. Their next assignment is to compare the song lyrics to the quote.

The students work in small groups again to complete the task as both teachers circulate the room to guide them through the analysis and comparison as well as offer language support to unpack some key phrases. The room is filled with the buzz of active discussions—students collaborate with one another making comments, asking each other questions, and working through the content. Some students speak in their home language to one another; some use print or electronic dictionaries, while others look for clarification from both teachers and peers.

This short vignette gives a glimpse into what a visit to an integrated social studies class looks and sounds like. Students whose first language is not English are not separated; the ENL teacher is working alongside her content area teacher counterpart, and the curriculum the ELs receive is identical with that of their general education peers. Yet there is ample opportunity for language and literacy development with rich, interactive learning opportunities and carefully designed scaffolds. In this chapter, we present a case study of the class in the opening vignette and offer a documentary account of the positive outcomes of its integrated ENL program in the secondary social studies context.

BACKGROUND

Integrated ENL services in New York State (NYS) are defined as (a) a co-teaching team consisting of one certified content area teacher (7–12) and one certified English for speakers of other languages (ESOL) teacher in a class or (b) one dually certified teacher in a content area (Grades 7–12) and ESOL. NYS has created mandates for integrated ENL instruction with

English language arts (ELA) as the instructional priority (NYSED, 2015). We know this content area is essential to help students acquire language; however it is not the only core subject necessary for students at the high school level. In some cases, districts focus on more than the minimum requirements mandated for integrated ENL programs in NYS and give ELs more opportunities to succeed and ultimately graduate. Therefore, some schools offer integrated classes in additional core subject areas.

Why did we select this high school to research? The school has over 1,700 students enrolled with 84% of them being White, 7.8% Hispanic or Latino, 5.2% Asian or Pacific Islander, 2% Black, and 1.3% Multiracial. At the freshman and sophomore levels, 57% and 54% respectively represent ELs at the entering, emerging, and transitioning levels of English acquisition in the social studies classroom. Of all freshman and sophomores, 90% received a passing grade of 65 or better on the Global Studies Regents in Year 2. New York State School Report Card Data (2017–2018) reports the graduation rate at 96% with a 4% dropout rate.

This district stands out from among the many others that we have visited and previously studied. They have seen their population of ELs increase in recent years, and they are facilitating co-teaching opportunities in integrated core subject classes to benefit ELs as well as mainstream and exceptional students. This district has and continues to dedicate funds to the co-teaching partnerships in high school content classes beyond the integrated ENL mandated requirements. The mandates for integrated services call for priority support in integrated ELA and ENL classes with between 90-minutes or 180-minutes per week. In addition, the mandates also include stand-alone services for entering and emerging students with flexibility between stand-alone and integrated ENL in the core content. Students at the entering and emerging levels receive additional units of study per week (NYSED, 2015). See Table 15.1 for more specific information about integrated ENL program mandates. The focus in this school has been to place students in co-teaching environments in all their core content area classes to ensure success. This means students are receiving between one and two additional units of study in integrated classes per week.

Case Study Participants

The co-teaching team consists of two highly committed educators who have been collaborating for less than two years at the time the case study was conducted. One is an ENL teacher multi-certified in ESOL, French, and Spanish who travels between two buildings daily. This ENL teacher has multiple co-teaching partnerships in both the middle school and high school and creatively carves out time to work with each co-teaching partner at least

TABLE 15.1 Units of Study Requirements

	Entering	Emerging	Transitioning	Expanding	Commanding
ENL Instructional Time (minimum)	3 Units of Study	2 Units of Study	1 Unit of Study	1 Unit of Study	1/2 Unit of Study
Stand-Alone	1 Unit of Study	1/2 Unit of Study			
Integrated ENL	1 Unit of Study ENL/ELA	1 Unit of Study ENL/ELA	1/2 Unit of Study ENL/Core Content	1 Unit of Study ENL/Core Content	
Flexibility	1 Unit of Study Stand-alone or integrated ENL in core content	1/2 Unit of Study Stand-alone or integrated ENL in core content	1/2 Unit of Study Stand-alone or integrated ENL in core content		1/2 Unit of Study Stand-alone or integrated ENL in core content

(NYSED, 2015)

	Entering	Emerging	Transitioning	Expanding	Commanding
District Provided Additional Services provided by this district	2 Units of Integrated core content	1 ½ Units of Integrated core content	1 ½ Units of Integrated core content	2-3 Units of Integrated core content	Varies from ½-2 Units of Integrated core content

District, 2017–2019

once a week, usually outside the confines of the school day. The other member of the team is a certified social studies teacher who works in one building and focuses specifically on social studies content. Due to scheduling challenges, this team has minimal planning time embedded in the school day; however, they do much of their collaborative planning online via technology using a dedicated website and Google Docs. In addition, the district has created a budget for summer curriculum work to foster collaborations for many of the co-teaching teams. The curriculum work has been offered each summer over the last few years to provide both new and experienced teams time to map out their overall plan to meet the needs of ELs in the integrated ENL classroom. This collaboration has specifically focused on building language through content and supporting student literacy.

How do these teachers feel about co-teaching? The team expressed their thoughts about the experience. In the beginning, they did not know what to expect but reported an overall positive experience. According to the ENL teacher, "Everybody agreed they wanted to work together, and they wanted to have this partnership. You see the change in the kids; you see the change in yourself, being together. So it's good. It's a good thing." The other teacher nodded in agreement. They also mentioned that they did not have summer curriculum planning time together before their first year, but they did the second. The ENL teacher added, "It helped us get off on the right foot and have a structured plan. It also helped us see where the language could be more of a focus for all the students." We also noted the collegiality of the pair during instruction. They had a positive rapport with one another as well as with their students. This collegiality transferred to the culture of the classroom. Students worked well with their peers and displayed multiple moments of success.

Context for Collaboration

The case-study team teaches two sections of integrated social studies. Both sections have 29 students. Approximately one third of each class consists of ELs. In preparation for their co-taught classes, the team sets aside their own time to plan weekly. Throughout the planning process, they select a quote of the week, a daily essential question, and a power phrase. These three components are established as a routine for both teachers and students. Technology also plays a vital role in the planning process, the class, and the structure of learning. Students have access to a teacher-created website, which is regularly updated to provide information for each lesson and additional resources to help students review key concepts and work with supplementary materials. These resources include partially completed graphic organizers, structured note-taking pages, embedded video clips, FlipGrid, and Padlet.

Although no formal co-planning time is included in the teachers' official weekly schedule, the team identifies collaborative planning as an essential component to the successful development and implementation of lessons and units. Social studies units are grounded in integrated studies and focuses on civic competence (Honigsfeld, McDermott, & Cordeiro, 2018; NCSS, 1994). Teachers emphasize the challenging concepts within the content of social studies for ELs as they may have been taught information from various points of view. Through purposeful planning, they work together to showcase the expertise each will bring to teaching the materials daily. Typical roles they take are aligned to their professional preparation; one focuses on the academic demands and the core content goals of the social studies curriculum, whereas the other focuses on the linguistic demands of the same curriculum and the ways students' language and literacy development may be systemically connected to the core content instruction. In some cases, the teachers plan on switching these roles depending on the needs of the students and the direction of the lesson. The team also uses collaboration time they carve out on their own to identify how they will differentiate the material and the roles the students will play in the classroom.

RESEARCH PURPOSE

Political constructs change through time and place (Parker, 2015) making social studies one of the most difficult content areas for ELs to master. For this reason, ESOL specialists need to collaborate with social studies specialists to help ELs master core academic content, language proficiency, and disciplinary literacy skills in English. Together, co-teaching teams address the complex needs of ELs by connecting language development instruction with the academic and linguistic demands of the content curriculum. This type of integrated instruction helps the team understand and respond to the needs of ELs while also feeling more prepared to meet the cultural, academic, and linguistic diversity (Yoder, Kibler, & van Hover, 2016) of students in the core content classroom.

The case study described in this chapter is a part of a larger, ongoing research project focused on social studies co-teaching teams and how they incorporate the six Cs of support for ELs: connection, code breaking, community and collaboration, culture, challenge, and classroom interaction (de Oliveira, 2016). The purpose of this research was to explore the process and professional learning outcomes of in-service social studies teachers collaborating with ENL teachers to help ELs master integrated content and language goals. The research focused on two main questions:

Research Question 1: *How did the participating co-teaching teams negoti-ate the integration of content and language instruction using the six Cs of support for ELs: connection, code breaking, community and collaboration, culture, challenge, and classroom interaction (de Oliveira, 2016)?*

1. *Connection:* Classroom instruction and curriculum were connected to students' backgrounds and experiences, making content ex-plicit.
2. *Culture:* Cultural and linguistic resources, or "funds of knowledge," that ELs already possess were used to support academic learning.
3. *Code-Breaking:* Co-teachers explicitly taught ways of engaging in school, academic literacy, and disciplinary, linguistic, and cultural codes of content learning.
4. *Challenge:* Classroom goals and activities explored disciplinary lit-eracy and higher-order thinking and reasoning.
5. *Community and Collaboration:* Learners socially co-constructed knowledge.
6. *Classroom Interactions:* Scaffolded classroom discourse was used to build academic oral literacy.

Research Question 2: *How did the participating co-teaching teams negoti-ate joint professional learning through collaboration and co-teaching?*

Data Sources and Collection

This case study is part of a larger research project focusing on integrated, co-taught social studies classes at the high school level. For the sake of this study, we collected a variety of data over the course of a year closely aligned to the research purpose. We conducted three site visits that included class-room observations, teacher interviews, and follow-up discussions and re-flections after each observation and visit. We also invited the participating teachers to complete questionnaires, which aimed at capturing their in-structional intentions regarding their students' academic and linguistic de-velopment. In addition, we collected relevant teacher and student artifacts including web-based planning documents such as lesson plans, teacher-cre-ated instructional materials, student work samples, and test scores.

OUTCOMES

Throughout most of the observations, we saw the social studies teacher and the ENL teacher introduce the lesson as a team. One practice the researchers noted was a daily do-now routine. As students entered the room, a do-now activity was displayed on the board for the students to begin working. For example, the teachers created an anonymous Padlet for the students to complete with the question, "What makes people dislike each other?" The teachers each had a role: The social studies teacher moved around the room to check student progress as the ENL teacher previewed the responses and approved them so they could be displayed for the class to see.

We also noted in this specific lesson that the social studies teacher took the lead focusing on the Arab–Israeli conflict in front of the class, and the ENL teacher purposefully taught on the side to those students who needed support. In one instance, the ENL teacher was supporting students with academic language and breaking the information down into smaller components to help them understand the meaning of the topic and the overall concepts of the conflict. On other occasions, we noted that these roles reversed depending upon the need or direction of the lesson. Throughout our time in the classroom, the teachers were flexible, constantly checking for understanding and encouraging students to remain focused and actively engaged in the learning process. The teaching team was organized and collaborated with one another, guided the students without dominating the conversation, and allowed students to navigate their own learning by using cultural and linguistic resources.

The team consistently helped students learn content through language by focusing on making connections to prior learning and experiences, bridging knowledge, and unpacking key concepts for understanding through scaffolding and differentiated techniques. They did this by engaging students in activities that were visual, scaffolded, interactive and relevant to the world around them. The classroom appeared to be a safe learning environment where students were comfortable and not afraid to take risks.

When the team discussed their experience with the students in the co-taught classroom, the ENL teacher stated, "We call on them, they're willing to participate. They're not afraid to have an accent or to even talk with other peers who are general education or special needs students. So, it's just a world of a difference with them." In response, the social studies teacher explained how it could be difficult when students and the content teacher do not receive the support they need in class. "You feel like you don't know what to do with them. You don't know what they're learning, if they're understanding anything." The learning turns more to hoping they get something out of what is being taught, "and whatever they could absorb, they absorb. But now with the interaction that we have, we involve them; we include them more. I think they're more comfortable. Which it's only going to help them learn more."

The teachers were also asked to report on how co-teaching impacted non-English learners. Although the strategies are meant for ELs, they also focus on the language and break down the content into more manageable pieces, which help all students filter the information in a way that makes sense to them. This scaffolded instruction helps all students to learn and retain the information over time. One teacher stated, "I think that's helpful. I think strategies can help every student." It also helps strengthen the classroom community and brings the students together in new ways. "I think it also gets them to realize that, hey there's another population of students in our building, and you should welcome them, embrace them as part of the family. And it gets them to know each other a little bit and break out of their shell." The other teacher pointed out the differences they see in the responses from students over the course of the year. In the beginning of the year, there was not a good amount of conversation or awareness among the students. As the year progressed, the teachers noticed "[a student] work with one of the ELs later on [in the year] and she was really trying to guide them along the way. She was almost modeling what we do with them. So it was interesting."

The teachers recognized that achieving success and both knowing and understanding the information are a challenge. Students are often learning difficult academic information through a new lens of language, content, culture, and collaboration. The team sets the example for collaboration and model working together as they build in the language, content, and culture of learning. According to the ENL teacher, "It does take a while to develop the culture of collaboration and help and working with everyone together. So it's a process. I don't think we've mastered it yet, but certainly we've improved." Collaboration takes time to make all of this work because it is a process, which builds and gets stronger over time. They both agreed that they are enjoying it. The social studies teacher added, "It's nice to see the kids utilizing all of these strategies that we're doing and it's rewarding, it's nice."

During the interview, the team reflected on the teaming during the lesson. The social studies teacher stated, "I think the groups were effective. We mixed the ELs with the mainstream students. It worked out really well." The ENL teacher stated, "The comparison question was really good too, and they came up with a lot of good stuff." As a follow up to this discussion a few days later, the teachers had time to take a closer look at student work. The social studies teacher noticed, "All the groups had some things written down. I think the stems worked." The teachers evidenced that students were able to use the language to convey meaning in the concepts.

IMPACT

Prior to the co-taught, integrated courses, ELs were placed in mainstream courses without support in the case study school. EL student achievement was lower, and students had limited success in passing courses or Regents exams. For instance, it was noted by one of the teachers that almost all of the ELs failed the midterm social studies exam and really struggled with the Regents exam in the years prior to co-teaching. This tendency negatively impacted opportunities for ELs to graduate with a high school diploma and continue with post-secondary education. As a result, this district focused on positively impacting student success through integrated co-teaching at the high school level. In the first year, 61% of the students in this co-taught course raised their grades from Quarter 1 to Quarter 4 by one or more letter grades. This number increased to approximately 70% in Year 2. Of this first year group of students, 75% of them passed the Regents exam at the end of the course. In addition, more than two thirds of the ELs demonstrated growth in their language proficiency level by at least one level.

In response to the positive impact on both students and teachers, administrators in this district have dedicated additional resources to increase the integrated co-teaching model in more classes at the high school and have also created a plan to begin rolling a similar initiative out at the middle school. One administrator noted, "Students have reached success from one quarter to the next in addition to the Regents exam. In response to this, we have decided to use a similar model at the middle school level in multiple content areas." It is evident that the administration also understands the importance of consistency. "We have decided to keep this co-teaching team together because of the success we have seen. All the students are benefitting and this is a good model. This team works very well together."

CONCLUSION

The study provided a deeper look into an integrated, co-taught social studies class and how this environment had a direct impact on ELs, general education, exceptional students, and teachers. Co-teaching in integrated classes gives students opportunities to learn content through language. It also fosters the teaching team's ability to learn through collaboration and co-teaching to reach ELs in meaningful ways by focusing on the 6 Cs of support for ELs in the integrated social studies classroom.

REFERENCES

de Oliveira, L.C. (2016). A language-based approach to content instruction (LACI) for English language learners: Examples from two elementary teachers. *International multilingual research journal, 10*(3), 217–231. https://doi.org/10.1080/19313152.2016.1185911

Honigsfeld, A., McDermott, C., & Cordeiro, K. (2018). Preparing social studies and ESOL teachers for integrating content and language instruction in support of ELLs. In L. C. de Oliveira & K. M. Obenchain (Eds.), *Teaching history and social studies to English language learners: Preparing pre-service and in-service teachers* (pp. 127–158). New York, NY: Springer.

National Council for the Social Studies. (1994). *National council for the social studies, expectations of excellence: Curriculum standards for social studies.* Washington, DC: NCSS.

New York State Education Department. (2015). *CR Part 154-2 (9-12) English as a new language units of study requirement.* Retrieved from http://www.nysed.gov/common/nysed/files/programs/bilingual-ed/enl-9-12-units-of-study-table-5-6-15.pdf

New York State School Report Card Data. (2017–2018). Retrieved from https://data.nysed.gov/essa.php?year=2018&state=yes

Parker, W. C. (2015). Social studies education eC21. In W. C. Parker (Ed.), *Social studies today: Research and practice* (pp. 1–13). New York, NY: Routledge.

Yoder, P. J., Kibler, A., & van Hover, S. (2016). Instruction for English language learners in the social studies classroom: A meta-synthesis. *Social Studies Research and Practice, 11*(1), 20–39.

CHAPTER 16

A CULTURE
OF COLLABORATION

How Do We Create The Greatest Thinkers for the World?

Marie Edgerton
Boeckman Creek Primary School

Jane Charlotte Weiss
Boeckman Creek Primary School

What does successful collaborative teaching and co-planning for multilingual students look like? What do educational leaders identify as the guiding principles for this work? In this chapter, we share our journey in pursuing answers to these questions, and the fundamental elements we have discovered to create a thriving schoolwide co-teaching model, including cultivating a culture of collaboration and collective wisdom, establishing the foundation of a strong workshop model, and creating an ecosystem of curiosity and authenticity around language and vocabulary. Our discoveries are informed by the brilliance and experience of our fellow collaborating teachers, our students, and the work of many authors and researchers.

Co-Teaching for English Learners, pages 185–198
Copyright © 2020 by Information Age Publishing
All rights of reproduction in any form reserved.

Teaching is an incredibly complex profession. In many careers that are as dynamic and intellectually demanding as teaching, professionals are given opportunities to collaborate throughout the day to discuss various approaches to tasks, ask for feedback, divide and conquer responsibilities, and learn from one another's individual experiences and expertise. Unfortunately, working as a teacher in public elementary schools in the United States often means long days isolated in classrooms with limited time to plan for the next day's lessons. When teachers do get the chance to come together, it is often in contexts that are overly structured and inauthentic. For example, some teachers might be asked to analyze data, such as abstract or outdated standardized test scores that do not necessarily guide instruction for the following day or give formative information about what students know and can do. In our school district, we often talk about *creating conditions for miracles to occur* where disenfranchised students transcend the opportunity gap that has traditionally written their story. As we see it, if we want this to happen for our most vulnerable learners, we are going to need to work together to build collective wisdom—exactly what teaching collaboratively has accomplished.

As a collaborating second-grade classroom teacher and a multilingual specialist, we were curious about what was happening for students categorized as English learners (EL) across Oregon and visited twelve different school districts to investigate. We observed teachers working tirelessly to help meet the diverse needs of their students but were left with profound questions about how often children truly engage in deep and meaningful work related to their lives. One in five children in Oregon currently speaks a home language other than English; yet by 8th grade, most linguistically and ethnically minoritized students in Oregon are more than a year behind their English-speaking peers in both reading and math (Hammond, 2015). Co-teaching for the sake of ELs is an emerging practice in Oregon schools, and English language instruction is often approached from a deficit perspective, focused heavily on remediation and taught in isolation, away from students' classrooms. The mission question for West Linn Wilsonville School District, Oregon, where we teach, is the following: "How do we create learning communities for the greatest thinkers and most thoughtful people...for the world?" What we were witnessing for multilingual children seemed antithetical to this mission, so we decided to try something new.

CULTURE OF COLLABORATION

"No matter how many years or how few you've been teaching, collaboration is one of the best tools you can use."

—Jean Fox, 4th-Grade Teacher, Boeckman Creek Primary School

Our school, Boeckman Creek Primary School (BCPS), is located in the town of Wilsonville, about 20 miles outside of Portland, Oregon. It is a diverse school in a rapidly changing community, where apartment complexes collide with luxury estates. Students whose parents work in agriculture learn alongside children whose families own the farms, and teachers are constantly challenged to address the needs of all types of learners. Perhaps the most exciting thing about our school is how closely it mirrors our country's demographics as a whole. The latest report from the National Center for Education Statistics (Kena et al., 2016) shows 21% of U.S. children live in poverty, while 36% at BCPS do. Likewise, 9.2% of Americans are categorized as English language learners (ELLs); 11% of our students at BCPS are ELLs (Kena et al., 2016). These statistics, combined with the striking range of life experiences amongst families, makes it a compelling environment for educational research. Teaching in such a community has forced us to diversify our skills and hone our practices to include only the most comprehensive and effective approaches.

Creating Collective Change

Before we started our collaborative teaching model at BCPS, students categorized as ELLs were pulled out of their classrooms to receive English language development (ELD) instruction in small groups. Both classroom teachers and ELD specialists worked hard in isolation to support students. Yet ELLs spent significant time outside of the classroom, were often the most disengaged, and did not seem to be making significant academic growth. As a school, we aspired to do better. Our district was determined to find ways to support students within the classroom instead of pulling them out. In May 2014, as the multilingual specialist, Jane (co-author 2) took a grassroots approach to building a collaborative teaching model. She started dropping by teachers' classrooms after school to see if they would be interested in trying the new model with her. She discovered other educators interested in collaborating and found many were passionate about improving access and opportunities for students categorized as ELL. Together, we looked at ourselves as teacher-researchers and approached the project from an inquiry perspective asking, "How can we work together so that students are growing in their language development all day while accessing complex academic content?" We used research from Stanford University's *Understanding Language Initiative* (http://ell.stanford.edu/) to cultivate excitement among teachers and build a shared vision for what it could look like to support language development in mainstream classrooms.

Drawing on Collective Wisdom

We would not have been able to launch our co-teaching model without the work of researcher Michael Fullan (2008) and his *Six Secrets of Change*. Fullan's first three secrets of change all focus on building meaningful relationships and recognizing the collective wisdom in your colleagues: love your employees, connect peers with purpose, and capacity building prevails. We know that without building real, meaningful relationships with each other and with our students, our collaborative teaching model would have never left the ground. The last three secrets of change—learning is the work, transparency rules, and systems learn—all focus on maintaining an esteeming, dynamic, and reflective perspective in our work with children, in which specialists and classroom teachers work as equals in collaboration for the same goals. Fullan's six principles were essential in guiding us to maintain a collective, open-minded, and grassroots approach to co-teaching.

A foundational goal of our work together has always been to recognize and build upon the unique talents and expertise of every individual teacher involved in the model. We have created space for this goal through frequent opportunities to co-plan, collectively reflect upon, and refine our work through a process called *lesson study* (Doig & Groves, 2011), and through intentionally prioritizing the *cross-pollination* of instructional approaches that most effectively support student learning. We have quickly realized that what we have been able to create and share with each other together has become much greater than anything we could have accomplished on our own.

Planning Together

One of the most important pieces to making co-teaching possible, yet such a difficult aspect to fit into the busy lives of teachers, is finding time to plan together. Without planning time, effective collaborative teaching is nearly impossible. In our school, we have found that planning works best when we make time for both informal weekly check-ins, as well as more in-depth half-day planning sessions across the year. During the weekly check-ins, classroom teachers sit down with specialists (individually or in grade-level teams) to talk about the following week's lessons. Some of the questions that guide our discussions are:

- What are you planning to teach these next weeks?
- What will be our purpose as co-teachers?
- What are your multilingual students struggling with most?
- How can we best work together to support them?

We work together to think about the content that specific students might find challenging and consider instructional moves to make it accessible and provide affordances for language development.

Planning together is also an opportunity for the specialist to connect and reference effective approaches she has seen in other classrooms and grade levels. In addition to weekly planning, we meet together for half-day sessions three times across the year. This allows specialists to have a sense of the scope and sequence of curriculum across the year, while considering how to best integrate the *English Language Proficiency Standards* (Council of Chief State School Officers, 2014) into core content to ensure that students are engaging in language throughout their day. As co-planning has become more fluid and natural, we have found that its impact on supporting students can be just as significant as the actual co-teaching.

LESSON STUDY: THE POWER OF TEACHERS AS RESEARCHERS

Another powerful aspect of our grassroots approach—and an important way in which we have built a collective vision—is through meeting two or three times a year to refine our collaborative teaching model using a process called *lesson study* (Doig & Groves, 2011). This protocol invites a group of classroom teachers to come together to develop lessons, observe them being taught, and analyze student outcomes (see Figure 16.1).

We use an inquiry model to frame our process, while research from Stanford University's *Understanding Language Initiative* (Bunch, Kibler, & Pimentel, 2012) also guides us. We focus on students categorized as ELs through a collaboratively designed lesson that includes an academic focus, a social interaction focus, and a language focus. We then spend time carefully observing individual students and teachers to gauge specific aspects of the learning,

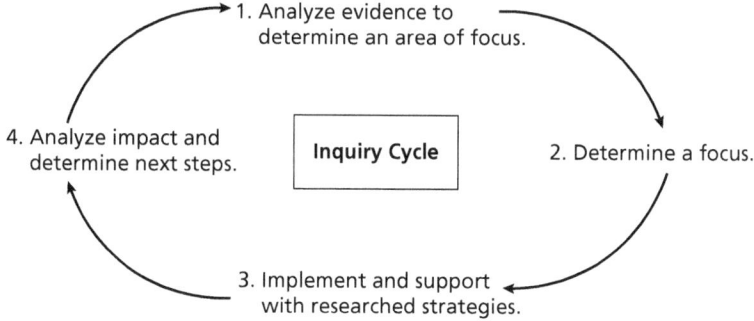

Figure 16.1 Inquiry cycle from lesson study.

while trying to analyze and improve the lesson as a group. This type of collaboration and action research has been some of the most profound work we have ever done. In our first year of co-teaching, Jane and her fifth-grade colleague co-taught a lesson on inferred meaning vocabulary with nonfiction texts from National Geographic. The lesson included teacher modeling of strong partnerships followed by students working with partners to use context clues and background knowledge to infer the meaning of words they did not understand in the text. A second-grade teacher reported that she noticed several things the fifth graders were doing that she could apply to her own classroom. Some of the approaches she saw were partner work, the use of complex text, and the inferred meaning vocabulary strategy (Harvey, 2008), which have since become common instructional practices across our school.

Cross-Pollination

One of our fundamental beliefs behind collaborative teaching is that every person in a school has individual strengths, experiences, and areas of expertise. When educators are immersed in an environment where they have frequent and authentic opportunities to draw from each other's wisdom, the collective becomes smarter. Jane is constantly taking videos and collecting tools and effective strategies from across classrooms and sharing them with other teachers. Collaborative teaching is and always has been about *our students* and responding to their individual needs, rather than monitoring whether classroom teachers are following a checklist of sheltered instruction strategies.

One of the benefits of the co-teaching model has been that now, when a child has significant success with one particular teacher, that educator's wisdom and insight can be shared with teachers in subsequent grade levels through co-planning, vertical articulation (the alignment of curricula across grade levels), and lesson studies. We find ways to collectively wrap our arms around children as they continue on their journey throughout the school (see Figure 16.2).

A STRONG WORKSHOP MODEL

We believe it is *essential* for our multilingual students to be *in* the classroom, engaged in rich work throughout the day. A growing body of research has identified numerous ways in which the classification of and services for students categorized as ELs can create a hierarchically tiered education system that parallels social inequalities in the larger society, and we certainly witnessed this in our prior pullout ELD model (Motamedi, Vazquez, Gandhi,

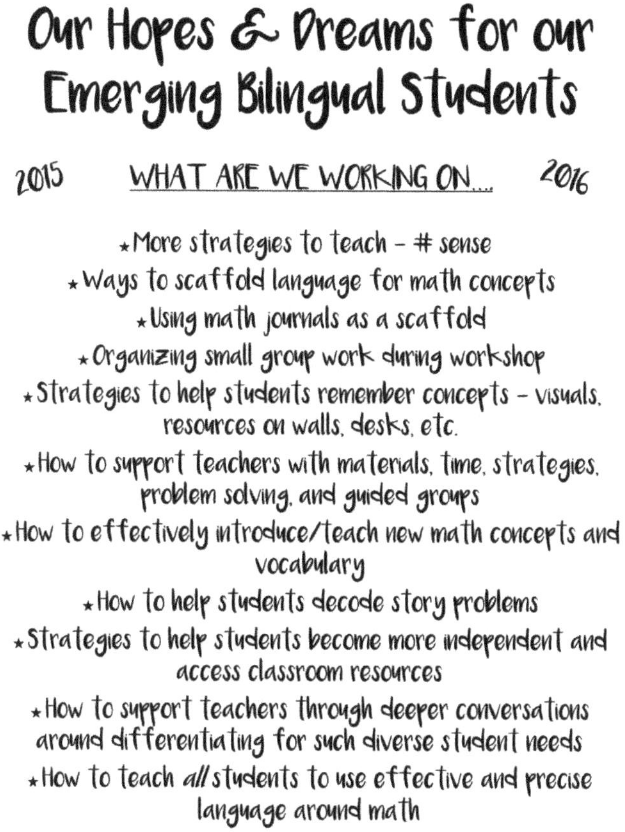

Our Hopes & Dreams for our Emerging Bilingual Students

2015   WHAT ARE WE WORKING ON...   2016

* ★More strategies to teach – # sense
* ★Ways to scaffold language for math concepts
* ★Using math journals as a scaffold
* ★Organizing small group work during workshop
* ★Strategies to help students remember concepts – visuals, resources on walls, desks, etc.
* ★How to support teachers with materials, time, strategies, problem solving, and guided groups
* ★How to effectively introduce/teach new math concepts and vocabulary
* ★How to help students decode story problems
* ★Strategies to help students become more independent and access classroom resources
* ★How to support teachers through deeper conversations around differentiating for such diverse student needs
* ★How to teach *all* students to use effective and precise language around math

Figure 16.2   Collective goals made by co-teachers.

& Holmgren, 2019; Umansky, 2016;). A few fundamental components of our workshop model have been to establish a culture of intellectual character and growth mindset, explicitly teach metacognition and thinking strategies, and give a voice to the diverse knowledge within the classroom. We have fostered academic independence through a gradual release model with lots of modeling, thoughtfully chosen texts to match readers, and time for students to explore content and new concepts.

What Does a Co-Teaching Workshop Model Look Like in Our Classrooms?

A lesson in a workshop model often follows a predictable pattern: mini lesson, independent work time, and reflection. The mini lesson is a short lesson that clearly models the expectations for the independent work time. In a co-teaching classroom, the interaction between co-teachers can look different depending on the lesson. In a lesson where students will be working in partnerships or groups, the co-teachers may model the interaction and ask for student input on what they noticed. It may also be a time where one teacher opens up his/her brain to model deep and explicit thinking aloud. The independent work time is when students are immersed in authentic tasks and teachers make sure there are enough scaffolds to help every child access the lesson, without limiting where students can take their learning. During this time, co-teachers confer with individual students/ partnerships, meet with groups working on similar objectives, and monitor the overall understanding of the learning target. It is important for teachers to analyze the task and processes they are asking students to do and to break it down into small steps, utilizing the catch-and-release model (Bennett, 2007; Tovani, 2011). If teachers notice a common misconception or area for growth amongst multiple students, they can briefly interrupt the work time to help clarify expectations or to highlight exemplars. This is an opportunity for teachers to notice individuals, partnerships, or small groups doing model work, or examples where students are changing their thinking and gives other students landmarks to help clarify and reflect on their own thinking. The final piece of the workshop model, and perhaps the one most easily omitted, is the time for reflection. This component is an essential part of the lesson during which students reflect on their learning, and teachers can formatively assess learning and consider implications for subsequent lessons. An authentic, co-taught workshop model in any content area can truly elevate the status of each child in your classroom and provide access to all learners.

Creating a Culture of Intellectual Character

Based on our own experiences and work by authors Keene (2011), Keene and Zimmermann (1997, 2007), and Miller (2013), we have found that one of the most important building blocks to creating a workshop model is establishing a classroom environment where students feel like important members of the community; where they feel safe to make mistakes, and look at themselves as readers, writers, mathematicians, scientists, and thinkers (Johnston, 2004). We recognize that growth mindset, perseverance, empathy, respect, and other aspects of social and emotional intelligence profoundly impact our students and their learning (Dweck, 2007). This whole-child approach to teaching and our understanding of how our language affects children's learning is an essential part of building a successful co-teaching model. Another element of helping students recognize and develop their intellectual character is teaching them explicit ways to be metacognitive. Based on Keene and Zimmermann's (1997) *Mosaic of Thought*, we introduce students to the *seven thinking strategies*, asking them to consider the metacognitive processes proficient readers and thinkers often use to comprehend. These strategies provide a framework across content areas to model and help students recognize the work they are doing as learners. Our goal is always to help students develop a sense of agency and academic independence while engaging with ideas and materials that are meaningful in their lives.

BELLA'S STORY

It is a strong workshop model that helps our most vulnerable students thrive. Before coming to second grade, Bella was disengaged with school and struggled academically. It was in Marie's (co-author 1) classroom that an important transformation occurred, especially in Bella's reading and her ability to express her thinking in English. She made 1½ years of growth and almost caught up with many of her peers in second grade. This academic growth itself was remarkable, but what struck Marie the most was how Bella's mindset changed. Through our ability as two collaborative teachers in the classroom to engage Bella in authentic learning experiences, and provide her with high expectations and scaffolds, Bella started recognizing herself as a learner and deep thinker. Our collaboration and persistence provided Bella with the mindset she might have needed in order to make such significant growth in one year.

CURIOSITY FOR LANGUAGE

"Co-teaching provides students with a strong model for discourse and academic conversations. With two teachers there is space and time to be able to coach emerging bilingual students in order to give them a more equitable voice in the classroom."

—Erin Hinshaw, 3rd Grade Teacher at BCPS

Education is fundamentally about the power of human connection. Our visionary principal, Lindy Sproul, often reminds us to "do a few things of great import; do them well and do them deeply." We believe one of these things of "great import" is to truly *believe* in each of our students, connect with and *know them* on a real, human, and personal level. One of the most fundamental ways you can know and love your students is to know their families; who they are as individuals, where they come from, and the languages and cultures through which they experience the world. Language is personal—it represents your mother and father, your grandparents, your family, and community. When teachers, schools, and assessments imply, through words or actions, that one form of speaking is superior to another, it can do lasting damage to a child's self-image and whether they ultimately see themselves as truly valued at school or not. Our approach to language development has also been founded heavily on a piece of advice our former superintendent, Bill Rhoades, often gave teachers, "First, do no harm." With this principle as our guide, we have tried to mindfully cultivate a classroom ecosystem of curiosity around language that increases time for children to collaborate with each other to explore and discuss real world content through hands-on experiences and a variety of rich and engaging texts.

Language as a Toolkit

There is currently much controversy about the term academic language, the myth of the million-word gap, and the oppressive consequences these ideologies can hold for students from marginalized communities (Rosa & Flores, 2015). We try to counter this narrative by approaching all languages as *toolkits* that we use to comprehend and navigate the world around us. We explore vocabulary and genres of text with curiosity—what types of words and concepts do scientists, authors, and mathematicians need to do their work deeply and authentically? We aim not to *curricularize* language development and instead hope to facilitate opportunities for language use in meaningful work throughout the day (Valdés, 2015). In addition to this, we spend lots of time working to make thinking visible for children with anchor charts, hand motions, table tents, sticky notes, text annotation, think alouds, sketches, and spur of the moment visuals when we, as co-teachers, realize students may need another access point to increase comprehension. Language acquisition cannot be achieved through one isolated strategy, but must instead be approached through creating an ecosystem of curiosity and collaboration that inspires authentic and purposeful discussion around meaningful experiences.

Collaborative Learning

One key to creating conditions for language development for some of our most vulnerable students has been to create space for children to engage socially with each other around real-world content in rich, hands-on ways. Opportunities to talk and work together are strategic and thoughtfully provided by monitoring student engagement and considering the depth of the content that has been delivered. We have found a lot of power in modeling explicit aspects of a productive and equitable conversation as co-teachers. Perhaps one of the most important aspects of collaborative teaching has been to carefully watch the dynamics of specific student partnerships and groupings to determine more effective configurations. We are constantly changing these flexible partnerships and are often surprised by the students who are most well matched.

Authentic Purpose and Engaging Texts

Providing students with opportunities to access and discuss copious amounts and varieties of text with photographs, text features, and engaging topics across content areas has been paramount (Kibler, Walqui, & Bunch, 2015). We often use Harvey's (2008) *Comprehension Toolkit* to guide us in this endeavor. One of her fundamental lessons teaches students to use context clues and their prior knowledge to infer the meaning of vocabulary words. Taberski (2017) also offered many ideas for increasing oral language in the classroom, including her *Words, Words, Words* strategy (drawing attention to useful vocabulary while reading aloud to students). In addition to finding ways to scaffold complex text, one key approach we have used to increase reading engagement and comprehension in general is through thoughtfully matching books to readers. We are constantly thinking about how to help students become passionate about reading by making book recommendations, doing book talks, and finding high-interest, culturally responsive books for read-alouds and shared reading.

JUSTIN'S STORY

Justin moved to our school in second grade and was a busy student from the start. He had a hard time staying engaged on the carpet and easily became distracted during the independent portion of the reader's workshop. Marie has a magical ritual that has captured the hearts of many of her students, including Justin—she writes personalized sticky notes to her students, recommending certain books. She is constantly on the lookout in our school library and book room for topics and titles that *hook* her most vulnerable readers. Whenever Marie finds something, she grabs it, writes a short sticky note to a student, and leaves it on his/her desk. After Justin received several of these special notes, he started making similar book recommendations to other students in the class, and his peers wrote them for him. This was a pivotal moment when Justin began to recognize his own intellectual character at school. Jane and Marie have now shared this technique with other teachers in our school.

CONCLUSION

When emerging bilingual students are in collaboratively taught classrooms where there is a strong workshop model, and teachers have a well-rounded understanding of language development, students make remarkable achievements (see Tables 16.1 and 16.2). Last year in one classroom, all eight emerging bilingual students made growth and most of them made more than a year's worth of growth according to the *Developmental Reading Assessment* or DRA (see Table 16.1). Similarly, in math the majority of the emerging bilingual students in the classroom met their projected growth according to the *Measures of Academic Progress (MAP) Growth Assessment*. And most of these students showed significant growth (see Table 16.2). This model creates a

TABLE 16.1   EL Reading Scores in Co-Taught Classroom

2nd Grade Students Categorized as English Learners DRA Scores (2016–2017)		
Student	Fall	Spring
EL 1	6	20
EL 2	4	20
EL 3	14	28
EL 4	6	14
EL 5	8	16
EL 6	3	8
EL 7	8	20
EL 8	10	24

TABLE 16.2   EL Math Scores in Co-Taught Classroom

2nd Grade Students Categorized as English Language Learners MAPS Math Scores (2016–2017)			
Student	Fall	Spring	Met Projected Growth
EL 1	167	n/a	n/a
EL 2	163	177	No (–1)
EL 3	174	192	Yes (+4)
EL 4	154	187	Yes (+17)
EL 5	164	194	Yes (+15)
EL 6	141	176	Yes (+17)
EL 7	156	189	Yes (+17)
EL 8	167	180	No (–2)

classroom environment where every child, especially the most vulnerable learners, can find success.

Through our experience, we have come to believe that when progress occurs, it is not because of one person's efforts, but because of a collective knowledge. Our intention was to provide a glimpse into some of the guiding principles we have discovered in creating our schoolwide collaborative teaching model, including establishing a culture of collaboration and a sense of curiosity for language, while maintaining the foundation of a strong workshop model for all children. We are grateful for the brilliance of our fellow collaborating teachers, our students, and the foundational work of the many authors and researchers. How do we create the greatest thinkers for the world? We hope we have inspired you to join this collective journey.

REFERENCES

Bennett, S. (2007). *That workshop book: new systems and structures for classrooms that read, write, and think.* Portsmouth, NH: Heinemann.

Bunch, G. C., Kibler, A., & Pimentel, S. (2012). *Realizing opportunities for English learners in the common core English language arts and disciplinary literacy standards.* Stanford, CA: Understanding Language Initiative.

Council of Chief State School Officers. (2014). *English Language Proficiency (ELP) Standards with correspondences to K–12 practices and Common Core Standards.* Retrieved from https://www.oregon.gov/ode/students-and-family/equity/EngLearners/Documents/ELPStandardsFinal.pdf

Doig, B., & Groves, S. (2011). Japanese lesson study: Teacher professional development through communities of inquiry. *Mathematics Teacher Education and Development, 13*(1), 77–93.

Dweck, C. (2007). *Mindset: The new psychology of success.* New York, NY: Ballantine Books.

Fullan, M. (2008). *The six secrets of change: What the best leaders do to help their organizations survive and thrive.* San Francisco, CA: Jossey-Bass.

Hammond, B. (2015, July 21). Racial achievement gap costs Oregon $2 billion a year, study says. *The Oregonian/Oregon Live.* Retrieved from http://www.oregonlive.com/education/index.ssf/2015/07/lagging_education_for_latinos.html

Harvey, S. (2008). *The primary comprehension toolkit: Language and lessons for active literacy.* Portsmouth, NH: Heinemann

Johnston, P. (2004). *Choice words: How our language affects children's learning.* Portland, ME: Stenhouse.

Keene, E. O. (2011). *Comprehension going forward.* Portsmouth, NH: Heinemann.

Keene, E. O., & Zimmermann, S. (1997). *Mosaic of thought: Teaching comprehension in a reader's workshop.* Portsmouth, NH: Heinemann.

Keene, E. O., & Zimmermann, S. (2007). *Mosaic of thought: The power of comprehension strategy instruction* (2nd ed.). Portsmouth, NH: Heinemann.

Kena, G., Hussar W., McFarland J., de Brey C., Musu-Gillette, L., Wang, X., . . . Dunlop Velez, E. (2016). *The condition of education 2016* (NCES 2016-144).

Washington, DC: U.S. Department of Education, National Center for Education Statistics. Retrieved from https://nces.ed.gov/pubs2016/2016144.pdf

Kibler, A. K., Walqui, A., & Bunch, G. C. (2015). Transformational opportunities: Language and literacy instruction for English language learners in the Common Core era in the United States. *TESOL Journal, 6*(1), 9–35.

Motamedi, J., Vazquez, M., Gandhi, E., & Holmgren, M. (2019). *English language development minutes, models, and outcomes.* Retrieved from https://education northwest.org/resources/english-language-development-minutes-models -and-outcomes-beaverton-school-district

Miller, D. (2013). *Reading with meaning: Teaching comprehension in the primary grades* (2nd ed.). Portland, ME: Stenhouse.

Rosa, J., & Flores, N. (2015). Hearing language gaps and reproducing social inequality. *Journal of Linguistic Anthropology, 25*(1), 77–79.

Taberski, S. (2017). *Comprehension from the ground up: Simplified, sensible instruction for the K-3 reading workshop.* Portsmouth, NH: Heinemann.

Tovani, C. (2011). *So what do they really know?: Assessment that informs teaching and learning.* Portland, ME: Stenhouse.

Umansky, I. M. (2016). To be or not to be EL: An examination of the impact of classifying students as English learners. *Educational Evaluation and Policy Analysis, 38*(4), 714–737.

Valdés, G. (2015). Latin@s and the intergenerational continuity of Spanish: The challenges of curricularizing language. *International Multilingual Research Journal, 9*(4), 253–273.

CHAPTER 17

CO-TEACHING
IN KINDERGARTEN

Connecting the Dots Between Content, Language Instruction, Oracy, and Writing

Kathryn Toppel
Tigard Tualatin School District

"The most damaging phrase in the language is: We've always done it this way."
—Grace Hopper

CHALLENGING THE NORM

In my suburban public school district located in the Pacific Northwest, English language development (ELD) instruction has been traditionally configured as a pullout program, serving approximately 1,000 students. At the elementary level, students leave their regular classrooms to receive language instruction in a different classroom for 30 minutes each day, and classroom teachers are directed to not teach any new content during that block of time. With the pullout model, there is often a sense of disconnect for both English learners (ELs) and their classroom teachers (Dove & Honigsfeld,

Co-Teaching for English Learners, pages 199–211
Copyright © 2020 by Information Age Publishing
All rights of reproduction in any form reserved.

2010) as a result of the fragmented instruction and interruptions associated with EL students leaving their general education classroom in order to receive language instruction from a different teacher in another location. Gibbons (2015) cautioned, "If children are following a separate EAL [English as an Additional Language] program, the risk is that there will be little relationship between the language being presented in the language class and the language required for children to access and participate in curriculum learning" (p. 208).

Often, ELs must stop in the middle of learning when it is time to leave their classroom for ELD. When they return, they have missed something and may be uncertain about what to do and how to rejoin the class. Sometimes ELs have to catch up on what they missed despite not having been present for the lesson or directions, which is particularly challenging for students who require linguistic and contextual support. Even if no new core content was taught in their absence, leaving and returning 30 minutes later can result in ELs feeling left out or disconnected from their classmates. Additionally, teachers can experience uncertainty about what to teach or have the remaining students work on during the ELD block that will not result in ELs falling behind their peers or feeling upset at having missed an activity they would have enjoyed.

In light of the discontinuity experienced by ELs as a result of the pullout model, a designated team of ELD teachers from my district, under the direction of district administrators, completed a review of instructional models during the 2015–2016 school year. In order to compare the respective benefits and challenges associated with a variety of language instruction models, they investigated (a) co-teaching, (b) pullout, (c) walk to language, during which all students, not just ELs, would receive leveled language instruction, and (d) coaching.

Following the review, it was decided that the pullout model would remain intact, but actions were needed to create consistency for ELD instruction across the district. At the time, ELD content and instruction varied from site to site because there was not an articulated curriculum with a scope and sequence for language development. To establish greater uniformity, district leaders designed a three-phase plan in the Spring of 2016, based around the concept of *Connected ELD*. The plan's main goal was to create instructional consistency for ELs by connecting classroom content and the topics/themes used in pullout ELD classes as the vehicle for language instruction. The alignment of content and language instruction would call for increased collaboration between classroom teachers and ELD specialists; yet, ultimately language instruction would still be delivered separately with ELs being removed from their regular classrooms for focused linguistic support.

Co-teaching was identified as a possible alternative to the pullout model; yet it was recognized that it would take time to shift to a co-teaching model because there are different stages of interest and readiness for the extent of collaboration required (Davison, 2006). District leadership decided that an immediate transition to the co-teaching model of language instruction could not be sustained and consequently, co-teaching was set aside as a long-term goal.

Although a district-wide transition to co-teaching was not imminent, my colleague and I were interested not only in the idea of collaborative partnerships with classroom teachers, but also exploring the benefits of co-teaching; rather than collaborate and continue to teach separately, we could collaborate and teach together. We strongly agree with Gibbons' (2015) assertion that, "the regular classroom is the best opportunity to learn a new language, because it provides an authentic context for a focus on the language most relevant for subject learning" (p. 207).

Because co-teaching was not yet an established model within the district, we sought permission to begin. District leaders wanted to be sure that we had a well-designed plan for delivering co-taught instruction including instructional goals, assessment practices, factors for determining success, and which content area(s) would be supported. We selected kindergarten as our target grade level because our kindergarten colleagues were also excited for the prospect of joining forces to improve instruction for ELs. Collectively, our main goals were to:

- foster greater continuity of instruction: fewer interruptions in ELs' school day,
- align content and language instruction,
- increase exposure to ELs' English-speaking peers,
- provide more opportunities for acculturation by having ELs integrated in their regular classes, and
- raise ELs' confidence in their ability to learn grade-level work.

We were granted permission to implement our plan and began co-teaching in kindergarten in mid-November 2016 in two classes (see Table 17.1).

TABLE 17.1 Comparison of Partnering Kindergarten Classrooms		
Class	Total Students	Total ELs
A	21	4
B	20	5

CONFIGURING COLLABORATION

Honigsfeld and Dove (2016) liken co-teaching to riding a tandem bicycle because teamwork and trust are critical for co-teaching success. My ELD colleague and I each formed partnerships with two kindergarten teachers so we could consistently work with our designated teachers and students and we created a plan to alternate between classrooms to co-teach with each kindergarten teacher for 45-minutes every other day. The information in this chapter pertains only to the collaborative and co-teaching work of my two co-teachers and myself.

It was beneficial to spend time observing the kindergarten teachers prior to any co-planning or co-teaching. For the traveling language specialist who may potentially collaborate with a number of different classroom/content teachers, it is pertinent to know and understand each teacher and classroom. It is also important to get to know the ELs in each classroom (TESOL, 2018) and to become familiar with their language levels and skill levels in reading, writing, speaking, and listening. Observing instruction, students, and teachers in respective classrooms can be a sneak preview of the instructional contexts. This glimpse can allow language teachers to consider what resources, strategies, and co-teaching models would be a good fit for each of their collaborative partnerships.

Reflection and Revisions for Collaborative Practices

One of the many benefits of self-study as part of action research is engaging in meaningful reflection on one's practice in order to revise future actions (Kitchen & Stevens, 2004). After a year of co-teaching, we have not run into any significant challenges associated with collaborating; however it is always wise to establish parameters for handling challenges should they occur. Our teams jumped into the process prior to laying some of the groundwork that helps to sustain positive collaborative relationships. We agreed that going forward, the creation of partnership agreements (Dove & Honigsfeld, 2018) would serve as an essential first step when establishing new collaborative relationships for co-teaching. Creating partnership agreements can support co-teachers in identifying agreed upon ways to resolve conflict when it arises and can lessen the difficulty of resolving conflict when both partners can refer back to the agreements they made together.

Co-Planning: Digitally Putting Our Heads Together

As a consequence of beginning co-teaching in November, the established school-wide schedule was not designed to provide time for co-planning, and time to meet in person to collaborate was not feasible. Conveniently, both pre-planning and post-planning, two of the phases of co-planning, are typically completed separately. Additionally, collaborative planning can take place in either face-to-face meetings or by using a virtual platform (Honigsfeld & Dove, 2016). Rather than allowing lack of shared planning time to become a roadblock, technology was a fundamental support for our collaborative planning. Email, Google Docs, and texting all allowed us to communicate about lesson planning and share in the process.

Because learning to read is a fundamental goal of kindergarten instruction in our district, our co-teaching focused on literacy instruction. More specifically, our intention was to connect rich language instruction to the reading curriculum so ELs could benefit from practice in all four of the language domains—reading, writing, speaking, and listening—within the context of what they were already learning. In the pullout model, language instruction was typically based on content that was different from the content being taught in the regular classroom.

Instructional alignment between the two kindergarten classrooms, in addition to the year-long kindergarten curriculum map and having access to the digital reading curriculum, were all advantageous for pre-planning. Curriculum maps and digital curriculum can support language teachers in keeping track of upcoming lessons and topics in order to conduct individual pre-planning. Viewing the digital content provides detailed information about what students will be learning during their content classes, which the language teacher can access independently.

Reflection and Revision for Co-planning

Initially, our collaborative planning was done exclusively through email; however, a visit to observe co-taught lessons at another school helped to highlight how we could improve our co-planning process. The teams we observed shared their lesson plans with us, which had been accomplished with Google Docs. Using Google Docs to co-plan has been a more effective and organized way to develop lessons. Engaging in shared planning with Google Docs not only helped us to clarify all the necessary elements to be considered for co-planning, but it also created an archive of lessons that were far easier to access and refer to than email chains. Anyone with access to edit the document could make additions, changes, post comments, or ask questions. Co-teachers could simultaneously work on lesson plans from different locations or could make contributions in their own time.

Co-Teaching: SWIRLing Our Way to Success

As suggested by Dodge and Honigsfeld (2014), we intentionally sought to create a connective thread between reading, writing, speaking, and listening by implementing routines that called upon students to engage in all four language domains in every co-taught lesson. The idea of SWiRL (speaking, writing, interacting, reading, listening) served as the foundation for our instructional delivery routine because giving students regular opportunities to read, write, and talk about academic concepts, supports them in understanding and articulating their understanding of classroom content (Schmoker, as cited in Motley, 2016). Although reading was our chosen content area of focus, lessons can be designed with SWiRL in mind for any content area. It is also important to note that the domains do not need to be utilized in the particular order they appear in the acronym.

Speaking

Typically the structure of our lessons began with explicit language instruction around a language form and function that supported the weekly reading theme. Utilizing co-teaching Model 2, two teachers teach the same content (Dove & Honigsfeld, 2018); we mainly kept the class as one group and taught together. This portion of the lesson involved introducing the language objective and target language. As the ELD specialist, I led the explicit language instruction and the classroom teacher sat close to me chiming in with pertinent information and clarifying or restating information if needed. We utilized my turn/your turn or choral response to have students practice the target language and use the sentence frames for repeated practice, changing elements each time (e.g., The horse has a mane and a tail. The pig has a snout and hooves). Oral language practice was particularly emphasized and was supported with visuals as well as printed sentence starters, sentence frames, and target words to scaffold for our ELs. As part of this lesson segment, students engaged in reading through the use of the printed content as scaffolds for their spoken output. If possible, the sentence frames used sight words included in the weekly lesson. The classroom teacher also supported lesson pacing by indicating if it was time to move to the next activity or interjecting to refer back to something she had taught the students prior to my arrival.

Interaction: Speaking, Listening, and Reading

To support language development, the kindergarten teacher and I acted as partners and modeled the target language for students, to demonstrate what a partner interaction should look and sound like. Depending on the task, we modeled how to agree and disagree with partners or demonstrated what to do if a partner answered incorrectly. We also modeled how to take turns alternating between asking and answering questions.

Language instruction was followed by opportunities for student talk (oracy practice) in order for students to utilize the target language with partners. They were also engaged in active listening because we intentionally planned activities that involved one student asking a question in which there was a changeable element (e.g., "Where is the bear?" as opposed to "Where is the chipmunk?" in a lesson incorporating animal habitats and prepositions), which required the other student to listen in order to answer accurately.

Oral language practice was intentionally planned to engage students in thinking and talking that would better prepare them for the subsequent writing tasks. Students had multiple opportunities to practice the target language so they would be confident when it was time to write. When students were engaged in partner practice, we both circulated and listened to the oral exchanges in order to informally check for understanding. We intentionally checked in with ELs at lower language levels in order to offer support, reteach, or provide additional scaffolding.

Writing

Lessons culminated with writing tasks that reiterated the target language in the context of the theme. My colleagues typically led writing instruction, providing directions around writing genre, letter formation, conventions, utilizing the class iPads to record language prior to writing (Toppel, 2014) and expectations for writing depending on the time of year. When the kindergarten teacher provided directions for writing, I supported with visuals or repeated information to ELs if needed. While students wrote independently, both the kindergarten teacher and I would circulate around the room to support students. My focus was on supporting ELs during this time because I wanted to ensure they had the necessary scaffolds to write. Since the writing task was directly connected to the oracy practice students just completed, I often used the pictures, sentence frames, and other visuals from the lesson to support and scaffold for ELs during their writing time. The kindergarten teacher checked students' work and provided students with directions for what to do when work was completed.

Speaking as a Scaffold for Writing

Students must simultaneously tie together numerous skills in order to compose written texts; therefore our intention was to connect oral language practice with writing so students would have multiple opportunities to practice the language and words needed for their writing prior to actually writing. By providing students opportunities to practice speaking about the topic with the support of visuals and sentence frames prior to writing, students were better prepared to write. We also incorporated the use of iPads as a scaffold so students could record their ideas before writing then listen and re-listen to their words in order to write them down on paper (Toppel, 2014). Allowing students to record also afforded us opportunities to evaluate students' language use and ideas, even when they were not yet able to write them all down. The inclusion of speaking skills as part of everyday classroom practice for all students correlated with exceptional writing growth.

Co-Reflection: Processing Together to Improve

Co-reflection typically took place in two ways. We either did a quick check-in before school to ensure everything was on track for lessons or we engaged in reflective conversations after lessons to process how they went. The second type of co-reflection was most significant to our success.

After co-teaching a lesson with one colleague, she and I often did a reflective check in to determine if any changes should be made before I co-taught the same lesson with the other kindergarten teacher the following day. Many lessons were improved based on those quick, reflective chats because we were able to jointly determine if there were any elements of the lesson that didn't go as planned or that needed to be improved upon. Pacing, the difficulty level of the planned activities, and student outcomes were all topics of these quick post-lesson reflective conversations.

Co-reflection is an integral part of co-teaching because it provides teachers the opportunity to process collaborative experiences and maintain trust by constructively discussing the shared instruction. Having co-reflection as part of the set routine makes it easier to provide constructive feedback to one another because we are continuously asking ourselves how lessons went and opening the door for feedback from each other.

Co-Assessment: The Missing Link

Given that much of our learning about co-teaching took place in the field as we experienced it, retrospectively it's clear that we were not successful in addressing all of the phases of the collaborative instruction cycle (co-planning, co-teaching, co-reflection, co-assessment). Our efforts were primarily dedicated to planning for instruction and lesson delivery, yet jointly planning for assessment was not part of our regular routine. Our knowledge of co-assessment needed further development, consequently, assessment in conjunction with co-teaching involved the kindergarten teachers conducting their own assessments of student performance on the content standards and me assessing ELs on their language development.

Summative assessment *of* learning was part of our process, yet assessment *for* learning, a distinction described by Gottlieb (2016) and Gibbons (2015) did not inform our co-planning as it should have (i.e., as an integral and consistent part of the cycle).

Beyond informal check-ins during lessons, co-assessment, as implied by the "co-" needs to involve careful co-planning as well as collaborative routines and practices that allow teachers to have a mutual understanding of what content and what language will be evaluated, how assessment will take place, how students will demonstrate proficiency, how development will be tracked/documented, and how the role of assessing will be shared among co-teachers. We were hearing the successful use of target language and seeing improvement in writing quality in addition to growth in writing skills; yet a formal plan around co-assessment practices was absent and proper documentation was lacking.

Reflection and Revision for Co-Assessment

Going forward, co-assessment needs to be part of our collaborative instructional cycle. Assessment is a necessary component of co-reflection in order to understand whether or not students met the content and language objectives of the lesson and to determine actions for subsequent lessons based on those results. Our new co-planning template includes space to more explicitly identify both the content standards and the language standards being addressed in each lesson. A helpful addition would be to create a space within lesson plans to explicitly note how students will be assessed and how often assessment will take place more formally.

Each lesson contains an opportunity for students to write independently, so we have also started to utilize the application, Seesaw, as a way to capture student writing in a digital portfolio as evidence of their skills. Even though the classroom teacher retains the hard copy of students' writing, the digital copies allow me to evaluate writing growth and use of target language on my own time in order to circle back and discuss students' progress with my co-teachers.

As many co-teachers lament, however, sufficient time to carry out all of the elements of the collaborative instructional cycle can be a challenge. Time to conceptualize and create a plan for assessment is something that would add value to our co-teaching process and must be prioritized. Dove and Honigsfeld (2018) offer some guiding questions around planning for assessment (e.g., What is our definition of success for ELs [and all our students] that will be valuable as we try to develop a better scope for assessment practices?).

EVALUATING SUCCESS: STUDENT GROWTH IN LANGUAGE DEVELOPMENT

We have identified co-assessment as an area marked for improvement in our collaborative instructional cycle (see *Co-Assessment: The Missing Link* above) because we didn't incorporate formative assessment, or assessment *for* learning, to the extent we should have. Yet, progress in the different domains of language development was evaluated through the use of several different assessment tools:

1. *The Dynamic Indicators of Basic Early Literacy Skills* (DIBELS) screener was administered three times during the school year to evaluate reading skills.
2. Formal writing tasks were administered three times during the year, once in each of the three writing genres (opinion, informative/explanatory, narrative) to evaluate writing development.
3. The English Language Proficiency Assessment (ELPA21) was used to assess ELs in reading, writing, speaking, and listening in February.

Dynamic Indicators of Basic Early Literacy Skills (DIBELS)

Although much of students' reading instruction was delivered outside of the co-taught lessons, it is remarkable to note that all of the ELs from our co-taught classrooms (nine out of nine) reached grade-level benchmarks in reading by the end of the year as determined by DIBELS compared to only three out of nine who met benchmark in the fall. There is not a direct correlation between co-taught lessons and reading achievement since the tested reading skills were not the focus of our co-taught lessons, however, this data is one example of ELs meeting grade-level expectations.

Writing Assessments

District-wide, each writing genre (opinion, informative, narrative) is the area of focus of study for a designated amount of time during the school year. In kindergarten, opinion writing was the focus in the fall, informative writing was the focus in the winter, and narrative writing was the focus in the spring. After learning about and practicing how to write in each genre, students were given a writing task as an assessment.

Table 17.2 shows our ELs' writing scores for opinion, informative, and narrative writing. A score of 2 indicates that a skill is developing, a 3 indicates that a student is meeting grade-level expectations, and a 4 indicates a student

TABLE 17.2 Outcomes for Writing Development Across Three Genres

Student	Language Level	Opinion	Narrative	Informative
1.	Beginner	4	4	4
2.	Beginner	3	3	2
3.	Intermediate	3	4	4
4.	Early Advanced	4	3	4
5.	Early Intermediate	4	4	3
6.	Early Intermediate	3	3	4
7.	Beginner	3	4	4
8.	Intermediate	4	3	3
9.	Early Advanced	4	4	4

is exceeding grade-level expectations. With the exception of one student who was developing in narrative writing, all ELs either met, or exceeded, grade-level expectations in writing. In addition to those excellent results from students who began kindergarten as non-writers, all of these ELs scored a 3 on the language standard requiring them to produce and expand complete sentences. We believe these exceptional outcomes are the result of our explicit focus on connecting content, oral language practice, and writing.

English Language Proficiency Assessment (ELPA21)

Table 17.3 shows initial language level scores for kindergarten students compared to scores capturing their skills after approximately 4 months of

TABLE 17.3 Comparison of ELs Language Proficiency Scores in September and February

Student	Pre-LAS			ELPA21				
	R/W	Oral	Comp.	R	W	L	S	Level
1.	1	1	1	4	3	4	5	Progressing
2.	1	1	1	1	2	2	2	Emerging
3.	1	3	3	5	5	5	5	Proficient
4.	2	1	1	3	3	3	3	Progressing
5.	1	2	2	3	3	3	5	Progressing
6.	1	2	1	3	2	3	3	Progressing
7.	1	1	1	3	3	3	4	Progressing
8.	1	3	3	5	3	4	4	Progressing
9.	1	4	4	4	3	3	5	Progressing

co-taught instruction. Scores were derived from the Pre-LAS language placement assessment, which was administered in September 2016 and ELPA21, which was administered in February 2017. The Pre-LAS results include a score for oral language skills (Oral), a score combining reading and writing skills (R/W), and an overall composite score (Comp.). Scores for ELPA21 include proficiency levels in reading (R), writing (W), listening (L), and speaking (S) as well as an overall language level category (Level). Although the language level data came from two different proficiency tests, in most cases, students showed more than one level of growth in respective categories. In many cases, for example Student 1 and Student 7, scores increased by several levels between the beginning of the school year and February.

CONCLUSION

Transitioning from a pullout model of language instruction to a co-teaching model district-wide would not be an easy feat, yet based on our experience co-teaching in kindergarten, we are convinced this is a direction in which we need to go. Having support from administration and collaborating with teachers who were flexible were certainly a huge part of our success, yet the ultimate success comes from what our English learners experienced as a result of co-teaching.

Intentionally connecting content, language instruction, oracy practice, and writing through the use of SWiRL as a consistent instructional routine provided ELs with the necessary components to achieve success. Students experienced language development as a meaningful practice to support their learning, thinking, and writing, and consequently, ELs were able to understand and engage with classroom content along with their English-speaking peers. Rather than feeling *different* or *inferior* as a result of their status as English learners, our ELs were an integral part of their classroom community and they thrived. Their linguistic needs were met without having to remove them in order to provide them with instruction that was markedly different from that of their non-EL peers. Fundamentally, the shift from pullout to co-teaching represents a shift in mindset from one in which both English learners and teachers that specialize in language instruction are siloed, to one in which learning language is viewed as an essential component of good instruction requiring teamwork between content and language teachers. Gibbons (2015) put it perfectly in saying effective language instruction "is not the icing on the cake, but the ingredients of it!" (pp. 220–221).

REFERENCES

Davison, C. (2006). Collaboration between ESL and content teachers: How do we know when we are doing it right? *International Journal of Bilingual Education and Bilingualism, 9*(4), 454–475.

Dodge, J., & Honigsfeld, A. (2014). *Core instructional routines: Go-to strategies for effective literacy teaching.* Portsmouth, NH: Heinemann.

Dove, M., & Honigsfeld, A. (2010). ESL coteaching and collaboration: Opportunities to develop teacher leadership and enhance student learning. *TESOL Journal, 1*(1), 3–22.

Dove, M. G., & Honigsfeld, A. (2018). *Co-teaching for English learners: A guide to collaborative planning, instruction, assessment, and reflection.* Thousand Oaks, CA: Corwin Press.

Gibbons, P. (2015). *Scaffolding language, scaffolding learning: teaching English language learning in the mainstream classroom.* Portsmouth, NH: Heinemann.

Gottlieb, M. (2016). *Assessing English language learners: Bridges to educational equity.* Thousand Oaks, CA: Corwin Press.

Honigsfeld, A., & Dove, M. G. (2016). Co-teaching ELLs: Riding a tandem bike. *Educational Leadership, 73*(4), 56–60.

Kitchen, J., & Stevens, D. (2004). *Self-study in action research: Two teacher educators review their project and practice.* Retrieved from https://pdfs.semanticscholar .org/0277/2d2866e5955cecb04e9dd209de3ea815cbab.pdf

Motley, N. (2016). *Talk read talk write.* San Clemente, CA: Canter Press.

TESOL International Association. (2018). *The 6 principles for exemplary teaching of English learners: Grades K–12.* Alexandria, VA: TESOL Press.

Toppel, K. (2014). *Accelerating learning: Making the most of iPads in kindergarten* (IRA E-ssentials series). Newark, DE: International Reading Association.

CHAPTER 18

CO-TEACHING TO SUPPORT PROJECT-BASED LEARNING

A Model United Nations Approach With Dual Language Learners

Samantha Chung
I.S.145Q School of Innovation and Applied Learning

Laura Baecher
Hunter College, City University of New York

William Hargrove
I.S.145Q School of Innovation and Applied Learning

Maria and seven classmates are seated on the inside circle of a double circle, about to begin a Socratic seminar. They have been studying the United Nations Convention on the Rights of the Child, reading related articles, and talking with classmates about the idea of children's rights. Now, their teachers have asked them to carry out a discussion with their classmates about why the United States is one of only two countries that has not ratified this convention. At first, they are not sure how this will work as they are so

Co-Teaching for English Learners, pages 213–222
Copyright © 2020 by Information Age Publishing

used to raising their hands and having the teacher call on them. But with their ESL teacher on one side of the circle and their ELA teacher on the other, Maria feels brave. She begins the conversation, "Why do you think the United States has not participated? Is it because children in the United States already have many protections?" From there, several other classmates respond. The discussion turns to whether students should be made to stand when the Pledge of Allegiance is read aloud. Some students feel strongly that this should be optional. Maria rejoins, "Is the Pledge of Allegiance about the flag? Or the president? Or some ideas of what it means?" At that moment, the loudspeaker crackles to life, and the voice announces it is time to stand for the pledge. Students and teachers look around at each other with expressions of surprise, and most students do not stand as they usually do. As Maria files past her ESL teacher, she asks if they will be doing this Socratic seminar style activity again. Her teacher responds, unsure if Maria wants to do this again or is dreading it. "Yes, Maria, we will be," to which Maria smiles with satisfaction.

As illustrated by Maria's (pseudonym) experience in the vignette above, this chapter explores how co-teachers can empower English learners (ELs) through project-based learning (PBL). Maria is filled with pride and a sense of responsibility and maturity due to the authentic, professional level of discourse she realizes she is capable of leading in this very different classroom experience. The setting is an 8th grade, Spanish/English dual-language, co-taught English Language Arts (ELA)/English as a second language (ESL) classroom. This classroom is situated in a large, urban middle school that has 21% ELs from predominantly Latin American and South Asian countries. Within the school, several smaller academies run concurrently as a way to increase students' sense of belonging and teachers' sense of a community of practice. The program we report on is the *Global Academy*. In this program, learners are recent immigrants from Central America with gaps in their prior education, and they are placed into a dual language program through which they learn English, continue Spanish learning, and access content through both languages.

The co-teachers presented in this chapter are an ELA teacher (William, the third author) and an ESL teacher (Samantha, the first author). The second author (Laura) is a faculty member at a partner university, which places student teachers for fieldwork in this setting; Laura served as a critical friend to the co-teaching partners. Samantha has worked as an ESL teacher, peer instructional coach, and teacher leader in this school and across the district. We focus here on Samantha and William's planning and teaching approaches of a class they co-teach that utilizes a Model United Nations (Model UN) approach for collaborative learning. William is an ELA/ESL teacher working with middle school students in both dual language and transitional bilingual programs; he is currently getting a master's degree in TESOL.

THE MODEL UNITED NATIONS AND PROJECT-BASED LEARNING APPROACHES

As an authentic, task-based curriculum, Model UN is situated under the umbrella of project-based learning (PBL). PBL is an instructional approach in which teachers create a learning environment and tasks that require students to engage in authentic learning that emphasizes inquiry and problem solving. PBL promotes 21st century workforce skills and asks students to engage in real-world critical thinking. For instance, in PBL students might be asked to solve an environmental problem as scientists do or to act as travel journalists and investigate an unknown place. In addition to the emphasis on rich critical thinking, it also engenders authentic language use, as "a project-based classroom allows students to investigate questions, propose hypotheses and explanations, discuss their ideas, challenge the ideas of others" (Krajcik & Blumenfeld, 2005, p. 318), and in so doing utilizes and expands students' speaking, listening, reading, and writing skills (Poonpon, 2011). PBL is seen as a powerful instructional practice for promoting autonomous learning (English & Kitsantas, 2013) as well as inspiring students' critical thinking in their writing (Kumar & Refaei, 2017).

Samantha and William's Model UN class is designed to provide students with a simulated experience of global issues deliberated in the United Nations with students taking on roles of the world's ambassadors and interacting in these roles. Model UN "introduces students to the world of diplomacy, negotiation, and decision-making . . . they prepare draft resolutions, plot strategy, negotiate with supporters and adversaries, resolve conflicts, and navigate the UN's rules of procedure—all in the interest of resolving problems that affect the world" (United Nations Association of the United States of America, n.d., para. 1). Students deeply engage in rich, authentic content as they research issues such as population growth, global warming, gender equity, and education, thus promoting global citizenship (Hazleton & Mahurin, 1986). Throughout the process, students also tap into and expand their English language skills as they learn to conduct research, construct arguments, and engage in collegial discussions around pertinent global issues. In the Model UN PBL classroom, the co-teachers act as facilitators of learning, modeling and guiding students through goal setting, collaboration, and reflection.

CO-TEACHING PRACTICES

Implementing a Model UN curriculum, and any PBL approach, requires skill and a sense of adventure for teachers. To do so with a class of 30 emergent bilingual students is even more challenging. For William and Samantha, this is the special benefit of collaborative planning and teaching. Through co-teaching, the EL and content teacher can truly build on each other's knowledge base, whether that knowledge is about the learners themselves, the Model UN curriculum, language teaching, or various literacy development strategies. William and Samantha shared their perspectives on their co-teaching relationship.

William: I have been teaching for several years now, and have done most of this teaching by myself. This is my first experience co-teaching, and I have found it enlightening, rewarding, and even fun. Importantly, I feel that I am improving my teaching practice by understanding the dynamics of co-teaching. Under the co-teaching model, I find myself constantly challenging previous notions of how I conduct my practice. Through collaboration I have found myself thinking about planning lessons differently. For instance, co-planning has pushed me to create more opportunities for inductive learning. Rather than deliver content as an authority figure in front of a room, I find myself thinking about ways to facilitate students' experience with content and encouraging them to reach their own conclusions.

Co-teaching has pushed me to think differently regarding ways of conducting discussions and questioning. I observed that Samantha pushes students not just to clarify their thinking, but also to situate themselves into the discussion. For example, in introducing concepts of human rights to the class, we conducted a discussion about the "headscarf ban" in France, and the class discussed how they might feel if our school adopted a similar policy banning religious items. Many students boldly claimed they would go to the principal's office and protest the treatment of their peers. While this was nice to hear, I noticed Samantha pushing the students, asking them to truly think about the repercussions of inserting oneself in a controversial situation. I noticed the students thinking and contemplating the importance, as well as the courage needed to take a stand for oneself or for others. This experience has encouraged me to further think about ways of making the content relevant to students.

Samantha: In our Model UN classroom, William and I are both positioned as the lead teacher. In this way, our students benefit from an equal emphasis on language and content as well as the guidance and support of two teachers in the room. For example, during the same Socratic seminar lesson cited above, we were able to transition between different co-teaching models to meet the needs of our students. During the mini-lesson, as we exposed students for the first time to writing higher order thinking questions in preparation for their discussion, we team taught. Team teaching allowed us to explain a complex idea to students in two different ways. For instance, we noticed that when we presented higher-order question writing as a task in class, we had different ways to explain it to our students:

> Samantha: Higher order thinking questions are often open-ended and don't lead to one single answer.
>
> William: You all have heard this before. I often call it a "philosophical question." People may see or interpret higher order thinking questions differently.

In this interaction, the students are able to benefit from hearing a concept clarified from two different positions. William, who is with the class every day, is able to tap into students' past experience with a reference to a similar term that he has already exposed the children to while I introduce a new term.

In other parts of the lesson, our co-teaching approach switches to meet the needs of our students. While William elicits student responses about the rights of the child, I begin to scribe on the board. Knowing that ELs benefit from seeing text in addition to hearing it aloud, we switch to an approach that is one-teach and one-assist. In this instance, William takes the lead, and I assist. Another moment in the class, during the launch of the Socratic seminar, I take the lead explaining a learning activity while William observes. In this way, William is able to take anecdotal notes of student engagement and participation that can be used later as we collaboratively plan for upcoming lessons.

One of the biggest benefits of working with a co-teacher is the ability to brainstorm and co-plan together. Through this collaboration, we are able to build off of each other's strengths while learning from one another. William, who comes from an ELA background and is highly interested in and motivated by the real world issues that are discussed in Model UN, is able to bring a critical eye towards content. In addition, because he has taught these students before and is with the class every day, he is able to anticipate student responses and can plan purposefully. I feel that this complements the emphasis on language and experience that I bring to the table.

It is essential that both teachers are able to engage in a collaborative discussion about their roles as educators within the classroom and also about student needs. William and Samantha centered their initial conversations using a collaborative planning tool they designed for collaborative co-teachers and also for other team teaching models. In using this tool (see Table 18.1), they were able to determine that they would both act as lead teachers, learn about the students in front of them, as well as set actionable planning and instructional goals.

DOCUMENTED OUTCOMES AND EVIDENCE OF SUCCESS

After the Socratic seminar, students were asked to reflect on their first experience with this type of learning in writing. These student reflections provide evidence of student success in growing language and content use within William and Samantha's Model UN class. For instance, Yesenia, a student who is approaching the advanced level of English, expresses her sense of accomplishment in participating in a student-led discussion. Below, she reflects on how the activity deepened her understanding of the content knowledge around controversial topics, the workings of the United Nations, all while setting her own learning goals:

> I feel satisfied and want to do more of these activities. I was able to keep going in on the conversation. My next steps are to pose more questions to my classmates so they can get involved in the argument. This helped me further understand how controversial this topic is and how the government works in the U.N. (Yesenia, 8th grade student)

The Socratic seminar as a classroom activity acted as an authentic language task, asking students to sustain a conversation for a substantial period of time with the goal of coming to a consensus on a controversial topic. With the support of both classroom teachers, the classroom transformed into a safe space where EL students were able to take intellectual and language risks. In Yesenia's reflection, she self-proclaims that she is "satisfied and want[s] to do more of these activities." A natural group leader, she states that she was able to "keep going in on the conversation," demonstrating

TABLE 18.1 Collaborative Work Plan		
C	**Teacher 1 William**	**Teacher 2 Samantha**
Who are our students?	32 students—8th grade ELA Spanish/English Dual Language Program.	10 Transitioning EL Students
		20 Expanding EL Students
		2 Commanding Students
What are their individual and collective needs?	• To prepare for Spring Model UN Conference. • Critical thinking skills that will enable them to engage in high level discussions around current events.	• To develop Cognitive Academic Language Proficiency (CALP) that will allow them access to the complex content of Model UN and to engage in high level discussions around world events.
What is our overall goal as a teaching team?	As far as Model UN, to prepare students for simulated UN conference.	Agreed. Also to provide them with language and literacy skills that will enable them to conduct research and to advocate for things they care about.
	To make students aware of issues around them and to interest them in taking action on issues they care about.	
I envision my role in this teaching team as... (during the mini-lesson, work-time, closing, etc.)	We can both be lead teachers. During planning time we can decide which part of the lesson to deliver depending on the content and on student needs.	I see myself as a lead on the language side of the content area you are addressing. I want to be an essential resource for you and the students.
I would like to contribute by... (during the mini-lesson, work-time, closing, etc.)	Bringing in my knowledge of my students.	Differentiate for the different language demands.
	Tying the learning back to other classes.	Work in small groups.
	Sharing my experiences as their ELA teacher and my understanding of current events.	Sharing my experiences as an ELA/ESL teacher.
I would like you to contribute by...	Share your experience with Model UN and teaching ESL to a Dual Language class. Provide feedback on how things could have been done better.	Provide me with a background of the students and the classroom, especially to catch me up on things that I might have missed when we aren't together.
What I need from you to do my best work is...	Flexibility with time. Distribution of preparation and grading. A real collaborative working relationship.	Meet with me regularly to plan and discuss student progress.
		Share with me the progress of students/curriculum on days that I am not in the classroom.
		Use digital tools (Google Slides and Google Docs) to plan collaboratively and share resources.
		Treat me like another lead teacher in the room.

her continued language use throughout the activity. In stating that the activity "helped [her] further understand how controversial this topic is," we can see the correct usage of target vocabulary, "controversial," and her understanding of the role of the United Nations in debating issues that have multiple perspectives.

In asking students to reflect, William and Samantha invite the students to become active participants in their own learning. This classroom routine moves students towards metacognition, which supports ongoing and lasting learning. We can see from Yesenia's reflection that this promoted critical thinking about her performance and learning style in regards to content and language learning. It is clear that although Yesenia was successful in initiating and maintaining discussion throughout the activity, she would like to "pose more questions" and invite others into the conversation. This short but powerful routine acts as formative assessment for Samantha and William and also as feedback on a classroom activity.

This student work provides valuable information for the classroom teachers that will later be used for collaborative reflection and planning. Centering planning sessions around student work ensures that conversations are low-inference and based on what actual learning is occurring in the classroom rather than on personal assumptions. It also grounds the conversation in a solution-oriented approach to viewing student work, asking both teachers to think about the students' language and content needs. In looking at Yesenia's sample, Samantha and William can see their successes from their first Socratic seminar implementation as well as where they need to go next with their content and language goals. Thus, a consideration for follow-up learning targets would focus on question formation that would support Yesenia's goal. In addition, it is clear that some students could benefit from further language supports during the Socratic seminar, specifically in regards to entering a conversation.

Socratic seminars act as an authentic building block within the PBL approach. Students are familiarized with the complexities of global issues while developing language and critical thinking, all skills needed for the culminating task. Within Model UN, this culminating task is the passing of their resolution amongst their peers. The resolution must be drafted using target language as modeled by the United Nations, with an emphasis on the strong action verbs depicted in accepted resolutions.

The second sample is an example of a student draft resolution in its beginning stages. In supporting both language and content in this culminating task, the content teacher reoriented students to the topic at hand, the role of women in STEM fields, and clarified the purpose of draft resolutions. The language teacher pointed out the use of the action verbs to state the issue at hand and to propose a solution.

THE GENERAL ASSEMBLY,

Reminding all nations of the celebration of the 69th anniversary of the adaption of the Universal Declaration of Human Rights, which recognizes the inherent dignity, equality, and inalienable rights of all global citizens,

Reaffirming its Resolution 34/180 of 18 December 1979, which encourages governments to work with the United Nations bodies aimed at the coordination and effectiveness of humanitarian assistance and gender equality around the globe,

Stressing the fact that the United Nations faces significant obstacles related to gender inequality in labor, particularly in the industries of science, technology, engineering and math (STEM),

Encourages all nations to increase wages for the female working class;

Urges member states to give scholarships to women who are interested in STEM careers in order to make a STEM education and career more accessible;

Requests that all nations develop a system in which STEM companies offer more opportunities to the women that are focused on pursuing STEM careers;

Calls for all advocates in promoting gender equality and the empowerment of women;

Stresses the importance of STEM jobs and the importance of women in STEM careers; and

Calls for the action of the accorded nations so that women are allowed to enter STEM careers with the same rights as men.

—Mauricio, Marcos, and Valentina, 8th grade students

William explained to the students that their resolutions should be widely agreed upon in order to pass. Samantha, as the language teacher, emphasized the use of present participle verbs such as *reminding, reaffirming,* and *stressing* to emphasize a need as opposed to simple present verbs such as *encourages, requests,* and *stresses* to introduce actionable propositions. The model text served as a guide for students during group work time as both teachers circulated and conferenced with individuals. As Samantha focused on language needs, William pushed students to consider their argument from multiple perspectives. The co-teaching model allowed the teachers to support and push students as they think critically about these real world issues.

CONCLUSION

Employing the methodology of practitioner research (Cochran-Smith & Donnell, 2006; Cochran-Smith & Lytle, 2009; Ghiso, 2016), the authors used data from student work samples, student interviews, classroom observation, teacher interviews and reflective notes to detail the process of collaboratively planning for learning English through the dynamic and authentic frame of Model UN and PBL. The research uncovered how Samantha and William made strategic decisions in the planning stages that allowed students a more hands-on experience in the classroom, and highlights their conferencing and reflection practices that support instruction. Initial findings suggest that PBL in tandem with a global citizenship focus such as Model UN are instructional approaches that can increase EL student motivation and dedication to their own learning. In addition, the co-teachers' collaborative work outside of the classroom allowed for the model to be implemented and support ELs as they develop in their learning and language development. Working in a co-teaching model that authentically functions as a shared planning, instruction, and reflective process (Honigsfeld & Dove, 2016) holds great promise for the implementation of PBL for English learner students.

REFERENCES

Cochran-Smith, M., & Donnell, K. (2006). Practitioner inquiry: Blurring the boundaries of research and practice. In J. Green, G. Camilli, & P. B. Elmore (Eds.), *Handbook of complementary methods in education research* (pp. 503–518). Mahwah, NJ: Erlbaum.

Cochran-Smith, M., & Lytle S. L. (2009). *Inquiry as stance: Practitioner research in the next generation.* New York, NY: Teacher College Press.

English, M., & Kitsantas, A. (2013). Supporting student self-regulated learning in problem- and project-based learning. *Interdisciplinary Journal of Problem-Based Learning, 7*(2), 127–150.

Ghiso, M. P. (2016). The laundromat as the transnational local: Young children's literacies of interdependence. *Teachers College Record, 118*(1), 1–46

Hazleton, W. A., & Mahurin, R. P. (1986). External simulations as teaching devices: The model United Nations. *Simulation & Games, 17*(2), 149–171.

Honigsfeld, A., & Dove, M. G. (2016). Co-teaching ELLs: Riding a tandem bike. *Educational Leadership, 73*(4), 56–60.

Krajcik, J. S., & Blumenfeld, P. C. (2005). Project-based learning. In R. K. Sawyer (Ed.), *The Cambridge handbook of the learning sciences* (pp. 317–334). Cambridge, England: Cambridge University Press.

Kumar, R., & Refaei, B. (2017). Problem-based learning pedagogy fosters students' critical thinking about writing. *Interdisciplinary Journal of Problem-Based Learning, 11*(2), Article 1. https://doi.org/10.7771/1541-5015.1670

Poonpon, K. (2011). Enhance English skills through project-based learning. *The English Teacher, XL,* 1–10. https://journals.melta.org.my/index.php/tet/article/view/258/155

United Nations Association of the United States of America. (n.d.). *Model UN.* Retrieved from http://www.unausa.org/global-classrooms-model-un

CHAPTER 19

CO-TEACHING TWICE-EXCEPTIONAL STUDENTS

Perspectives From ESOL/Special Education Teacher Education

Ebony Terrell Shockley
University of Maryland College Park

Kia Myrick McDaniel
McDaniel College

"The mere imparting of information is not education."
—Dr. Carter G. Woodson

Today's classrooms include multiple opportunities for teachers to reach students with a wide range of learning differences, including those with varied skill sets. Educating children requires a unique set of skills, and educating multilingual learners and children with exceptionalities requires more than simply imparting information. This chapter examines the policies that influence diverse learners and the core teacher competencies and research-based instructional strategies needed to effectively co-teach students who are twice-exceptional; that is English learners (ELs) with a high-incidence

Co-Teaching for English Learners, pages 223–233
Copyright © 2020 by Information Age Publishing
All rights of reproduction in any form reserved.

disability identification according to the Individuals with Disabilities in Education Act (IDEA) of 2004.

Drawing from a culturally relevant pedagogy framework (Ladson-Billings, 1995b), this chapter uses an interpretive case study methodology for practitioners to draw upon the existing knowledge related to teaching English learners in special education (EL-SE). We explore which co-teaching model teachers of English for speakers of other languages (ESOL) and special educators employ. We describe the most frequently used model and the rationale for co-teaching, specifically in two elementary EL-SE classrooms and two middle school EL-SE classrooms during summer school. The findings and recommendations are strategies for assisting school districts and universities that prepare teachers to support the unique needs of students learning a second language who also need scaffolding for their disability in a co-teaching setting.

POLICY: AN OVERVIEW OF TWICE-EXCEPTIONAL LEARNERS

There is limited research that addresses how mainstream teachers and special educators can work together to address the intersection of language needs of English learners and their academic needs in co-teaching settings. Case law (Castaneda v. Pickard, 1981; Lau v. Nichols, 1974) and Title III outline the core requirements for supporting English learners, while the IDEA of 2004 provides all of the requirements for servicing students with disabilities. However, specific legislation for servicing students who are twice-exceptional is not outlined in federal or state guidelines (McDaniel, 2017).

Effective instruction for twice-exceptional learners, such as English learners with disabilities, is also overlooked in much of the co-teaching literature. Twice-exceptional learners are sometimes defined as children in gifted and talented programs; however, we consider EL-SE students as those who are "trapped in between two worlds" (King, 2005, p. 17) in the same way that other exceptional learners are described. While existing research highlights co-teaching outcomes for ESOL teachers and for special education teachers, the literature on teacher competencies focuses on tailoring instruction to develop either students' academic language, co-teaching models for an ESOL educator, co-teaching models for a special educator, or in addressing English learners or the needs of learners in special education in separate environments.

CORE-TEACHER COMPETENCIES FOR ELs
IN SPECIAL EDUCATION

In order to ensure that EL-SE students receive instruction in the least restrictive environment (LRE) as articulated by the IDEA of 2004, Nguyen

(2012) suggested that general educators and special educators collaborate in order to meet the language and special needs of their students simultaneously. Similar to the aims of Nyugen's (2012) study, we maintain that the instruction occurs as sheltered instruction for English learners and within the context of a culturally relevant pedagogy. In order to provide sheltered instruction, teachers should know the English language proficiency (ELP) levels for their students and consider students' background knowledge and previous experiences. Teachers should also adjust their curricula to align with the lives of their students (Gay, 2010). Culturally relevant pedagogy laid the foundation for culturally responsive teaching, which Gay (2010) defined as "using the cultural knowledge, prior experiences, and performance styles of diverse students to make learning more appropriate and effective for them; it teaches to and through the strengths of these students" (p. 29). Likewise, Terrell Shockley (2017) maintained the importance of positive dispositions for diverse learners. Students' home language and cultures are assets that teachers must acknowledge, value and build upon rather than ignore. A culturally relevant pedagogy draws upon students' culture as a component of pedagogy (Howard & Rodriguez-Scheel, 2017; Ladson-Billings, 1995a, 1995b).

Given the cultural and linguistic diversity of English learners in special education, understanding students' culture and valuing their language is critical (Ladson-Billings, 1995a, 1995b; McDaniel, 2017). Teachers should also consider past schooling in order to identify students' instructional needs (Abrams, Ferguson, & Laud, 2001; Terrell Shockley, 2017). However, national surveys continue to show that teachers of EL-SE students feel underprepared to work with this population (Hernandez Finch, 2012).

TOWARD EFFECTIVE INSTRUCTIONAL STRATEGIES FOR ELs IN SPECIAL EDUCATION

To prepare in-service and pre-service teachers, we investigate the practices of the teachers of ELs in special education. To the best of our knowledge, effective co-teaching models for EL-SEs are similar to models implemented with other learners in special education. As we aim to expand the literature on EL-SE students by studying co-teaching in elementary and secondary classrooms, we researched the following established models from the special education literature: models: (a) team teaching; (b) parallel teaching; (c) one teach, one drift; (d) station teaching; and (e) alternative teaching (e.g., see Figure 19.1; Cook, 2004).

Team teaching includes one teacher leading while the other teacher models and demonstrates. Parallel teaching happens when the class is divided into two, with teachers teaching the same lesson. One teach, one

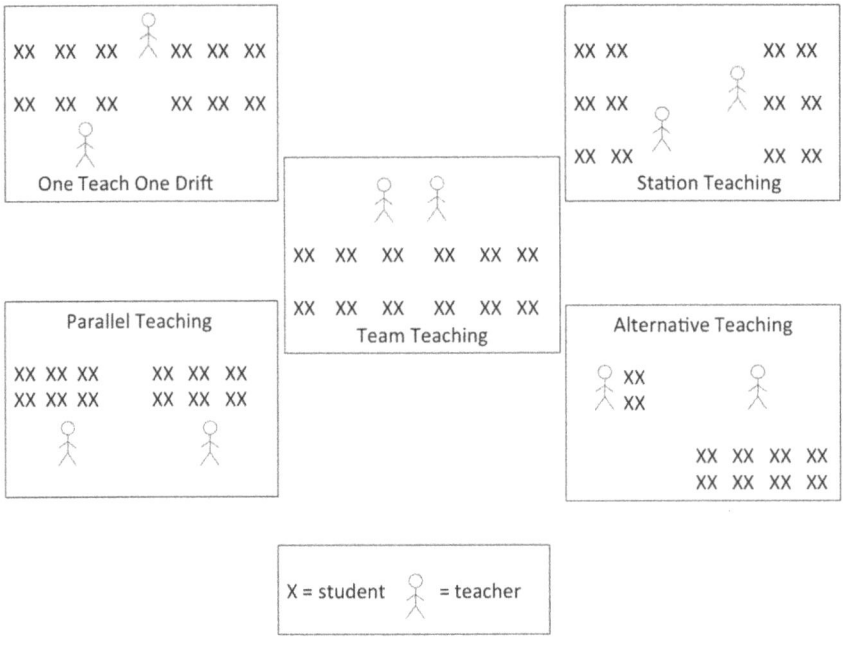

Figure 19.1 Five co-teaching models.

drift occurs when one teacher leads the lesson and the other teacher assists students. Station teaching is when two teachers monitor particular stations. Alternative teaching includes one teacher working with a small group and another with a large group. Coupled with the research from culturally responsive pedagogy (CRP), these are the five co-teaching models that we examine in this chapter in order to identify the most frequently used models, the rationale for specific models and instruction that support a positive outcome for EL-SE students.

In classrooms with English learners with disabilities, instruction should incorporate research-based, high quality instructional strategies validated with diverse populations (Hernandez Finch, 2012). Barrera and Liu (2006) defined an instructional strategy as a set of systematic activities utilized by an educator that consists of clear directions or steps to achieve a specific outcome for students. In the case of English learners with disabilities, the outcomes may include student participation and language development (Abrams et al., 2001; McDaniel, 2017; Nguyen, 2012). In order for an instructional procedure to be an instructional strategy, it must be replicable (Barrera & Liu, 2006).

Key instructional strategies that support culturally and linguistically diverse students overlapped with the culturally relevant pedagogy framework (Piazza, Rao, & Protacio, 2015). Effective strategies include (a) collaboration, defined as a "cooperative relationship between two or more individuals working toward a mutually agreed upon goal" (p. 9); (b) dialogue, the ability to "use language as a tool to mediate actions and interactions" (p. 8); (c) explicit instruction defined as a "structured, systematic and effective methodology for teaching academic skills" (p. 11); and (d) visual representation identified by charts, graphs and photographs that promote understanding (Piazza et al., 2015). Given the cultural and linguistic diversity of ELs in special education, these strategies provided a background to describe co-teaching methods in the EL-SE classroom.

THE EL-SE CLASSROOM CONTEXT AND CO-TEACHING METHOD

The study took place in four classrooms in a large school district in the mid-Atlantic region of the United States. We used purposive sampling to select the teachers, conducted semi-structured interviews with the educators, and completed six classroom observations per group of students over a 4-week summer session. The summer school period offered the most consistency with attendance from both teachers and students in the school district and as such, became the session of choice.

Incorporating a qualitative case study method (Stake, 1995; Yin, 2013) included the gathering of information regarding the co-teaching models used by general, special education, and ESOL educators. According to Stake (1995), the case study approach allows the researcher to (a) pull together key issues and components in order to determine focus of the study; (b) identify the phenomena, themes, or issues; (c) triangulate key observations in order to interpret meaning; and (d) develop generalizations about the case. In both the interviews and observations the grand tour research question for this case study remained:

1. What co-teaching practices are teachers of English learners in special education employing in their classrooms?
2. What co-teaching practices lead to positive outcomes for English learners in special education?
3. What evidence of CRP is present in classrooms of teachers of English learners in special education?

FINDINGS: CO-TEACHING MODELS IN ACTION

In response to the research questions, we describe the observation and interviews of teachers, their practices, and co-teaching settings (Table 19.1).

TABLE 19.1 Observations of CRP and Rationale for Co-Teaching Model

Class #	Level and Educator Role	Evidence of CRP	Most Frequent Co-Teaching Model	Rationale for Co-Teaching Method	Student Outcomes/ Responses to Model
1	Elementary • Special Educator and ESOL Educator	Visual Representation • Multicultural images • Bilingual resources	Station Teaching, Alternative Teaching	Students "We tried parallel teaching during the first week, but students were distracted by both voices. We used stations to focus our activities based on student assessment scores."	Increased Participation
2	Elementary • ESOL Educator and General Educator	Collaboration • Buddy system • Positive messages • Building authentic relationships	Alternative Teaching, Team Teaching	Students "With a class of 27, we pulled students into large and small groups for reading and mathematics. I focus on students with mathematics IEP goals and he focuses on reading IEP goals and language development."	Increased Progress Towards IEP Goals Increased DRA Scores
3	Middle • Elementary Educator and Para-Professional	• Buddy system • Multicultural topics	One Teach, One Drift	Timing/Resources "Depending on the availability of the para-professional, I organized students with a partner that spoke the most English and put them in stations. When the para-professional was here, I would lead and she would walk around to see if students had questions."	Did Not Observe Positive Outcomes
4	Middle • ESOL Educator and Bilingual Aide	Dialogue and Visual Representation • Multicultural books/topics • Interest-based topics	Station Teaching, One Teach, One Drift	Resources/Students "Most of the students in our class speak Spanish, we wanted to include the one student who spoke French because he was not participating, even though our aide is a Spanish speaker we rotated our time and themes to give him resources in his L1. We noticed that he participated more frequently in the reading groups."	Increased Participation Use of Native Language to Explain Concepts

The table shows the classroom number, the educator information, evidence of culturally relevant pedagogy, the most frequent co-teaching method, and the rationale for the co-teaching method. In addition, we organized the responses into common themes when teachers described their rationale for their co-teaching method. The themes were: students, resources, and timing.

As described in Table 19.1, the station teaching model allowed for the widest range of differentiation between the teachers, the alternative teaching model offered whole group instruction, and the team teaching model allowed educators to work in their comfort zone. The significance of the findings is in the details of which teachers employed which co-method, and why. Most teachers indicated students were the rationale for their co-teaching model. The elementary educators incorporated a buddy system for accountability, which appears in the culturally relevant pedagogy research (Ladson-Billings, 1995b), and other teachers and aides focused on multicultural images and themes throughout the summer. The middle school educators integrated multicultural books. Other teachers documented [limited] resources as a rationale, the teacher in Classroom 3 responded that one teach one, was most convenient. We maintain that given the linguistic diversity with students who speak various English varieties and other students who are under-identified for one or both of these programs, that an EL-SE pairing may work outside of these contexts, even in low-incidence settings (Coady, Harper, & De Jong, 2016) in order to meet the needs of children in general education and special education classrooms.

Regarding instructional strategies, we observed collaboration as described previously by Piazza and colleagues (2015) in each context except Classroom 3. Based on the instructional strategies, CRP, and co-teaching models in Figure 19.1, alternative teaching was the most frequently observed co-teaching model, and in addition to other factors (e.g., instruction and co-teacher background), it led to increased participation. Visual representation as a culturally relevant instructional strategy, along with ESOL and special educators assigned to the same grade level (e.g., ESOL and special educators matched consistently to the same Grade 6 curriculum and classrooms daily), showed positive outcomes for learners. Other findings unique to each classroom included the following:

- Students appeared frustrated in Classroom 1 when teachers employed a parallel teaching model, where more than one teacher spoke at a time, even if one of the educators spoke in the students' first language (L1).
- Each visit to Classroom 2 included the majority of students participating in literacy and numeracy activities; and with the students' use of oral language in addition to content-specific language (i.e., aca-

demic vocabulary), the teachers reported progress toward all students meeting their IEP goals.

- Classroom 3 tasks were mostly worksheets, with limited direct instruction, and with rotating paraprofessionals. In other words, the support personnel in this classroom varied; the class regularly used the one teach, one drift model with different support people. This may have contributed to the lack of observable or reported positive outcomes.
- Classroom 4 students attempted speaking English at an increasing rate. Teachers also noticed an increase in student participation and use of their native language to explain concepts.

Remarkably, each classroom context included some form of CRP to meet the needs of their students, such as visual images and bilingual resources integrated into instruction (Classroom 1), a buddy system and authentic relationships in the joint literacy and numeracy instruction occurring in Classroom 2, multicultural topics in Classroom 3, and multicultural books and interest-based topics in Classroom 4 (see Table 19.1).

FEEDBACK FROM TEACHERS OF EL-SE STUDENTS IN CO-TEACHING CLASSROOMS

Regarding the impact of co-teaching for students, we also learned the following:

- The educators shared their quantitative data (e.g., language proficiency test scores and student learning objectives [SLOs]) and qualitative data (informal teacher-created formative assessments, such as anecdotal records during guided reading groups), and within the co-teaching model, the smallest possible group for newcomers in ESOL classrooms offered the most opportunity for growth in literacy skills. The teachers noticed that students would take risks (e.g., speaking English and reading English aloud) in these smaller groups, increasing their literacy skills.
- EL-SE educators explained that instruction provided to the groups was just as important as the co-teaching structure and co-teaching relationship between the two educators, which appears in the effective co-teaching literature (Pratt, 2014).
- Educators stated that flexible homogeneous (same ESOL level) groups for EL-SE proved effective for literacy instruction and improvement. Once students met an objective in their leveled group, they could move to a different group with a different objective and

higher level of literacy skills. This was not a counter to the literature that highlights that students should pair with a more English proficient peer (Santamaria, 2009; Tomlinson, 2014); it was an alternative to the literature, particularly when learners were working in small groups (not pairs) focused on the same objective.

- Notably, Classroom 3 paired students with a higher scoring peer and did not report positive outcomes. One teach, one drift may be the most available strategy but not the most effective.

IMPLICATIONS FOR TEACHERS: CULTURE, COMPETENCE, AND SHARED RESPONSIBILITY

The expertise and shared responsibility of each professional shapes the educational plan for each student (Ortiz et al., 2011). We reported earlier in the chapter that a high-quality instructional strategy should be replicable (Barrera & Liu, 2006); as such, we provided the teacher background to the study to add insight to co-teacher matching for EL-SE students. For instance, simply placing an ESOL educator and special educator in the same class does not always yield a wide range of positive outcomes, and using multicultural topics in the form of worksheets without instructional support or the intended student connection also does not prove beneficial. Teachers reported that a positive co-teacher relationship was key to successful co-teaching that yields positive outcomes for students (Pratt, 2014) and most referenced attending to students' cultural background and literacy background as critical components that supported students' instructional goals. Arranging and adjusting co-teaching to include and to assist each group of learners, and the knowledge they bring was essential. Such awareness provided the opportunity to identify specific strategies and practices that would positively influence students' academic performance (Terrell Shockley, 2017). Appropriate instructional strategies, small, leveled groups, a supportive co-teaching relationship, and co-teaching models that attend to students' language and culture were vital for student success in EL-SE classrooms.

REFERENCES

Abrams, J., Ferguson, J., & Laud, L. (2001). Assessing ESOL Students. *Educational Leadership, 59*(3), 62–65.

Barrera, M., & Liu, K. K. (2006). Involving parents of English language learners with disabilities through instructional dialogues. *Journal of Special Education Leadership, 19*(1), 43–51.

Castaneda v. Pickard, 648 F.2d 989, 5th Circuit. (1981).

Coady, M. R., Harper, C., & De Jong, E. J. (2016). Aiming for equity: Preparing mainstream teachers for inclusion or inclusive classrooms? *TESOL Quarterly, 50*(2), 340–368.

Cook, L. (2004). *Co-teaching: Principles, practices, and pragmatics* (New Mexico Public Education Department Quarterly Special Education Meeting Participant's Guide). Retrieved from https://files.eric.ed.gov/fulltext/ED486454.pdf

Gay, G. (2010). *Culturally responsive teaching: Theory, research, and practice.* New York, NY: Teachers College Press.

Hernandez Finch, M. E. (2012). Special considerations with response to intervention and instruction for students with diverse backgrounds. *Psychology in the Schools, 49*(3), 285–296.

Howard, T. C., & Rodriguez-Scheel, A. (2017). Culturally Relevant Pedagogy 20 years later: Progress or pontificating? What have we learned, and where do we go? *Teachers College Record, 119*(1), 1–32.

Individuals with Disabilities Education Improvement Act of 2004, P.L. No. 108-446, 20 U.S.C.

King, E. W. (2005). Addressing the social and emotional needs of twice-exceptional students. *Teaching Exceptional Children, 38*(1), 16–21.

Ladson-Billings, G. (1995a). But that's just good teaching! The case for culturally relevant pedagogy. *Theory Into Practice, 34*(3), 159–165.

Ladson-Billings, G. (1995b). Toward a theory of culturally relevant pedagogy. *American Educational Research Journal, 32*(3), 465–491.

Lau v. Nichols, 414 U.S. 563 (1974).

McDaniel, K. M. (2017). Beyond compliance: Supporting the transition of English language learners with special needs. In A. L. Ellis (Ed.), *Transitioning children with disabilities: From early childhood through adulthood* (pp. 43–59). Rotterdam, The Netherlands: Sense.

Nguyen, H. T. (2012). General education and special education teachers collaborate to support English language learners with learning disabilities. *Issues in Teacher Education, 21*(1), 127–152.

Ortiz, A. A., Robertson, P. M., Wilkinson, C. Y., Liu, Y. J., McGhee, B. D., & Kushner, M. I. (2011). The role of bilingual education teachers in preventing inappropriate referrals of ELLs to special education: Implications for response to intervention. *Bilingual Research Journal, 34*(3), 316–333.

Piazza, S. V., Rao, S., & Protacio, M. S. (2015). Converging recommendations for culturally responsive literacy practices: Students with learning disabilities, English language learners, and socioculturally diverse learners. *International Journal of Multicultural Education, 17*(3), 1–20.

Pratt, S. (2014). Achieving symbiosis: Working through challenges found in co-teaching to achieve effective co-teaching relationships. *Teaching and Teacher Education, 41*, 1–12.

Santamaria, L. J. (2009). Culturally responsive differentiated instruction: Narrowing gaps between best pedagogical practices benefiting all learners. *Teachers College Record, 111*(1), 214–247.

Stake, R. E. (1995). *The art of case study research.* Thousand Oaks, CA: SAGE.

Terrell Shockley, E. (2017). Field notes: Strategies to encourage positive disposi-
    tions toward exceptional students. *Educational Leadership, 12*(6). Retrieved
    from http://www.ascd.org/ascd-express/vol12/1216-shockley.aspx
Tomlinson, C. A. (2014). *The differentiated classroom: Responding to the needs of all learn-
    ers.* Alexandria, VA: ASCD.
Yin, R. K. (2013). *Case study research: Design and methods.* Thousand Oaks, CA: SAGE.

CHAPTER 20

IMPROVING ELLs' SCIENTIFIC WRITING THROUGH CO-TEACHING

Collaboration Between ESL and Science Teachers in a Secondary School in Canada

Brandy Gibb
Crofton House School in Vancouver, British Columbia

with

Guofang Li
University of British Columbia

Teresa Schwartz
Vancouver Public Schools

Throughout the 2016–2017 school year, my colleague, Teresa Schwartz, a high school science and physics teacher in Vancouver, BC, Canada, was concerned about her students' misunderstanding of how to write scientific

Co-Teaching for English Learners, pages 235–244
Copyright © 2020 by Information Age Publishing

lab reports, despite the fact that she had provided her Grade 9 and 11 students with lab report outlines, ample front-loading readings and exercises, and guided practice in class. For scientific writing, students are required to move fluidly between the verb tenses, effectively use the passive voice, and be precise on word choice. However, Teresa noticed that the language errors of overuse of personal pronouns, errors with verb tense, including not understanding passive voice, and over-use of modifiers, especially -ly adverbs, were the same between English language learners (ELLs) and mainstream students. Teresa's situation speaks to the challenges faced by many content area teachers who have both ELL and native English speakers in their mainstream classes. With the move towards inquiry-based assessments in science, students are being called upon to explain their results and hypotheses in greater detail through writing—a challenging task for many ELLs. Typically, writing lessons are not part of the science curriculum, and Teresa concedes that science teachers have an expectation that students know how to write in accordance with the requirements of the discipline. She acknowledges that content area teachers like herself need to access language and writing specialists in their schools to help fill the gap between what students actually know and what teachers expect them to know.

I (Brandy) am an English as a second language (ESL) teacher with a background teaching senior English, and have been on a journey to help students understand and eventually master the art of writing between the disciplines. This chapter explores how collaboration between Teresa and me helped support students as they worked towards mastery of scientific content while also addressing the language requirements of scientific writing, particularly objectivity and concision.

While many schools do an excellent job teaching students the grammar and writing skills required for humanities courses, these same skills do not transfer directly to the sciences. In fact, writing for the sciences asks students to adopt the voice and grammar structures verboten in an English class. For example, when writing a literary analysis, students are required to use the active voice and the literary present tense. Conversely, for scientific writing, especially lab reports, students are asked to use the passive voice and the simple past tense. When students apply the writing strategies they have worked so hard to master in English class to the writing of a scientific lab report, the writing reads as subjective, wordy, and highly imprecise.

Realizing that ELL students needed to be able to distinguish between the two different writing styles required for the specific disciplines, Teresa and I set to the task of designing a scientific writing lesson that explored the differences between writing for English versus writing for science following the pedagogical recommendations of Zwiers (2014) in his book, *Building Academic Language*. Our first lesson focused on providing students with writing strategies that could be modified to fit the content of any science class.

In order to test the crossover capabilities of the lesson, we created the first lesson for a Grade 9 unit on mitosis and then modified this for a Grade 11 physics lesson on power and energy.

The majority of ELL students in the class were from Mainland China, and all possessed grade-level fluency in their mother tongue: Mandarin. The profile of our ELL student community follows: They must possess a high level of oral fluency, also known as Basic Interpersonal Communication Skills or BICS (Cummins, 1999) developed in elementary school over the 2 years (Grades 6 and 7) prior to their entry into our Grade 8 program; they must understand that the goal of our school is to support their acquisition of academic English, also known as Cognitive Academic Language Proficiency or CALP (Cummins, 1999); and finally, they must understand that language acquisition is a five–seven year process when students are in a high immersion/high support schooling situation.

THE CO-PLANNING PROCESS

A review of previous student lab reports and writing in Grades 9 and 11 revealed some consistent errors across the grades and across the language levels: lack of concision; over use of personal pronouns; heavy reliance on adverbs to link different ideas within one clause or a series of clauses, especially -*ly* adverbs; and a misunderstanding of how to use passive voice to describe procedure. Based on this review, we designed a content-based scientific writing resource package that combined the challenging Tier 3 scientific vocabulary and content from a Grade 9 unit on mitosis with the specific grammar skills needed to write a well-crafted lab report. The lesson focused on three grammar skills that are *must do's* when writing science lab reports: (a) no personal pronouns, (b) omitting -*ly* adverbs, and (c) effective use of the passive voice. After a successful lesson with the Grade 9 students, this unit was modified to fit the content of the Grade 11 physics unit on power and energy. Both lessons were designed to allow students time to apply the grammar skills to their writing: The Grade 9 students edited their mitosis charts, while the Grade 11 students were given the opportunity to revise and resubmit the procedures section of their recent lab reports.

Prior to the delivery of the lesson, we agreed that chunking the lesson according to a cumulative development of skills, combined with front-loading *chalk and talk*, was essential to student success. This chunking included explaining some easily identifiable grammar skills through direct instruction or *chalk and talk* that the students could quickly recognize and change in their own writing. This *chalk and talk* was adequately paced to allow students time to collaborate and discuss each stage of their learning. Editing and collaboration time was built into the lesson in order to help students recognize errors and edit their own and their peers' work. This time for collaborative learning was successful as students reported to us an increase in their confidence as developing writers.

In order to reinforce the learning for the Grade 9 students, the lesson was followed up with independent editing of a chart that explained the stages of cell division (see Figure 20.5 later in the chapter). This chart was completed on a Google doc and shared with both teachers. I edited the doc for style and grammar while Teresa ensured the accuracy of the scientific content. Students were allowed to edit and then resubmit their mitosis charts. The Grade 11 students were also provided with time to edit in class. They applied their learning by completing edits of their lab reports (procedures section) and resubmitting these to Teresa for assessment.

CO-TEACHING

The co-teaching took place in two Science 9 blocks and two Physics 11 blocks and included both ELLs and native-English speaking students. The classes were 80 minutes long; the first 35 minutes were used to front-load the students with the specific grammar skills needed for effective scientific writing, and the last 45 minutes were left for students to self-edit, collaborate with their peers, and ask clarifying questions: grammar questions for me; scientific content questions for Teresa.

Each class began with a chalk-and-talk front-loading session to address the easily recognizable writing traits that create a lack of concision, clarity, and authoritative voice in scientific writing. For example, avoiding the use of personal pronouns was an easy starting point for the students, who all recognized their tendency to overuse personal pronouns and were able to confidently and quickly make changes in their writing. Having students reflect on their overuse of personal pronouns was also humor inducing, as several publicly conceded to overusing personal pronouns in their recent lab reports.

The front-loading session also included key vocabulary to help students focus their language use during the lesson (see Figure 20.1). Definitions for vocabulary were either taken directly from the Science 9 or Physics 11 textbooks and in some cases were simplified for the purposes of supporting student comprehension and understanding of higher level concepts that students were finding challenging.

The next stage of front-loading activities (see Figure 20.2) included explaining why overusing adverbs, especially *-ly* adverbs, creates wordiness in lab reports and written responses. Students were asked to look through their papers for *-ly* adverbs. This accessible task worked to build their confidence as young writers and editors. Asking students to reflect on *why* they were making the editing choices they were making was an essential part of

---

Science 9
The grammar and language of science
Mitosis

Purpose: The exercises, examples, and descriptions that follow have been designed to help you build your scientific writing skills.

Task: This unit will ask you to demonstrate your knowledge, explain the process of mitosis, relate, and compare

Unit vocabulary:
- Cancer: a serious disease in which growth of cells, also called cancers, form in the body and kill normal body cells. The disease often causes death.
- Cell cycle: the process by which a cell divides into two cells.
- Genes: a unit inside a cell that controls the qualities of a living thing.
- Cytokinesis separates the two nuclei and cell contents into two daughter cells.
- Interphase is the stage in which cells carry out the functions.
- Prophase is the stage in which chromosomes in the nucleus condense. Pairs of centrioles move to opposite sides of the nucleus. Spindle fibers begin to form a bridge between the ends of the cell.
- Metaphase is the stage in which the sister chromatids are aligned by the pushing and pulling of the attached kinetochore microtubules. Both sister chromatids stay attached to each other at the centromere. The chromosomes line up on the cell's equator, or center line, and are prepared for division.
- Metaphase plate: the chromosomes meet in the middle.
- Anaphase: moving apart to either pole.
- Telophase: the end.
- Mitosis divides the duplicated contents of the cell's nucleus into two equal parts.
- Replication: when the two new daughter cells contain the same genetic information as the parent cell.
- Spindle fibres: protein structures that divide the genetic material in a cell.
- Haploid (one copy of the DNA: N): A sperm and egg are both haploid.
- Diploid (has two copies of the chromosomes: 2N)
- Dinoflagellates: A type of algae. Single-celled algae that can reproduce at astounding rates if conditions are favourable.

Note: Definitions have been taken from your science textbook, *Simple English Wikipedia*, and the *Oxford Online Learner's Dictionary*. Please see these as useful resources that can assist with your comprehension of complex scientific concepts.

Tips when writing for science:
Walking your reader through the process of your test or experiment is relatively straightforward. But what type of language should you use when you are asked to do the following, "Explain how you made your decision."

This is a question from your recent readings about mitosis. Keep in mind that although this question uses the second person pronoun "you," it is important to resist the impulse to respond using phrases like "I/we think" "I/we think that." When writing for science, omit all personal pronouns from your responses unless you are being asked to personally reflect on something. This is a standing rule that you must remember even if the question uses personal pronouns . . .

Figure 20.1   The grammar and language of science, grade 9.

each stage of this process as it helped to remove the stigma and fear of discussing their work with a partner. This movement between front-loading information and student-led discussions created a collaborative atmosphere that was motivating (Dornyei, 2014).

Once we built the students' confidence and comfort with these tasks, we moved to the more complex grammar skill of the effective use of passive

(Grade 9)
Some differences to keep in mind when writing for science:

- The language of science is clear, concise, sharp, and to the point. To that end, be aware of how you are using adverbs, especially -*ly* adverbs. Take some time now to go back through your lab reports and circle, underline, or highlight any -*ly* adverbs. Re-read the sentence and ask yourself, "If I remove this word, does my writing still make sense? Does it sound better?" Share your findings with a partner. Read your first version, with the -*ly* adverb to your partner, and then read your second version, without the -*ly* adverb. Discuss which one sounds better and why. We will be looking for two to three examples from the class before we move on.

- Now go back through your paper and do the same thing, but this time look for the adverbs *very*, *also*, and *even* (used as an adverb). These words may be a bit tricky, as not all of these will need to be removed from your write-up. Discuss with a partner whether or not the word could be omitted and why.

(Grade 11) Editing exercise:

Before we begin, please open your most recent lab report in a Google doc. Go into "Suggesting mode" (top right corner of the doc). This will allow you to strike through words while still being able to see what you had previously written. Now, re-read your lab report and strikethrough (delete) the following:

1. All personal pronouns
2. All -*ly* adverbs
3. The words
    a. *Well*
    b. *Being*
    c. *Very*
    d. *Then*
    e. *Next*
    f. *First, second, etc.* (By the way, *Firstly, Secondly, etc.* are incorrect)
    g. *To conclude*—we will work together to come up with better transitions. If you are looking for suggestions for transitional words, go to the *Canadian High-School Writer's Guide*, (Harris & Pilz, 2003, p. 59). But keep in mind that not all of these transition words are appropriate for every subject.
4. Now that you have crossed out words from the list above, take a moment to slowly re-read your lab report. What do you notice? Does your writing sound more clear and concise? How? Why?
5. Now let's work on some transitions.
6. Would someone be willing to share their before and after sentence(s)? (you can take over the Air Play to do this).

Figure 20.2   Example front-loading handout for grades 9 and 11 (adverb section).

voice in scientific writing. Figure 20.3 is an example of the content-based explanation of how to use passive voice. The example sentences were modified directly from the Science 9 textbook in order to create relevance and familiarity with the content and new grammar skill they were about to learn. In addition, references to pages were included in their style guide so that students could refer to it when they were at home working independently.

The final, and most complex skill, was providing students with an example of how to move between the tenses. This is important in scientific writing when students are moving between explaining *what* something is (the present tense) and *how* an experiment was done (passive voice; see Figure 20.4):

Effectively using the passive voice in scientific writing:

- Scientific writing uses the passive voice construction: the verb to be (*is, are, was, were, been*) + the past participle (*-ed* form of the main verb, or an irregular past tense form of the verb). Remember that this is very different from the active voice that is required when writing for English class, and the simple past and past progressive forms that are used when writing about historical events in social studies.
  - The language of science tends to "use large amounts of passive voice construction—for example, 'The transformation **is carried** out in just a few seconds. Then the compound **is subjected** to intense heat'" (Zwiers, 2014, p. 96).
  - Be conscious of the discipline you are writing for recognizing that each requires a different mode of voice.
  - Each of you has a copy of the *Canadian High School Writer's Guide*. Please take the time to look at how voice is used on the following pages: 47, 56–57, 129 (example at the bottom of the page), 357 (definition and example).

Figure 20.3 Handout on how to use passive voice in lab reports.

Moving between tenses:

- For scientific explanations, use the simple present or another appropriate tense (Zwiers, 2014). The tense you choose will be dependent on what you are explaining. Consider the following explanation of cytokinesis from the chapter on mitosis:
  - "The final stage of the cell cycle **is called** cytokinesis. Cytokinesis **separates** the two nuclei into two daughter cells. These new cells **are** identical to the original parent cell" (McGraw Hill Ryerson, Unit 2 Reproduction, p. 158).
    - Notice the combined use of the **passive voice** and the **present-tense** verb forms in this explanation.
  - This next explanation of anaphase only uses the present tense: "The spindle fibres **begin** to contract and shorten. This action **pulls** the centromere apart, allowing the sister chromatids to move to opposite poles of the cell" (MHR, Unit 2 Reproduction, p. 157).
  - In short, it is important to be consciously aware of what you are being asked to do and to make sure that you are choosing the appropriate writing mode for the task.

Figure 20.4 Handout for moving between verb tenses (grade 9).

POST-TEACHING REINFORCEMENT: HOMEWORK AND TEACHER FEEDBACK

In order to reinforce the classroom learning, it was important to provide students with the opportunity to independently edit their work and then receive teacher feedback. The Grade 9 students were assigned a homework task for which they first edited a chart where they had to accurately identify the cell cycle stages and then write explanations for each stage (see Figure 20.5). Not only did this work help reinforce the classroom learning, but it also taught students about the importance of organizing and pre-planning their writing.

Interphase

Interphase is when the cell prepares to split in half. The cell duplicates its organelles and increases in size. The DNA breaks in half, and those **halves** ~~halfs~~ grow the rest of them back using what they have already as a guide. The cell **then** ~~also~~ produces ~~many~~ proteins **needed** ~~for~~ by the new cells when they ~~eventually~~ split apart. ~~Later on~~ d During interphase, mitosis occurs. Mitosis is when the **chromosones inside** ~~innards of~~ the nucleus split. ~~First, to~~ To prepare for division, the two sets of chromosones join together to create the sister chromatids~~,~~**, which are** held together by the centromere.

Figure 20.5 A student example of editing for overuse of adverbs and correct use of passive voice, grade 9. *Note:* not all errors were corrected.

Student 1: Procedure

The experiment that the ~~my~~ **group** designed can measure the amount of power that students, with different mass, can develop when walking on the same incline and at the same time. ~~We first~~ **First,** ~~collect~~ the group members weight ~~mass~~ **was collected** by standing on a Newton scale and record**ing** it on a shared doc. Then ~~we~~ the group ~~had~~ found a belcher in the PE gym and ~~measure~~ measured its ~~it's~~ height. After collecting the all the basic data, ~~we~~ **the group** began **the** ~~our~~ experiement. ~~One person had their timer on, and timed the amount of seconds that it takes for all the group member to climb up the stairs. Four of our~~ **The group** members held ~~hold~~ **their** ~~our~~ hands together and walked up to the top of the belcher **with the same speed** ~~while trying to keep at the same pace~~. Once person in the group ~~member~~ had her timer on during the walk~~,~~ and ~~had~~ recorded the amount of time that the group took to reach the top. ~~When we got to~~ **At** the top, the timer stopped ~~the time~~ and record**ed** the time. With all the data ~~we~~ collected, the group ~~can~~ calculate**ed** ~~we can~~ how much power and work each member exert**ed** while walking up the incline.

Student 2: Procedure. This student was focusing on editing for concision and correct use of passive voice.

~~First, three~~ Three physics students **were chosen** to run **up** the stairs 3 times for 3 trials at different speed**s** each time. ~~Then, the~~ The students' weights **were measured** in Newtons on a kilogram/Newton scale. **as independent variables and** ~~The~~ the height of the staircase **was** ~~being~~ **measured** in meters as a controlled variable. ~~After a~~ The first student was timed **running up the flight of staircase** using a stopwatch once in 8.00 seconds for the first trial, ~~once in~~ 6.00 seconds for the second trial, and ~~once in~~ 42.00 seconds ~~run up a flight of stairs~~ for the third trial. This step **was** ~~being~~ **repeated** 2 more times for the two other students. All data collected from the experiment **was** ~~being~~ **recorded.** ~~Then, with~~ **With** the students' weights, the work done and the power used by ~~the the students~~ each of them, all of which are the dependent variables, **the results were** ~~being~~ **calculated**.

Figure 20.6 Two student examples with student edits, grade 11. *Note:* not all errors were corrected.

The Grade 11s were assigned a homework task for which they had the opportunity to begin editing the procedures section of their most recent lab reports, and complete this editing work for homework (see Figure 20.6).

LESSON OUTCOME AND STUDENT GROWTH

Each lesson ended with a debrief session where students provided us with their immediate feedback about the co-taught lesson. The results were overwhelmingly positive, and both ELL and native English-speaking students expressed an increased understanding of how to use the necessary grammar and style elements required for scientific writing. Both groups of students, particularly the ELLs, also noted that they felt more confident about writing future lab reports. Once the writing lessons were completed and the lab reports were submitted and marked, Teresa saw a dramatic improvement in the quality of the students' writing. The Grade 9 pre-writing-lesson lab reports (Lab 1) averaged 83%, and their post-writing-lesson lab reports (Lab 2) averaged 90%. The Grade 11 students saw similar improvements where the pre-writing-lesson lab reports (Lab 1) averaged 80%; the post-writing-lesson lab reports (Lab 2) averaged 87%; and their third lab reports averaged 90%. Teresa noted that while students were still working on mastery of the scientific concepts and writing skills, mainstream and ELL students omitted all personal pronouns, showed effective use of the passive voice, and produced concise lab reports by reducing their reliance on adverbs to describe procedure.

Given the success of the Grade 9 science lesson and the Grade 11 physics lesson, I (Brandy) have repeated the same lessons to assist two Grade 11 AP Physics 1 classes and a Biology 11 class. The results were again overwhelmingly positive with students submitting higher quality writing that adopted the grammar skills required for scientific writing.

CONCLUSION AND REFLECTIONS

What began as a conversation between a science teacher and an ESL teacher about the challenges ELL students face writing scientific lab reports has blossomed into a larger collaborative project that now includes several members of the senior science department. Now, our collective mission is to improve the scientific writing skills of ELL and mainstream students through Grades 8–12, and by doing so, increase their confidence and reduce their stress levels around the writing of tests, lab reports, and scientific research papers.

Despite the success and the collective motivation to collaborate, we experienced several challenges. Like other teachers documented in Li, Sweeney, Protacio, and Ponnan's (2013) research on co-teaching, a lack of time for co-planning during the school day has been the biggest obstacle to continuing our co-teaching initiatives. Throughout the planning stage, Teresa and I scrambled to find time to meet and plan. Our co-planning process was spliced between quick conversations in the workroom and Google doc collaborations. As with those teachers in Li et al.'s study, a "lack of time to meet and talk [was the] top barrier" (p. 46).

Finding time for teachers to collaborate is also highly dependent on the administration and whether or not they value the co-teaching/co-planning experience as something beneficial to students and the school community. Li et al. (2013) noted that "administrative and funding support for [such] effort[s]" (p. 37) is seen as essential to the success of ELLs in mainstream classrooms. While time continues to be a challenge, Teresa and I had an administrator who told us to "go for it!" and a science department head who welcomed the collaboration. In addition to this administrative support, however, we would have benefitted from release time specifically for such collaboration. As Li et al. pointed out, in order for co-teaching initiatives to be successful,

> Teachers need to have a built-in block of time for such cross-disciplinary collaboration wherein they might meet to update one another on the progress of ESLs in their classroom, share ideas of how to better meet the needs of ESLs, and provide feedback on classroom strategies they want to try out with their ESLs. (p. 51)

Teresa and I continue to collaborate despite the obstacle of time and there is no doubt that each new venture brings new discoveries, for us and our students. If co-teaching is something that you think will benefit your students, we encourage you to go for it. In my experience, the job is simply more fun when we are co-teaching.

REFERENCES

Cummins, J. (1999). *BICS and CALP: Clarifying the distinction.* Retrieved from https://eric.ed.gov/?id=ED438551

Dornyei, Z. (2014). Motivation in second language learning. In M. Celce-Murcia, D. M. Brinton, & M. A. Snow (Eds.), *Teaching English as a second or foreign language* (4th ed.; pp. 518–531). Boston, MA: National Geographic Learning.

Harris, M., & Pilz, J. (2003). *Canadian high-school writer's guide.* Don Mills, Ontario: Pearson.

Li, G., Sweeney, J., Protacio, M. S., & Ponnan, K. (2013). A team-training approach to professional development: Perceptions and practices of in-service teachers of ELLs in two urban high schools. In Y. Bashevis & Y. Weidenseld (Eds.), *Professional development: Perspectives, strategies and practices* (pp. 1–25). New York, NY: Nova Science.

Oxford Online Learner's Dictionaries. (n.d.). Retrieved from https://www.oxfordlearners dictionaries.com/us/

Simple English Wikipedia. (n.d.). Retrieved from https://simple.wikipedia.org/wiki/Main_Page

Zwiers, J. (2014). *Building academic language* (2nd ed.). San Francisco, CA: Jossey-Bass.

CHAPTER 21

COLLABORATIVE CONVERSATIONS

Jennifer S. Daddino
Harrison Central School District

Kimberly Grogan
Harrison Central School District

Marina A. Moran
Harrison Central School District

My expertise and role in the classroom are not considered as an "add-on" or "supplementary," but a crucial component of a shared responsibility to create the most effective learning environment for all students.

—Jennifer Daddino, ENL Co-teacher

Our conversations are never about your students and my students. Rather, our conversations are always about OUR students and our shared responsibility and commitment to meet the needs of ALL learners in our classroom.

—Kimberly Grogan, ELA Co-teacher

Co-Teaching for English Learners, pages 245–260
Copyright © 2020 by Information Age Publishing
All rights of reproduction in any form reserved.

The shared classroom between the ESOL and content teacher provides the most ideal environment for emergent bilinguals to achieve in rigorous academic settings while continuing to develop their academic language skills. Language and content take turns, scaffolding each in the service of knowledge and creativity.

—Marina Moran, Director of ENL and World Languages

We embarked on documentary research to explore the collaborative conversations necessary for successful partnering and co-teaching in the secondary English language arts (ELA) classroom. The research is centered around the co-teaching partnership of Jennifer Daddino and Kimberly Grogan as they taught a unit on the novel *The Great Gatsby* by F. Scott Fitzgerald (2004), during the 2016–2017 school year. Dr. Daddino and Ms. Grogan have been working together in collaboration with and supported by Mrs. Moran, the director of world language and English as a new language (ENL), since 2012 and in 2016–2017, co-taught a diverse group of 16 English learners (ELs) in two separate ELA 11 classes at Harrison High School in Harrison, New York. Throughout this chapter, we demonstrate how the collaborative discussions and a shared interest in supporting the needs of *all* students guides the creation of supports for emergent bilingual students and their mainstream counterparts.

The collaborative conversations are framed around three fields of research: differentiation and purposeful curriculum design (Tomlinson, 1995, 1999; Wiggins & McTighe, 1998), co-teaching (Honigsfeld & Dove, 2015; Honigsfeld & Dove, 2019), and making content comprehensible for culturally and linguistically diverse learners (Echevarria, Vogt, & Short, 2017; Gottlieb, 2016; Vogt, Echevarria, & Short, 2010; Zwiers & Crawford, 2011). The co-teaching model from Honigsfeld and Dove provides the framework for co-teaching that is documented throughout this chapter. The collaborative conversations occur at each step of the co-teaching cycle—co-planning, co-instructing, co-assessing, and shared reflection (Honigsfeld & Dove, 2015, Honigsfeld & Dove, 2019).

EMBRACING EQUITY, ACCESS, RIGOR AND ADAPTABILITY THROUGH CO-TEACHING

The Harrison Central School District is a high-performing medium-sized suburban district located in southern Westchester County, 25 miles north of New York City. Harrison encompasses several micro-communities comprising a socioeconomically and culturally diverse student population. The district has experienced significant growth in its EL population and currently EL students comprise 10% of the total population. There are 27 languages from 52 nations spoken, with Japanese and Spanish being the highest incidence primary languages. The faculty and staff are committed to the district's mission of equity, access, rigor, and adaptability for *all* of its students, and these core values have informed every aspect of the district's work contributing to the creation of a culture of inclusion for all learners. Through collaborative co-teaching practices between English to speakers of other languages (ESOL) and content professionals, our ELs have been able to perform successfully in our most rigorous classes. Harrison started offering co-taught classes for ELs in 2008 in one ninth grade global studies section. Today, we offer co-teaching for ELs in ELA 9, ELA 10, ELA 12, and International Baccalaureate (IB) Language and Literature. Additionally, we continue offering co-taught courses in Global Studies 9 and 10, and U.S. history.

Harrison High School is ranked among the most competitive high schools in New York State and the nation according to The Washington Post, Newsweek, and the U.S. News and World Report. It provides a comprehensive, rigorous, college and career preparatory curriculum through the offering of Advanced Placement (AP), and IB. 95% of students in the class of 2017 enrolled in at least one AP or IB course. The disaggregated data for the achievement of ELs indicated that in the last 3 academic years 80% of ELs passed the ELA Common Core State Standards (CCSS) Regents. Our district ranked 13th in NY State for EL passing rate of CCSS Regents and 2nd highest in Westchester County. Approximately 40% of our ELs are enrolled in an AP and/or IB course.

COLLABORATIVE CONVERSATIONS

The remainder of the chapter focuses on the different types of collaborative conversations that we continually engage in to meet the needs of the many diverse learners in their classroom. We start the discussion with an explanation of what guides our practice and how we view student readiness. We then go into detailed descriptions of the types of supports that we create for all students based on their readiness.

The Framework and Student Readiness

Our approach relies on constant communication combined with our shared expertise to meet the needs of all students in our classrooms. Figure 21.1 represents the essential elements we consider when planning for student readiness. Our collaborative discussions around creating materials, designing lessons, and assessing students always take *student readiness* into consideration, and as a result, we constantly consider the three components

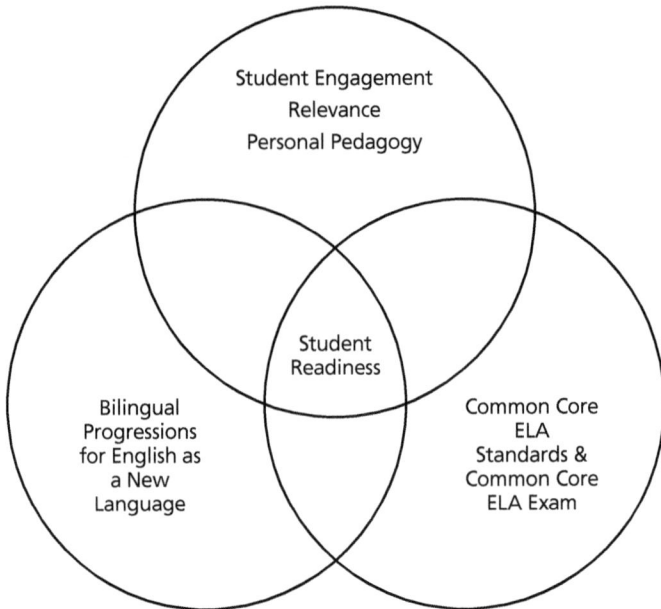

Figure 21.1   Collaborative Conversation Foundational Framework.

as outlined below. It is in those different components that we trust in both our separate and combined expertise.

In the ELA 11 class, the content teacher focuses on incorporating the New York State Next Generation Standards and a knowledge of the English Regents exam into planning. We now include more nonfiction, complex supplementary texts into our units and incorporate more argumentative writing tasks. We strive to align the classroom tasks to those on the English Regents exam—multiple choice questions, argumentative synthesis writing, and text analysis writing.

The ENL teacher focuses on incorporating the Bilingual Common Core Progressions (NYSED, 2014) in order to meet the needs of culturally and linguistically diverse students. These standards are used as a starting point to guide how to provide comprehensible input as well as tailor assessments based on our students' English language proficiency (*New York State Bilingual Common Core Initiative*, NYSED, 2014). We have found that supports outlined in the progressions also serve our lower readiness general education students.

The final component we address is student engagement, relevance, and personal pedagogy. Amidst the need to prepare students for standardized assessments, it is important to us that students have an engaging and rich experience in the classroom. Though students are practicing skills and tasks related to standards and assessments every day, we know that the best work happens in the classroom when students have *buy-in*. We want our students to be active agents in their own learning and to feel confident to assert critical, evidence-based claims about a text. An inquiry-based approach to instruction is an integral part of our personal pedagogies as teachers.

Conversations Around Reading and Writing

Many consider *The Great Gatsby* to be a challenging text due to its elevated language and complex syntax. While the story itself is engaging, it can be difficult for students to understand the nuances of meaning within the text. As we prepared to teach this unit, we found ourselves at a crossroads: Do we assign reading homework that we are confident will not be completed or do we respond to the student readiness levels and find a way to make this text more accessible from the start? Ultimately, we decided on the latter, knowing well that this meant a tremendous amount of work was about to take place.

Everyone Is Reading Gatsby!

To address our concerns regarding the complexity of the text and to meet the needs of different readiness levels as it related to reading, we created leveled student reading guides for each chapter. Each reading guide came with a prompt to which students would respond in paragraph form at the end of reading the chapter. Each prompt was framed similar to the following: How does F. Scott Fitzgerald's use of (literary technique) help to support the central message of the chapter? For the first few chapters, we selected the literary technique based on what was most relevant in the chapter, starting at first with techniques such as setting, conflict, and characterization. As the chapters progressed, we challenged our students to identify the most important literary technique to discuss. In Chapters 6–9, the prompt for the reading guide asked students to respond in a paragraph to the following prompt: Based on specific evidence from the chapter, does money buy happiness?

In our reading guides, we selected pages from the text and added annotation boxes that guided students toward noticing key features and ideas in the text and also prepared them for the culminating writing tasks. We also asked students to create *independent observations* for each page, and we provided them with ideas for what those annotations might look like. As we got further along in the chapters, we provided less guidance and more opportunities for independent observations.

During our first year of experimenting with the reading guides, we had one version that was distributed to students. However, our second year of co-teaching allowed us to build upon the success of the previous year and we began to tease out the guides into as many as four different readiness levels. All students were reading the same text and being prepared for the same writing prompt, but with different, appropriate levels of support based on their readiness. For example, when guiding students to analyze the opening paragraph in Chapter 3 of *The Great Gatsby* (Fitzgerald, 2004), we highlighted the following key sentence for some of the students, "On week-ends his Rolls-Royce became an omnibus, bearing parties to and from the city between nine in the morning and long past midnight, while his station wagon scampered like a brisk yellow bug to meet all trains" (p. 46), whereas others were presented with the entire paragraph. Table 21.1 summarizes the differentiated guiding tasks and prompts we developed on four readiness levels. While much of the task was differentiated, all students were expected to engage in independent annotations and also complete the following writing task: "Page 46 contains examples of metaphor and simile. Choose one and describe the author's purpose for including this technique."

In addition, each reading guide offers varying supports in the form of visuals, definitions, more direct or indirect questioning, and so on. We carefully tracked the levels that students received. After each chapter, we discussed each student's progress and adjusted the level of guide they received for the next chapter. This cycle of providing appropriate scaffolds, tracking student progress, and adjusting supports as needed guided our conversations around the writing assessments at the end of each chapter as well.

TABLE 21.1 Differentiating Tasks and Prompts Based on Student Readiness Levels

Readiness Levels	Differentiated Tasks	Differentiated Prompts and Supports
Lowest Readiness	Describe the setting at Gatsby's house.	How do these lines support the claim that Gatsby was a good host? A host is someone who is throwing a party. (Additional supports: Visual scaffolds, underlined key words, evidence underlined in text)
Low Readiness	Describe the setting at Gatsby's house.	How do these lines support the claim that Gatsby was a good host? A host is someone who is throwing a party. (Additional supports: Key words and evidence underlined in text)
Medium Readiness	Describe the setting at Gatsby's house.	Would Gatsby be considered a good host? What is the best evidence to support your response?
High Readiness	Based on this description of setting, what would be your impression of Gatsby if you were his neighbor?	To what extent is Gatsby indirectly characterized by the way in which he hosts his parties?

That's Right, Six Versions of the Chapter 2 Writing Assessment

It is important to note that in our first year of teaching *Gatsby,* we did not have six versions of each assessment. Initially, we created versions of assessments that supported the linguistic abilities of ELs based on the bilingual progressions (NYSED, 2014). We began by creating high and low readiness versions aligned to the reading guides. Our new goal was to purposefully align the reading guides to the writing assessments. We measured readiness for writing in terms of language proficiency and readiness for organization and structure, thus with these two lenses in mind, we typically had five to six versions of any given writing assessment based on four different levels of support (in addition to the original, non-modified version of the assessment task—see Figure 21.2). Before each assessment we would discuss the readiness of students, reflect on their past writing, and assign them a version of the assessment. The four different scaffolds outlined here were combined in different ways to meet the specific needs of all of the students in our class. These different combinations resulted in six different versions of this assessment.

The Level 1 scaffolds addressed readiness for organization and structure and include sentence frames. Higher readiness ELs and lower readiness English proficient students received this type of support (see Figure 21.3). The Level 2 scaffolds incorporated content support as well as the organization support similar to those in Level 1. This version was for lower readiness English proficient students as well as lower readiness ELs. Claim support as well as an evidence grid were provided for this level (see Figure 21.4). The Level 3 scaffolds offered content and organization support for the lowest readiness ELs. This level also included the Level 1 organizational support. More scaffolds were given for

---

Part A (10 SUMMATIVE POINTS):

Write a well-developed, text-based response of **one paragraph** (you will be required to write 2–3 paragraphs for the Regents exam at the end of the year). In your response, **identify a central message in Chapter 2 of *The Great Gatsby* by F. Scott Fitzgerald and explain how the author's use of characterization, conflict, OR setting (NOT ALL OF THEM) helps to support the message.** Use strong and thorough evidence from the text to support your analysis. Do not simply summarize the text. Write your response IN PEN.

Guidelines:

Be sure to:
- Identify a central message in the text
- Analyze how the author's use of **characterization, conflict, OR setting (NOT ALL OF THEM)** helps to support that message.
- **PUSH IT—WEAVE IN OTHER LITERARY ELEMENTS AS PART OF YOUR ANALYSIS.**
- Use strong and thorough evidence (at least two quotes) from the text to support your analysis
- Organize your ideas in a cohesive and coherent manner
- Maintain a formal style of writing
- Follow the conventions of standard written English

Figure 21.2 Non-adapted writing prompt.

Below are some sentence frames to help you organize your work. **THEY ARE NOT IN ORDER SO DO NOT JUST COPY THEM DOWN:**
- In the work, _____(TITLE)_____ by _____(AUTHOR'S NAME)_____, the author's use of _____(DEVICE)_____ helps to reveal the central message that _____(CENTRAL MESSAGE)_____.
- The author's use of _____ supports the central message by…
- This is significant because it demonstrates how…
- For example the author states, "quote." In other words… (rephrase)
- The author's use of _____ connects to the central message because…
- In addition,…
- Therefore, through the use of _____, the author…

Figure 21.3   Level 1 writing support.

Evidence & Central Message Organizer

Step 1: Create a claim statement. You can choose one of the following central messages to help you write your claim. Remember your claim has TWO parts: **ONE** literary technique and the central message. The author's use of _____ (characterization, conflict, setting) helps to reveal the central message that_____.

Possible Central Message		
Money cannot buy happiness	Money can buy happiness	Having money can change how people act

Step 2: Choose **ONE** piece of evidence from this grid to support your claim. Choose your **second piece of evidence from the TEXT.**

"Some time toward midnight Tom Buchanan and Mrs. Wilson stood face to face, discussing in impassioned voices whether Mrs. Wilson had any right to mention Daisy's name. 'Daisy! Daisy! Daisy!' shouted Mrs. Wilson. 'I'll say it whenever I want to! Daisy! Dai--!' Making a short deft movement, Tom Buchanan broke her nose with his open hand." (p. 44)	"Mrs. Wilson had changed her costume some time before, and was now attired in an elaborate afternoon dress of cream-colored chiffon…With the influence of the dress her personality had also undergone a change. The intense vitality that had been so remarkable in the garage was converted into impressive hauteur." (p. 37)	"'I want to get one of those dogs,' she said earnestly. 'I want to get one for the apartment. They're nice to have—a dog.'…'I think it's cute,' said Mrs. Wilson enthusiastically. 'How much is it?'" (p. 33)

Figure 21.4   Level 2 writing support.

the creation of claim statements and a full evidence grid was provided to students. The cognitive load for students with this level was to be able to connect "given" best evidence to chosen claim statements (see Figure 21.5). The Level 4 scaffolds provided more organizational support for the lowest readiness ELs and English proficient students. Depending on student readiness, Level 2 or Level 3 scaffolds were also included. This scaffold provided a paragraph frame for students to use in order to write their paragraphs (see Figure 21.6).

Directions: Create a detailed claim statement, and then choose the best evidence to support your claim.

Step 1: *Create a claim statement by choosing one of the given statements and providing more details to make it more detailed by adding specific characters and/or locations.*

The author's use of the conflict between _____ helps to support the central message that money cannot buy happiness.

The author's use of setting of _____ helps to support the central message that money can buy happiness.

The author's use of characterization of _____ helps to support the central message that having money can change how people act.

Step 2: *Choose the two best pieces of evidence from this grid to support your claim statement.*

"Some time toward midnight Tom Buchanan and Mrs. Wilson stood face to face, discussing in impassioned voices whether Mrs. Wilson had any right to mention Daisy's name. 'Daisy! Daisy! Daisy!' shouted Mrs. Wilson. 'I'll say it whenever I want to! Daisy! Dai--!' Making a short deft movement, Tom Buchanan broke her nose with his open hand." (p. 44)	"Mrs. Wilson had changed her costume some time before, and was now attired in an elaborate afternoon dress of cream-colored chiffon…With the influence of the dress her personality had also undergone a change. The intense vitality that had been so remarkable in the garage was converted into impressive hauteur." (p. 37)	"The only *crazy* I was when I married him. I knew right away I made a mistake. He borrowed somebody's best suit to get married in, and never even told me about it, and the man came after it one day when he was out…This is the first I ever heard about it. But I gave it to him and then I lay down and cried to beat the band all afternoon." (p. 42)
"'Get some more ice and mineral water, Myrtle, before everybody goes to sleep.' 'I told that boy about the ice.' Myrtle raised her eyebrows in despair at the shiftlessness of the lower orders. 'These people! You have to keep after them all the time!'" (p. 38)	"At 158th street the cab stopped at one slice in a long white cake of apartment-houses. Throwing a regal homecoming glance around the neighborhood, Mrs. Wilson gathered up her dog and her other purchases, and went haughtily in." (p. 34)	"'I married him because I thought he was a gentleman,' she said finally. 'I thought he knew something about breeding, but he wasn't fit to lick my shoe.'" (p. 41)
"Catherine leaned close to me and whispered in my ear: 'Neither of them can stand the person they're married to.' 'Can't they?' 'Can't stand them.'" (p. 40)	"…I was standing beside his bed and he was sitting up between the sheets, clad in his underwear, with a great portfolio in his hands." (p. 45)	"'I like your dress,' remarked Mrs. McKee, 'I think it's adorable.' Mrs. Wilson rejected the compliment by raising her eyebrow in disdain. 'It's just a crazy old thing,' she said. 'I just slip it on sometimes when I don't care what I look like.'" (p. 37)

Figure 21.5 Level 3 writing support.

Model Paragraph

In the work, *The Great Gatsby* by F. Scott Fitzgerald, the author's use of _____ (characterization/setting) helps to reveal the central message that _____(CENTRAL MESSAGE)_____. The author's use of _____ (characterization/setting) supports the central message by _____ (describe 1–2 sentences of context). For example the author states, "quote." In other words _____ (rephrase the quote). This is significant because it demonstrates how the author's use of (characterization/setting) supports the central message. In addition the author states, "quote". In other words _____ (rephrase the quote). This is significant because it demonstrates how the author's use of _____ connects to the central message because _____. Therefore, through the use of _____ (characterization/setting), the author reveals the central message of _____.

Figure 21.6 Level 4 writing support.

Conversations Around Listening and Speaking

The Socratic Seminar Is for ELs Also

A typical Socratic seminar involves a group of students sitting in a circle, engaging in a dialogue about text without teacher participation. Students are held accountable for oral interactions during the seminar. As co-teachers, our conversations about student readiness include English language proficiency, lowering the affective filter, language production, and content readiness. Initially, we focused on how to hold our ELs accountable during class discussions. We had created more comprehensible input for the content of the discussions by embedding more supports into the reading guides; however, we realized that these efforts did not address how to support listening and speaking in the classroom (Echevarria, Vogt, & Short, 2017). As such, Socratic seminars became our primary way to practice speaking and listening skills with ample supports for both content and language.

To meet student readiness in terms of content, we created direct connections between the reading guides, the writing tasks, and the preparation for Socratic seminars. Knowing that a deep knowledge of the text would be key to a productive class discussion, the importance of preparation for a Socratic was critical. Mirroring the annotations from the reading guides and replicating the *best evidence* emphasis of the writing tasks, students identified evidence to support key motifs and topics within the text and explained how that evidence supports a particular topic across a set of three chapters. All students were encouraged to create discussion questions and higher readiness students were challenged to generate a claim to assert how a particular topic changed or stayed the same across the set of three chapters. See Figures 21.7 and 21.8 as examples of Socratic seminar preparation sheets on two different levels.

Directions: Complete the Socratic Seminar Organizer below using best evidence from Chapters 7-9 to support your point. Create two discussion questions too!

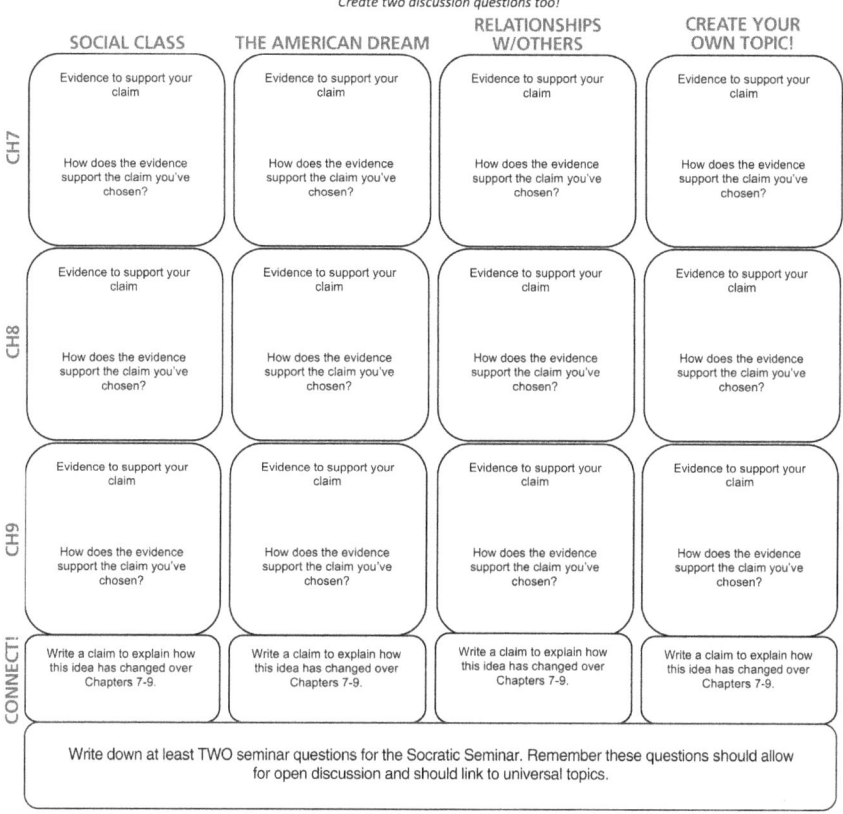

Figure 21.7 High readiness sample Socratic preparation sheet.

To support classroom discussions, we engaged in "mini-Socratics" before most full class Socratics. In these mini-Socratics, we made groups of four students of varying readiness levels. Each student was given a card that assigned a role in the conversation and designated appropriate sentence stems to use (see Figure 21.9).

During practice rounds of *purposeful participation*, students engaged in the discussions in the order of the role they received, using their assigned sentence frames. Questions were provided to students at the lowest readiness level: one low-risk, non-academic question (What is your favorite show on TV or Netflix right now?) and one low-risk, academic question (Do you like *The Great Gatsby* so far?). After students engaged in one-to-two practice rounds of purposeful participation, we chose one group to model their conversation chain while the rest of the class observed. This activity allowed students to not only practice some of the content associated with the

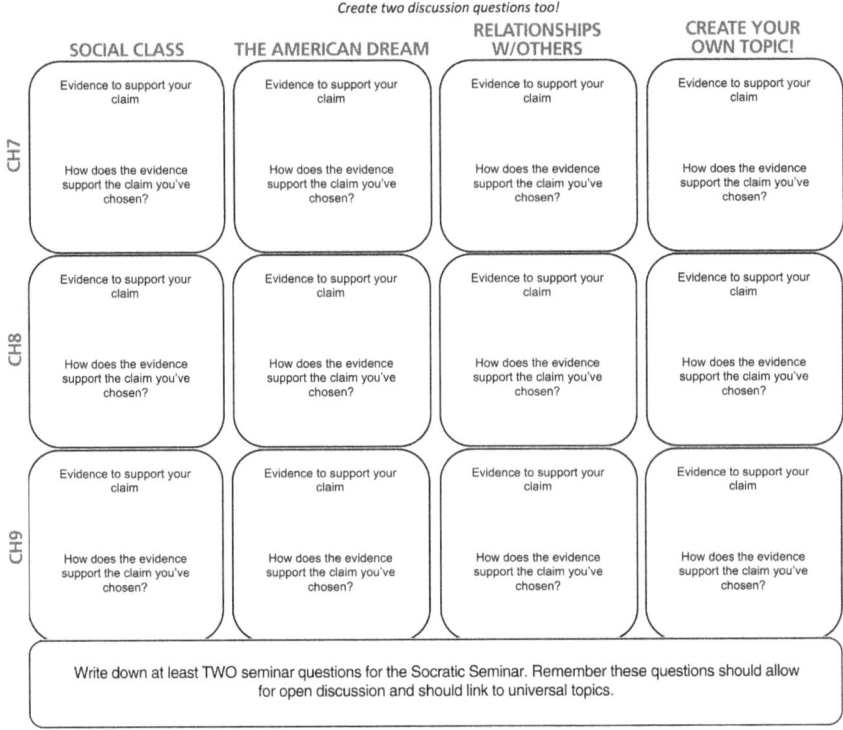

Directions: Complete the Socratic Seminar Organizer below using best evidence from Chapters 7-9 to support your point. Create two discussion questions too!

Figure 21.8 Low readiness sample Socratic preparation sheet.

full-class Socratic, but to also practice the language components associated with a class discussion.

Once we moved into our full-class Socratic, we designated an inner circle, which focused on participating verbally, and an outer circle, which focused on participation by listening. Our circles varied from being heterogeneously or homogeneously grouped, and all students were held accountable for being active listeners, regardless of their position in the inner or outer circle. Students were required to record evidence to support a claim and to record the types of participation strategies they heard.

At teacher-directed times, students in the inner circle turned to the student directly behind them in the outer circle to debrief the conversation, sum up key ideas, or ask for opinions or reactions. Most importantly, the inner circle was always asked to bring back an idea from the outer circle to start the next conversation. This back and forth flow of information ensured that all students were held accountable for participating in the Socratic. Periodically, we asked the outer circle to reflect on what kinds of participation strategies were done well by the inner circle and to offer

1

ASK A QUESTION!
Your job is to start the
conversation with the following
question:

Do you like the novel, The Great
Gatsby?

Lowest Readiness

2

RESPOND TO THE QUESTION
WITH EVIDENCE!
Your job is to continue the
conversation with evidence.
Consider using these sentence
stems:

In my opinion… because…
I think… because…
Based on…, I believe…
According to…
An example of this is…

Low-Middle Readiness

3

ADD TO THE RESPONSE WITH
EVIDENCE!
Your job is to add to the
response before you using
evidence. Consider using these
sentence stems:

Another example is…
Yes, and I also think…because…
Yes, but I don't think…because…
Even though…, I think… because…

Middle-High Readiness

4

ASK A QUESTION ABOUT THE
RESPONSES YOU'VE HEARD!
Your job is to ask a question to
clarify, make sense of, or to
extend the responses. Consider
using these sentence stems:

What do you mean when you say…
What made you think that…
What would happen if…
What do you think… reveals about…

Highest Readiness

Figure 21.9   Purposeful participation roles.

feedback on what could be improved upon for next time. In this way, again, all students were held responsible for working towards knowledgeable, academic conversations in the classroom.

REFLECTING ON THE COMPLEXITY
OF COLLABORATIVE CONVERSATIONS

From a teacher's perspective, we have come to realize that shared pedagogy, constant conversations, and countless hours of time and effort outside of the classroom are the biggest contributors to our success in the classroom. On a fundamental level, our co-teaching partnership works because we not only acknowledge the diverse learning needs in our classroom, but we deeply and philosophically believe that it is our *shared* responsibility and duty to figure out the best way to meet these readiness needs. On a more practical level, we understand that such a deeply held commitment requires a judicious amount of time, work, and flexibility in order to truly put our beliefs into practice. Working together for nearly six years has certainly helped, but we also know that our success relies on more than just consistency. We arrive at school by 6:00 a.m. most mornings; we text ideas to each other throughout the day; we e-mail handouts and slides back and forth late into the night. This is our reality—the conversation never stops. Sometimes we are able to create supports and find success in our first go-around of a differentiated lesson or assessment, but many times we have found that it takes us a lot of reflections and revisions to get to where we want to be.

From a leadership perspective, the implementation of the collaborative co-teaching instructional model for ELs has required the thoughtful placement of ELs in small clusters of five to seven students in sections. Particular consideration was given not only to the linguistic level and literacy readiness of the students, but also their ethnicity and primary languages. The cluster of ELs in each section should not surpass 30% of the entire group. When building teaching partnerships, personalities and teaching styles were considered. However, we found that with training and support, most content and ENL teachers were successful co-teaching.

One of the most significant structural supports for co-teaching is the opportunity for regular joint planning time for collaborating colleagues. Summer curriculum writing hours for teachers are provided, and we strive to maintain the partnerships for a few years to optimize growth over time as a unit. Additionally, ongoing professional development in sheltered instruction and the expectation of differentiation practices for ELs for content teachers is paramount. Teachers engage in extensive training in differentiated instruction and assessment that focuses on the use of linguistic, multisensory, graphic, and interactional scaffolds as well as strategies to essentialize content based on students' levels of English proficiency.

FINAL THOUGHTS

The collaborative co-teach model has enabled the Harrison Central School District to realize its mission of inclusion for all learners and has strengthened its four core values of equity, access, rigor, and adaptability. By being included in content classes with their peers, emergent bilingual students have been able to attain at high levels in the most rigorous content classes while continuing to develop their academic language skills in English. This model has also provided a great opportunity for acculturation and socialization with many students of diverse backgrounds in settings where their uniqueness has become a source of empowerment and self-realization.

As teachers, the collaborative co-teach model has enabled us to find great personal satisfaction in using our distinct professional expertise to help students find success. During the first year of our partnership, we learned how to navigate the curriculum. In our second year, we were able to create many more supports for students, and we were able to see the evidence of our hard work in their state exam results. At the time this chapter was written—following the 2016–2017 school year—16 ENL students were enrolled in our co-taught class. Of the 16, only two students—transitional-level English language proficiency per the NYSESLAT exam—did not pass the ELA exam with a 65% or better. One student received a 65% and another earned a 69%. All other students earned scores 79% or higher, with three students earning 90% or above. During the 2018–2019 school year, we were co-teaching our second round of IB Language and Literature Year 1. There were six ELs enrolled in the class. We saw a similar trend in student scores, only two students—transitional level per the NYSESLAT exam—did not pass the exam with a 65% or better.

While we love to see success on state exams and assessments, the greatest highlights for us tend to be in the smaller day-to-day moments in class. What kept us going were: (a) seeing a student participate for the first time in a Socratic, (b) watching a student's reaction to understanding a critical moment in a novel, or (c) reading a student's organized paragraph when they received one less language support on that assessment. As we take on the challenge of co-teaching a rigorous, new IB course in our district, we are excited to see how we can continue to implement our fundamental pedagogical beliefs to achieve student success.

REFERENCES

Echevarria, J., Vogt, M. E., & Short, D. (2017). *Making content comprehensible for English learners: The SIOP model* (5th ed.). Boston, MA: Pearson.

Fitzgerald, F. S. (2004). *The great Gatsby.* New York, NY: Shribner Paperback Fiction.

Gottlieb, M. (2016). *Assessing English language learners: Bridges to educational equity connecting academic language proficiency to academic achievement* (2nd ed.). Thousand Oaks, CA: Corwin Press.

Honigsfeld, A., & Dove, M. G. (2015). *Collaboration and co-teaching for English learners: A leader's guide.* Thousand Oaks, CA: Corwin Press.

Honigsfeld, A., & Dove, M. G. (2019). *Collaborating for English learners: A foundational guide to integrated practices.* Thousand Oaks, CA: Corwin Press.

New York State Department of Education. (2014). *New York State Bilingual Common Core Initiative.* Retrieved from https://www.engageny.org/resource/new-york-state-bilingual-common-core-initiative

Tomlinson, C. (1995). *How to differentiate instruction in mixed-ability classrooms.* Alexandria, VA: ASCD.

Tomlinson, C. (1999). *The differentiated classroom: Responding to the needs of all learners.* Alexandria, VA: ASCD.

Vogt, M. E., Echevarria, J., & Short, D. (2010). *The SIOP model for teaching English language arts to English learners.* Boston, MA: Pearson.

Wiggins, G., & McTighe, J. (1998). *Understanding by design.* Alexandria, VA: ASCD.

Zwiers, J., & Crawford, M. (2011). *Academic conversations: Classroom talk that fosters critical thinking and content understanding.* Portland, ME: Stenhouse.

ABOUT THE EDITORS

Maria G. Dove, EdD, is professor in the School of Education and Human Services at Molloy College, Rockville Centre, New York, where she teaches and mentors pre-service and in-service educators in the graduate education TESOL program and the doctoral program, Educational Leadership for Diverse Learning Communities. Before entering the field of higher education, she worked for over 30 years as an English-as-a-second-language teacher in public school settings (Grades K–12) and in adult English language programs in New York. She frequently provides professional development for educators throughout the United States on the teaching of diverse students. She has published broadly on collaborative teaching practices and instruction for English learners. With Andrea Honigsfeld, she coauthored six best-selling Corwin Press books, including *Co-Teaching for English Learners: A Guide to Collaborative Planning, Instruction, Assessment, and Reflection* (2018) and *Collaboration for English Learners: A Foundational Guide to Integrated Practices* (2019). The same writing team also co-edited, *Co-teaching and Other Collaborative Practices in the EFL/ESL Classroom: Rationale, Research, Reflections, and Recommendations* (2012), published by Information Age.

Andrea Honigsfeld, EdD, is associate dean and professor in the Division of Education at Molloy College, Rockville Centre, New York. She directs a doctoral program in Educational Leadership for Diverse Learning Communities. Before entering the field of teacher education, she was an English-as-a-foreign-language teacher in Hungary (Grades 5–8 and adult) and an English-as-a-second-language teacher in New York City (Grades K–3 and adult). She also taught Hungarian at New York University. She has published extensively on working with English learners. In the past 12 years, she has been presenting at conferences across the United States, Great Britain, Denmark, Sweden, the Philippines, and the United Arab Emirates. She frequently offers staff development, primarily focusing on effective differentiated strategies and collaborative practices for English-as-a-second-language and general education teachers. She coauthored *Differentiated Instruction for At-Risk Students* (2009) and co-edited the five-volume *Breaking the Mold of Education* series (2010–2013), published by Rowman and Littlefield. She is also the co-author of *Core Instructional Routines: Go-To Structures for Effective Literacy Teaching, K–5 and 6–12* (2014), and her latest book, *Growing Language and Literacy* (2019), published by Heinemann.

ABOUT THE CONTRIBUTORS

Felice Atesoglu Russell, PhD, is an assistant professor in the Department of Educational Leadership, Policy, and Instructional Technology at Central Connecticut State University. Her teaching and research focuses on the professional learning and support of culturally and linguistically responsive teachers and leaders. She is particularly interested in collaboration, advocacy, and supports for teachers and leaders to meet the varied needs of multilingual students.

Laura Baecher, EdD, is associate professor of TESOL at Hunter College, City University of New York. Her research interests and publications relate to ESL teacher preparation including content-language integration, teacher leadership, the use of video for teacher learning, and practicum and supervision in teaching English learners.

Leia Bruton, MS, is an elementary ESL teacher in Salisbury, North Carolina. She has been teaching ESL for 6 years and has co-taught for 1 year. She has her Masters in Education and continues to learn so she can support and train other educators in best practices for supporting ELs. She lives in Salisbury with her husband, her toddler son, and their animals.

Samantha Chung, MS, began her teaching career as an 8th grade ELA/ESL teacher and now is an instructional coach at I.S. 145Q. She is also currently a doctoral candidate at Teachers College, Columbia University. She is passionate about educational equity for students and supporting schools and teachers in achieving success.

Co-Teaching for English Learners, pages 263–268
Copyright © 2020 by Information Age Publishing
All rights of reproduction in any form reserved.

Beth Clark-Gareca, PhD, is an assistant professor in the School of Education at SUNY New Paltz. In addition to coordinating the MSEd TESOL program, she directs a NYSED-funded grant designed to certify practicing content teachers in ESOL. Implementing successful co-teaching models and strategies is a focal point in all the work that she currently does in teacher preparation. Her research interests include educational assessment, bilingual education, and teacher education in K–12 contexts.

Debra Cole, MS, is a long-time K–12 language educator. Since moving to St. Louis in 2009, she has taught ESOL in St. Louis public schools, and worked as an adjunct professor in the TESOL program for the University of Missouri, St. Louis (UMSL). From 2012–2018 she worked as a Migrant English Language Learners (MELL) Instructional Specialist at the St. Louis Regional Professional Development Center (RPDC), and is currently the coordinator for English Learner and Immigrant Education for the Hazelwood School District. She is working to complete her PhD in TESOL at UMSL evaluating the impact of co-teaching for English learners.

Adam Cooper, EdD, is an ESOL teacher at Withrow University High School, in Cincinnati Public Schools, as well as an adjunct professor at Xavier University. After initial work with Navajo families in Arizona, Dr. Cooper taught and consulted with a variety of schools serving diverse populations in the Cincinnati area. He currently co-teaches content-based language courses for refugee and immigrant children in Grades 7–12.

Jennifer Daddino, PhD, has been working with multilingual learners (MLLs) at Harrison High School since 2009 and co-teaching with Kimberly Grogan since 2013. Dr. Daddino's work has focused on creating appropriate curriculum and assessments for multilingual learners as well as working to create an environment for purposeful collaboration amongst colleagues who work with MLLs.

Marie Edgerton, MA, is a 4th grade teacher at Boeckman Creek Primary School in Wilsonville, Oregon. She studied Spanish and lived abroad both during and after her undergraduate years at Oregon State University. She is passionate about creating a classroom community that honors each individual student, as well as creates an environment where each student looks at him- or herself as a thinker and problem solver.

Amy Frederick, PhD, is an associate professor of literacy education at the University of Wisconsin–River Falls. Her work focuses on teaching literacy in elementary schools, particularly for children who are learning English or who have reading difficulties.

Brandy Gibb, MA, TESOL Dip, is the English+ program coordinator at Crofton House School in Vancouver, British Columbia, Canada. The English+ program focuses on the development of academic language skills for advanced ELLs.

Amanda Giles, PhD, teaches English as a second language and has her doctorate from the Department of Curriculum and Instruction at the University of Alabama. She has taught English/Language Arts and Spanish. Her research interests include collaboration between ESL and mainstream content teachers, literacy, language policy, and assessment practices for ELs.

Kimberly Grogan, MA, has been teaching at Harrison High School since 2012 and co-teaching ENL classes with Jennifer Daddino since 2013. With additional experience as a creative writing teacher and literary magazine adviser, Ms. Grogan strives to incorporate her creative and multifaceted approach to language in all of her work.

William Hargrove, MS, is an 8th grade teacher at I.S.145Q. He recently obtained a master's degree in TESOL at City College, City University of New York. He is interested in using literature to expose students to different people and experiences, as well as how language shapes our thinking and perspectives.

Anne Ittner, PhD, is an assistant professor of literacy education in the Division of Education and Leadership at Western Oregon University in Monmouth, Oregon. Her research interests include literacy education for emergent bilinguals in elementary schools, literacy coaching, professional learning and teacher education.

Stephen Kroeger, EdD, is an associate professor at University of Cincinnati, whose experience includes international professional development among teachers working in the Palestinian West Bank. His recent work has focused on developing cultural competence in pre-service teachers to unleash the learning potential of ethnically diverse students. He taught in St. Lucia, West Indies, in Peru among the Quechua Indians of the Andean Highlands, and in a high school in Detroit, Michigan.

Joan R. Lachance, PhD, is an associate professor in teaching English as a second language at the University of North Carolina at Charlotte. Dr. Lachance's research agenda encompasses dual language teacher preparation, academic literacy, and authentic assessment with multi-language learners, including research specific to the context of co-teaching.

Guofang Li, PhD, is a professor and Tier 1 Canada research chair in Transnational/Global Perspectives of Language and Literacy Education of Children and Youth in the Department of Language and Literacy Education, University of British Columbia, Canada. Li is a leading researcher in immigrant children's language and literacy education internationally. Her program of research aims to improve the life success of immigrant and minority students by addressing the cultural, linguistic, instructional, and structural barriers in their literacy learning and academic achievement both in school and at home.

Greg McClure, PhD, is an associate professor in the Department of Curriculum and Instruction at Appalachian State University. His teaching and research focus on the ways language, culture, and power intersect to influence teaching and learning. He earned his PhD in Language and Literacy Education at the University of Georgia.

Kia Myrick McDaniel, EdD, is currently the coordinating supervisor for specialty programs, in Prince George's County Public Schools, Maryland. She also serves as an adjunct professor and consultant. Throughout her career in education, she has held positions as a classroom and ESOL teacher, reading specialist, and ESOL instructional supervisor.

Carrie L. McDermott, EdD, is an assistant professor, coordinator of graduate TESOL programs, and director of bilingual and ESOL grants in the School of Education and Human Services at Molloy College, Rockville Centre, New York with concentrations in cultural and linguistic diversity, ESOL methodology, theory, language acquisition, and action research. In addition, Carrie is an international speaker and presenter, author, national grant writer, curriculum writer, instructional coach, and researcher.

Marina Moran, MS, started her career as an ESOL teacher and staff developer in the United States, specializing in differentiated instruction and assessment for ELs. She is an adjunct professor at SUNY New Paltz and provides in-service training in various areas of pedagogy related to the academic achievement of ELs.

David Mumper, MA, is a doctoral student in urban education at the CUNY Graduate Center and a specialist for the Hudson Valley RBERN, where he supports educators and multilingual and immigrant students in New York's public schools. He has worked in secondary and higher education since 2001, and formerly taught high school English and ESOL.

Jennifer Norton, EdD, spent several years as an elementary school teacher and since then her work has focused on English learner policy, professional development, and assessment. This research was conducted as part of her dissertation study at The George Washington University.

Lucia Perez-Medina, EdD, is an ELL services administrator at the New York City Department of Education, where she provides compliance and instructional support to school administrators and teachers regarding the instruction of English language learners. Lucia served as a director for school quality, an elementary school principal, ELA instructional specialist and teacher. Lucia holds a doctorate in educational leadership from The Sage Colleges of Albany, a master's degree in special education and a bachelor's degree in education with bilingual extension from Brooklyn College. In addition, she completed postgraduate studies in organizational leadership at College of Staten Island, and earned her certification in TESOL at St. John's University.

Holly Porter, EdD, director of language supports and services for the Cherry Creek School District, has over 21 years of specialized experience ranging from preschool teacher of the deaf to principal consultant at the Colorado Department of Education. She holds several degrees including in bilingual/bicultural education, special education, and educational leadership.

Teresa Schwartz, BA, has taught junior sciences and physics in both public and private schools for 34 years. She is a graduate of Western Washington University with a Bachelor of Education majoring in biology. She has diplomas from Simon Fraser University in teaching with technology and environmental science.

Ebony Terrell Shockley, PhD, is an associate clinical professor, director of teacher and leader education, and director of the master's certification program at the University of Maryland College Park. Although formerly in a K–12 position, she currently researches under-represented groups in STEM, literacy, and exceptional education contexts.

Kathryn Toppel, EdD, is currently a K–5 English language development specialist in Oregon. Katie's instructional background includes experience teaching kindergarten and first grade in addition to being a K–12 support services teacher at the Franconian International School in Germany. She is also a co-founder of #EllChat_BkClub on Twitter.

Jane Charlotte Weiss, MA, has taught multilingual students for 11 years and holds an MA in policy, organization, and leadership at Stanford University. She is currently on a Fulbright Distinguished Award in Teaching fellowship researching language-aware pedagogical innovations and collaborative teaching models for immigrant and refugee students in Finland.

Karrie Woodruff, MS, is an ELD teacher in a dual immersion elementary school. She has been teaching K–12 ELD and Spanish for 20 years, and co-teaching for the last 4 years. She is also a PhD student in the Language,

Equity and Educational Policy (LEEP) program in the College of Education at Oregon State University. Her research interests include co-teaching and culturally responsive pedagogy.

Bedrettin Yazan, PhD, is associate professor of applied linguistics in the Department of Bicultural Bilingual Studies at the University of Texas at San Antonio. His research is focused on language teacher learning and identity, language policy and planning, World Englishes, and collaboration between ESL and mainstream teachers.

Lightning Source UK Ltd.
Milton Keynes UK
UKHW050407241020
371994UK00006B/139